D0193890

Illness and culture in contemporary Japan

Illness and culture in contemporary Japan

An anthropological view

EMIKO OHNUKI-TIERNEY
Department of Anthropology
University of Wisconsin, Madison

CAMBRIDGE
UNIVERSITY PRESS

Published by the Press Syndicate of the University of Cambridge
The Pitt Building, Trumpington Street, Cambridge CB2 1RP
40 West 20th Street, New York, NY 10011-4211, USA
10 Stamford Road, Oakleigh, Victoria 3166, Australia

© Cambridge University Press 1984

First published 1984
Reprinted 1986, 1987, 1989, 1992,1993

Printed in the United States of America

Library of Congress Cataloging in Publication Data

Ohnuki-Tierney, Emiko.
Illness and culture in contemporary Japan
Bibliography: p.
Includes index.
1. Medical anthropology – Japan. 2. Folk medicine –
Japan. 3. Medicine care – Japan. 4. Japan – Social
life and customs – 1945–   . I. Title.
GN635.J2046   1984   362.1′0952   83–14415

ISBN 0-521-25982-7 hardback
ISBN 0-521-27786-8 paperback

In loving memory of my father, Kōzaburō Ohnuki

Contents

List of illustrations

Acknowledgments

This is the first step in my odyssey back to my own culture. In so many ways, my life in the United States has been like living on a tightrope. My miraculous deliverance from major falls is due to many individuals, both in and out of academe, who have extended their understanding and generosity. It would be difficult to acknowledge even those who contributed directly to this book, not to mention the others.

The fieldwork for this project, both in 1979 and 1980, was supported by a grant from the Japan Foundation, for which I am most grateful. My trip back to Japan in 1980 as well as my fieldwork among the Japanese in Madison in 1980 were supported by the Research Committee, University of Wisconsin Graduate School. Their funding and encouragement have been a source of strength in my research since I started my career at the University of Wisconsin.

Countless Japanese have contributed to this work. Although I cannot name my individual informants, in order to protect their privacy, I am most indebted to them. My special thanks go to Drs. I and S, as I refer to them in my book, who let me observe their clinical practice for an extended period of time. During both 1979 and 1980, the National Museum of Ethnology in Osaka extended its hospitality and supplied me with an office and access to various facilities. Most of all, I cherish the staff's generosity and willingness to share insights and discuss Japanese culture. In particular I extend my appreciation to Professor Tadao Umesao, director of the museum. Despite the heavy demands on his time, he generously offered me his keen observations of Japanese and Western cultures. Professor Mikiharu Itoh shared his lifelong work on Japanese religions with me and made my stay most enjoyable by extending gracious hospitality.

If I must choose one individual most responsible for preventing me from vanishing from the field of anthropology, it is Professor Jan Vansina of the University of Wisconsin, Madison. He first knew me as a foreign student, ignorant both of anthropology and the culture of the American graduate school. He has kindly read all my writings and continuously encouraged me in my slow and feeble endeavor in anthropology. He also read the manuscript for this book and gave valuable criticisms and suggestions. Over the years, he has offered me original theoretical insights that have enriched my anthropology enormously. Words cannot express my gratitude.

Some years ago, I had *kaiun* (good luck) in meeting Professor Robert J. Smith of Cornell University, a most respected *genrō* (master) in Japanese anthropology. Since then he has generously helped me in countless ways. Professor David Plath of the University of Illinois read a draft of this book and offered detailed criticisms and suggestions. I asked his assistance not only because of his intimate knowledge of Japanese culture, but also because he worked in the same region of Japan where I did my fieldwork. Professor Roger Sanjek of the City University of New York also read a draft of this book with meticulous attention and then offered me generous support as well as constructive criticisms and suggestions. To all those who suffered through the reading of the manuscript at one stage or another, I am most appreciative. Their criticisms and suggestions have improved the final version of this book enormously. I remain responsible for its shortcomings.

Shortly before I received the contract for this book, my father passed away. He was an unusual father who wrote to me every single day for four years during college and for several more years during my stay in the United States, and less frequently after he realized I intended to stay in the United States. Although I was too busy with my life fully to appreciate his effort, I have no doubt in my mind that it was his love that kept me innocent of the negative side of life and that kept me going without fear and discouragement. A book is indeed a poor substitute for the personal care I could not give him in his final years. Nevertheless, I dedicate this book to his memory. My appreciation is no less to my mother, whose love and concern are always shown in the most helpful ways. My husband Tim, with his enormous sense of integrity and tolerance, has kept our home a peaceful place in which to engage in my obsession with anthropology. Our sons Alan and Roderic and their cheerful outlook on life have been a major source of strength to me; without their bright eyes and smiles, life would not be this beautiful.

E. O-T

Madison, Wisconsin

1   Introduction

This is a book on the contemporary health care system in urban Japan. It is not, however, the usual social science study containing only "facts" and statistics. Nor does it present cures for specific illnesses or descriptions of the effectiveness of certain herbs. Instead, it focuses on a culturally defined concept of hygiene, urban magic, deities and buddhas as medical doctors, and family involvement in the care of the sick, as well as clinics and hospitals. The book consists of descriptive data and my interpretations of the sociocultural patterns underlying the concepts of illness and health and the health-related activities of contemporary Japanese. The book illustrates that, despite industrialization and significant advances in modern science, including biomedicine, in contemporary Japan, Japanese concepts and behavior regarding health and illness are to a large extent culturally patterned, even when they are couched in biomedical idioms.

A latent but more ambitious aim of the book is to lay the groundwork for a future undertaking: the critical appraisal of some of the assumptions made in the social sciences about the effects of modernization on a culture and society. Data about the health-related behavior of contemporary urban Japanese, as presented in this book, challenge the view held by some social scientists that modernization produces a "rational" individual whose behavior loses symbolic dimensions. For this larger aim, then, the choice of the modern Japanese health care system as a subject for study is a strategic one. The contemporary Japanese are a non-Western population among whom both industrialization and the development of science have reached a high degree. Nevertheless, their thought patterns and behaviors are deeply symbolic; they are not simply "rational" or "utilitarian" in nature.

This book, then, attempts to make a contribution not only to the fields of anthropology called ethnomedicine and symbolic anthropology, respectively, but also to an understanding of Japanese culture. It provides an interpretation of Japanese culture and society based on examination of the health-related activities and beliefs of the Japanese.

The book consists of two parts. Part I describes daily hygiene practices and beliefs of ordinary people, as well as their concepts of health, illness, and related matters. Part II describes the various medical systems practiced today. The purpose of describing these systems is twofold: First, to illustrate how each system is embedded in Japanese culture and society; and second, to present a descriptive model of a pluralistic system of medicine, in which several systems of health care exist side by side within a single society – a pattern common to many societies of the world.

The primary emphasis in this book is on day-to-day health care, including daily hygiene and relatively minor illnesses. Except for a brief discussion in Chapter 3, serious illnesses do not receive an extensive treatment. This emphasis should be kept in mind in reading the book.

Throughout the book, I have labeled thought processes and behavioral patterns as "Japanese" or "urban Japanese," but these labels are not intended to mean that the patterns, taken individually, are unique to Japanese. For example, cultural sanctioning of illness (Chapter 3) is found among other peoples, including American Jews and Italians (Zborowski 1952), and a Catholic priest praying for the recovery of the sick in the United States is not too dissimilar from a Buddhist priest reciting a sutra for the sick (Chapter 6). To give another example, the continued care by the family of hospitalized patients (Chapter 9) is a common practice among many peoples with strong emphasis on kinship or human relationships in general, including many African peoples, and among Westerners, Italians. Folk cultures in the United States are just as rich in symbolism as they are among the Japanese described in this book (see Summary).

Thus, the various "Japanese features" described in this book are not uniquely Japanese, when taken separately. The uniqueness that distinguishes Japanese culture from other cultures emerges with "a unique combination of factors which are not unique in themselves" (Vansina 1970:177). A systematic examination of "historical regularities" is often useful in demonstrating the uniqueness of a particular culture (Vansina 1970). I have therefore explored the historical background of certain aspects of contemporary Japanese health care. Without a more systematic examination of the history of Japanese culture and a broader coverage of Japanese culture, however, the book can only suggest how culture patterns the health-related behavior and concepts of contemporary Japanese.

Although the book is basically comparative in perspective, it by no means presents a systematic comparison. Only passing references are made to beliefs and practices in the United States in order to provide some basis for comparison for those familiar with health care systems in the United States. In addition, the book is not aimed at a highly specialized audience. More specific critiques of anthropological approaches to medicine (the field of so-called medical anthropology) and of theories of symbolic anthropology are presented in an earlier work, *Illness and Healing among the Sakhalin Ainu: A Symbolic Interpretation*

(Ohnuki-Tierney 1981a). Since this book is addressed to people interested in medical anthropology, as well as to those interested in symbolic anthropology and Japanese culture, there are sections that may be essential but not directly tied to health-related issues. For example, one section in Chapter 2 discusses early world view and the classification of people. It is included because it is vital to understand that categories of thought operative in the medical domain are related to thought governing other domains of Japanese culture, and that these categories show historical continuity. The details in these sections may be meaningful to the reader interested in Japanese culture; for others, only the main thrust of the argument may be significant.

The basic approach of the book

After professing not to address a specialized audience, I must briefly engage in a somewhat technical discussion here in order to explain my basically symbolic approach. I use the term *symbolic* broadly, and my approach is closest to that of Sahlins (1976:55) when he stated that "human action in the world is to be understood as mediated by cultural design, which gives order at once to practical experience, customary practices, and the relationship between the two." This approach, which he calls the cultural paradigm, contrasts with the praxis or utilitarian paradigm, which sees cultural order "to be conceived as the codification of man's actual purposeful and pragmatic action." I use the term *symbolic* in order to emphasize the cultural paradigm, since "cultural" has been too commonly and broadly used in anthropological literature to carry any specific meaning.

The main focus of the book, then, is the conceptual structure or categories of contemporary Japanese thought, using some historical perspective. I examine health-related practices and concepts from the perspective of how they are organized according to the "logico-meaningful" structure of the culture. This approach contrasts with the approach that emphasizes the "technical" or "causal-functional" integration of acts and objects (Peacock 1975:4) – the approach that approximates the praxis paradigm of Sahlins and is frequently used by biomedically oriented medical anthropologists.

In a technical sense, "symbol" should be reserved for situations involving metaphors. Strictly speaking, an object, a phenomenon, and the like becomes a metaphor when it stands for another object, phenomenon, and so on through its connotative meaning, while the designative, or literal, meanings of the two belong to two separate semantic categories (Basso 1979). Using "symbol" more broadly, I follow Geertz (1973: 91), who explains: "It [symbol] is used for any object, act, event, quality, or relation which serves as a vehicle for conception – the conception is the symbol's 'meaning.'..."

By choosing this definition of symbol, anthropologists do not confine themselves to an examination of formalized and/or religious rituals alone. In fact, the approach obliterates the distinction between secular and sacred ritual. Every behavior, object or phenomenon, be it in a temple or a factory, is subject to examination for its symbolic dimension (for an excellent theoretical explication of "ritual," "symbol," "meaning," and "categories of cognition," see De Craemer, Vansina, and Fox 1976; for a detailed discussion of "secular" versus "sacred" ritual, see Moore and Myerhoff in Moore and Myerhoff 1977).

Anthropological approaches to health care systems

Until fairly recently, anthropologists often failed seriously to consider such cultural institutions as witchcraft and sorcery and shamanistic healing practices as parts of the medical systems of their host societies. Instead, these were seen primarily as magicoreligious practices, or as methods of social control. This lack of recognition of the actual medical systems of host societies seems to reflect a not-so-surprising cultural bias among anthropologists, who are now increasingly aware of the fact that they cannot entirely escape their own cultural and personal biases in their attempts to record and understand other societies. As Carstairs (1977:1) points out, it might be true that even for anthropologists, the advancement of scientific medicine was "of such compelling importance that traditional concepts of illness seemed positively irrelevant."

In recent years, biomedicine has clearly failed to live up to its almighty image, even in the Western societies where it originated. Public demand for alternative health care has placed considerable pressure on the medical profession. Medical anthropologists have been assigned the role of providing information on alternative medical systems elsewhere in the world, especially in the Third World. As a result, there is a growing body of anthropological literature on medical systems in other societies. The majority of anthropological writings, however, are about "folk medicine," either in nonindustrialized sectors of the Third World or among "ethnic minorities" and rural populations in industrialized nation-states.

The work of medical anthropologists, then, follows an anthropological tradition – providing a sympathetic account of folkways, of which the medical system is a part. These folk systems are usually not institutionalized, and their practitioners, such as shamans, are not professionalized. There are as well a few studies of institutionalized nonbiomedical traditions, such as *kanpō* (Chinese-derived medicine) in Japan, Chinese traditional medicine in Taiwan and the People's Republic of China, and Āyurvedic, Yunānī, and homeopathic medicines in India. Most of these studies deal with medical systems of societies that are not in the forefront of the industrial or postindustrial sectors of the world.

In short, little exists in the way of a comprehensive overview of medical systems in a society comparable to some of the Western industrialized nation-states. This book, then, is intended to fill the gap in available publications by describing the medical systems of contemporary Japan, whose society is modernized in every sense of the word, and yet whose medical systems in many ways present striking contrasts to those of Western societies dominated by the biomedical tradition.

The book is not, however, intended to provide answers to the problems of medical systems in the United States or elsewhere. Since medical anthropology, at least in part, has grown out of dissatisfaction with biomedicine among the general public, many anthropologists feel, either implicitly or explicitly, that their task involves helping to solve the problem by presenting ideas for alternative health care. This trend has two unfortunate consequences for the rigorous theoretical development of medical anthropology as a field. First, the medical system under study often becomes idealized to suit the image that both anthropologists – who often are romantics – and lay people look for. Second, in order to legitimize their quest, anthropologists sometimes resort to simplistic medical positivism – proving "medical efficacy," for example, by presenting the chemical constituents of a few herbs, and thereby elevating the medical system in toto to scientific legitimacy. Legitimacy may also be based on how their system, as opposed to ours, meets the needs of "individuals," as defined and perceived in a Western society.

As Lewis (1981) chides, anthropologists become shamans who journey to distant realms "in search of enlightenment and knowledge" which, upon acquisition, they transmit to the people for their salvation. Unfortunately, this "what can we learn from them" approach often results in anthropological work that falls short of total understanding, since the utilitarian questions predispose the anthropologists to emphasize only those features of the culture that are directly relevant to the questions.

My goal in this book is to understand and describe the specific medical systems and general health care system of contemporary Japan, and to demonstrate how they are embedded in the Japanese sociocultural milieu – especially in their value systems and their patterns of interpersonal relationships. Indeed, if there is a message at all, it would be that the importation of any alien medical system is not a simple process; any imported medical system goes through a profound transformation in the recipient culture before it becomes a viable cultural institution.

Another goal of this book is to contribute to our understanding of medical pluralism. In recent years, a number of publications on medical pluralism in the Third World have appeared. Many of them focus on the problem of how people in a society with plural systems of medicine choose among the options available to them. Romanucci-Ross (1977) describes the strong competition between indigenous and biomedical systems among the Admiralty Islanders, and discusses how the people choose between them. In Lieban's work (1977) on sorcerer-healers among lowland Christians on the Philippine Island of Cebu, the decrease in the importance of sorcery is attributed to the modernization process. Press's (1978) work in Seville also points to the decline of folk medicine, as biomedicine, through its burgeoning bureaucracy, has expanded its roles to include a wide range of functions beyond the simple amelioration of symptoms. Janzen's work (1978), on the other hand, indicates that medical systems in Zaire fulfill not competitive, but complementary roles. Several other studies show that indigenous healers can remain viable or even successful, through skillful role adaptations, in a modern urban environment (see Landy, ed. 1977).

In some anthropological studies, indigenous medicine and biomedicine are often seen as distinct systems, or at least described as such, and the patient must choose between them in order to maximize his or her goal of obtaining the best health care available. Such studies often involve a situation in which Indian or black African medicine with "native healers" is juxtaposed against white people's biomedicine, administered by white doctors or native doctors trained by white doctors. Many such societies studied by anthropologists are former European colonies, adding the important negative factor of antagonism between the native medicine and biomedicine. Furthermore, except in a few cases, such as those of Lieban and Press, the studies often deal with remote rural areas of the Third World, where indigenous medicine is usually neither institutionalized nor professionalized. Thus, aside from the very brief overviews of Indian and other Asian medical pluralism by Leslie (1974, 1975, 1976), we have few ethnographies of medical pluralism that deal with urban medical systems that are institutionalized and professionalized.

Some of the inferences of these studies are misleading, since they depict a pluralistic system of medicine as consisting of several independent systems. This picture is inaccurate in most cases because within a given society, all the medical systems interact closely and are transformed through the interaction. Biomedicine, for example, which has been introduced to almost every society in the world, acquires a distinct form and color in each recipient society because it is transformed by the sociocultural milieu of that society, a milieu that includes other medical practices in the society. Part II of this book describes how the different medical systems in contemporary urban Japan complement and interact with one another. The more general aim is to provide a descriptive model of a pluralistic system of medicine in a modern society. The mechanism for successful coexistence is traced to a thorough patterning or embedding of each medical system in the Japanese sociocultural milieu.

As a work in ethnomedicine, this book presents a sociocultural analysis and interpretation of health, illness, and medical treatment among the Japanese.

Useful for an understanding of the ethnomedical approach taken in this book is the distinction between illness and disease made by Fabrega, who uses the term *illness* to refer to a socioculturally defined departure from health (see also *cultural disease* in Obeyesekere 1976), and *disease* as a category defined in biomedicine. Fabrega (1975:971) explains that "biomedical diseases are defined on the basis of deviations and malfunctions of the chemical and physiological systems of the body and any number of processes and structures can be implicated in disease." He emphasizes that biomedically defined disease is "an abstract biological 'thing,' " divorced both from the human individual who suffers from it and from the sociocultural milieu (Fabrega 1975:969). This distinction is useful in clarifying the basic difference between the ways disease is defined in biomedicine and illness is defined in other cultures. Nevertheless, I concur with Stein, who claims that the concept of disease in biomedicine in itself reflects cultural bias: "The mechanical-biological, pathogen-specific or organ-specific disease *is* the illness" (1977:15, italics in the original). My concern in this book is cultural germs and cultural illnesses, which never precisely correspond to microbes or diseases as defined in biomedicine.

In describing the way in which the Japanese manage health and illness, I prefer the phrase "health care system" to "medical system." The former covers a broad range of practices, including management of the body, beliefs about health maintenance, and both formalized and nonformalized medical treatments. The phrase "medical system," on the other hand, implies formalized medical treatments only, often excluding nonformalized systems such as healing at temples and shrines or healing by shamans.

Following Dunn (1976:135), many medical anthropologists prefer the term "cosmopolitan medicine" to "biomedicine," which I chose for this book, as well as such other labels as "Western medicine," "scientific medicine," and "modern medicine." Although I agree that biomedicine is cosmopolitan in distribution, I chose to use biomedicine in order to emphasize that the theories and practices of biomedicine undergo transformations in each recipient society; I avoided the possible inference from cosmopolitan medicine that this form of medicine, practiced in most societies of the world, is identical wherever it is practiced.

Scope of the book

Daily hygiene is basic to the understanding of any health care system, and yet it is rarely covered in anthropological literature. Chapter 2 provides a detailed description of Japanese daily practices and beliefs. This chapter, entitled "Japanese Germs," best illustrates my own sociocultural or symbolic approach to the Japanese health care system. I argue that daily hygienic behavior and its underlying concepts, which are perceived and expressed in terms of biomedical germ theory, in fact are directly tied to the basic Japanese symbolic structure. Contemporary concepts of dirt and cleanliness derive from symbolic notions of purity and pollution, which have been basic themes of Japanese symbolic structure throughout history. The same symbolic structure that generates the concepts of purity and pollution also governs the classification of space, time, and people.

Just as germs are culturally defined, so are illnesses, as described in Chapter 3, "My Very Own Illnesses." In addition to describing Japanese illnesses, this chapter also examines Japanese attitudes toward the body and death. These descriptions reveal that the Japanese are "indulgent" in recognizing and caring for relatively minor illnesses. The cultural sanction of illness is explained within the dualistic world view of the Japanese, in which both good and evil, like health and illness, exist in complementary opposition.

Chapter 4 explains a prominent and important feature of the Japanese concept of illness; that is, the Japanese attribute causes of illnesses to objects and phenomena, such as nerves (in a physical sense), blood types, and aborted fetuses – a type of causal logic called *physiomorphism*, or *somatization*.

Part II, consisting of six chapters, describes the pluralistic system of medicine in urban Japan in the postindustrial era. It begins with a description in Chapter 5 of *kanpō* medicine, introduced from China by the sixth century. Basic theoretical premises of *kanpō* diagnosis and treatment are contrasted to those of biomedicine in order to demonstrate that the two systems, which the Japanese use simultaneously, are in fact diametrically opposed in their basic approaches. After an examination of the causes of its enormous popularity in recent years, *kanpō* is described in its various forms and at the several levels at which it is delivered: by biomedical doctors, by licensed paramedics, by priests and nuns at temples, by pharmacists and drugstore sales personnel, and by people in their own homes. *Kanpō* is indeed omnipresent in Japan, available not only as a highly professionalized medicine, but also as a part of daily health care, often in forms unrecognized by the people themselves.

The succeeding two chapters discuss the role of religions in health care. In Chapter 6, two case studies illustrating the use of shrines and temples are presented to demonstrate the importance of religions in contemporary Japanese health care. Chapter 7 examines the past and present "medical specializations" of Japanese deities and buddhas. A certain buddha or a deity, for example, may be known for healing children's illnesses, while another is known for illnesses of the ear. In contemporary Japan, just as in the past, some of these supernaturals serve as pediatricians, gynecologists, or general practitioners. The difference between past and present practices is that the contemporary Japanese no longer formally acknowledge the medical role of religions, despite the fact that they still resort to them. An examination of the medical functions of these supernaturals in a historical perspective is also meant as a contribution to the current controversy among scholars of Japanese culture over whether or not various religions (Buddhism, Shintoism, Taoism, and folk religions) constitute a multilayered structure or a single fused structure.

The next two chapters are devoted to a description of biomedical health care in Japan, with primary emphasis on its transformation within the Japanese sociocultural milieu, which renders it quite different from the way it is practiced in other countries. Chapter 8 starts with a brief history of the development of the medical profession in Japan to illustrate how the profession of biomedical doctor today is in large measure a product of history. After an overview of the current biomedical profession, the remainder of the chapter is devoted to descriptions of visits to doctors' offices and clinics. The absence of an appointment system at Japanese clinics and hospitals, the spatial arrangement of the examination room, the use of "surrogate patients" (someone representing a patient in the doctor's office), and various other aspects of visits to doctors' offices and clinics are interpreted against the background of Japanese culture and society. In the last section of the chapter, pregnancy and childbirth are described to illustrate how biomedicine is combined with traditional religious beliefs and practices.

The hospitalization process is evaluated in Chapter 9. The feeding of the patient by the family and visitors, despite the provision of three meals by the hospital, the extensive visitation allowed by most hospitals, and the gifts brought by visitors are all examined in relation to the values assigned to the state of illness and to the Japanese codification of the patient role. The chapter ends with a case study of the actors involved in the human "drama" of hospitalization, to complement earlier sections that emphasize hospitalization as a cultural system.

Chapter 10 concludes Part II by drawing together the information on pluralistic systems to seek the mechanisms that have sustained and promoted the successful coexistence of medical systems with quite distinct basic approaches. The success of the pluralistic system lies in the thorough embedding of each system in the Japanese sociocultural milieu. Further analysis of biomedicine, introduced only about a hundred years ago from the West, is undertaken to illustrate this point.

Although each of the medical systems, formalized and nonformalized, has always had its own place in the pluralistic system, there have been clear fluctuations in the popularity of each system. These shifts in popularity can be roughly charted through the developmental stages of Japanese society from the premodern to the modern postindustrial period. In order to avoid a simplistic explanation for the shifts in popularity, I seek factors responsible for the phenomena other than the narrowly defined medical efficacy of any given system. I attempt to link the phenomena to broader perspectives such as the Japanese world view and, in particular, the Japanese view of the collective self in relation to the outside world. The brief Summary discusses the effect of modernization on the symbolic dimension of human behavior. It presents a critical commentary on anthropological theories of modernization and the so-called primitive versus civilized mentality.

I omit traditional folk medicine (*minkanyaku*) and the medicine of contemporary popular culture, both of which are mentioned briefly in Part I. Also excluded from the present treatment are two types of massage (*anma* and *shiatsu*) and various other folk practices, some of which are popular versions of *kanpō*. A comprehensive treatment of nonformalized medical systems should also include dietary practices, as well as the use of baths and hot springs, and various other cultural practices. Indeed, hot springs are still used extensively for medical purposes, with each hot spring considered beneficial for the treatment of particular illnesses. Home manuals on medicine often have extensive lists of famous hot springs all over Japan and describe the medical efficacy of each (see Ariyoshi, ed. 1978). In fact, almost all cultural practices have some medical dimension, so that an exhaustive treatment of nonformalized medicine would have to examine all aspects of Japanese culture – an impossible task. Here I confine myself to a description of three medical systems: *kanpō*, religious systems, and biomedicine.

Fieldwork and methodology

When I initially conceived the plan for an ethnomedical study in Japan, I planned to conduct research on the health care system in a city rather than in a rural area. Japanese rural communities are rapidly being engulfed by urbanization, and they are also experiencing depopulation as younger people are drawn into cities. I envisioned my research as somewhat similar in methodology to a highly celebrated work by Dore (1973) based on the study of a ward in Tokyo. However, as several Ph.D. dissertations by young anthropologists on Japanese ethnomedicine started to appear, I realized there was no overall study of contemporary urban health care in Japan to provide a broader perspective for these microstudies.

When I began my fieldwork in 1979 in the city of Kobe in western Japan, it immediately became apparent that the artificial municipal boundary of the city was totally irrelevant in the health care of the people; the Keihanshin area thus became the unit for the study. Keihanshin is a term comprised of the initial characters of the three principal cities in the area – Kyoto, Osaka, and Kobe. In many ways, the three cities are very different from each other. Kobe, the smallest of the three, had a population of 1,366,397 in 1977 (Kōbe-shi Eiseikyoku, ed. 1978:2). Although its economic development since World War II has been slow due to a lack of industries, the city has been characterized by a unique international flavor since the opening of Kobe harbor in 1868, the first year of the Meiji Restoration. The harbor brought numerous foreign visitors to the city, and some stayed there permanently, creating their own "quarters." Westerners, for example, had their own section (*kyoryūchi*) with a school, hospitals, and a cemetery; the Chinese had a Chinatown; and Koreans had their own section. The foreign population in 1975 in the city of Kobe alone, excluding the surrounding area, where many Westerners reside, was 32,427: 22,961 Chinese, 6,471 Koreans, 594 Americans, and 2,401 other foreign nationals (1975 national census reported in Bureau of Statistics, Office of the Prime Minister, ed. 1977:142).

Osaka, the most heavily industrialized and most populous of the three cities, had a population of 2,723,752 in 1977 (Kōbe-shi Eiseikyoku, ed. 1978:5). Its development began much earlier than that of Kobe, and it played a key role in international trading before the country was closed to the outside world toward the end of the feudal period. Osaka is characterized by early urbanization and development of a capitalist economy, and later by industrialization. Nevertheless, it also maintained traditional values and practices. It is in this city that we see the strong and continued use of herbs and other traditional medicines, and also of religious healing. In fact, the eastern outskirts of the city, at the foot of the Ikoma Mountain range, is where we see a heavy concentration of temples and shrines with specific medical functions, as well as the greatest number of shamans.

Kyoto, best known to outsiders for its temples, shrines, and castles, was the capital of Japan between A.D. 794 and 1868, when the capital was moved to Edo (present-day Tokyo). Its population in 1977 was 1,464,964 (Kōbe-shi Eiseikyoku, ed. 1978:5). Without the extensive development of business or heavy industry, the city has retained much of its traditional culture; as Lock's work (1980a) shows, *kanpō* is more professionalized in this city than in others.

Despite these clear and widely recognized differences between the cities, people freely cross municipal and prefectural boundaries in seeking health care. Residents of Kobe seem to rely more heavily on services in Osaka and Kyoto than residents of these two cities rely on Kobe.

In order to cover the entire geographic area, as well as to gain a broader perspective, I used numerous research techniques. Systematic fieldwork was carried out at several clinics and hospitals. Intensive fieldwork, conducted almost every other day for three months, was undertaken at a medium-sized private hospital, which I refer to as hospital X. Founded in 1935, it is situated in a suburb of Kobe. Hospital X has 226 beds and 300 employees, among whom are 25 doctors and 140 nurses. It has an obstetric and gynecology clinic, where I spent most of my time, and pediatric, ear-nose-and-throat, surgery, ophthalmology, internal medicine, and radiology clinics. Another major field site was a clinic to the west of Kobe, where an M.D., whom I refer to in this book as Dr. I, practiced *kanpō*, the Chinese-derived Japanese medicine. In order to understand the range of types of hospitals, I spent several days at two large hospitals in Osaka. One is a large university hospital founded by the Japanese government in 1887. Referred to in this book as university hospital Y, it has 1,219 employees, including 287 doctors, 38 pharmacists, 372 registered nurses, 21 midwives, 49 practical nurses, and 53 nurse's aides. It has 17 clinics and 1,011 beds. In 1977, hospital Y accommodated 212,266 inpatients and 630,672 outpatients. It used to have a reputation of being fairly "dirty," as did many public hospitals in Japan. However, with completely new buildings, it provides the best of facilities and biomedical expertise. Another large hospital I visited was the National Center for Circulatory Diseases, which specializes in cardio-vascular diseases, the category of disease that now claims the highest death toll in Japan. It was built by the Japanese government in 1977 and boasts the best facilities and medical expertise in this field. It accommodates both outpatients and inpatients, and has 600 beds. In 1979 it had 128 doctors, 426 nurses, and 140 paramedics and pharmacists.

There were a number of other hospitals and clinics of various types and sizes that I visited with my family, relatives, and friends. Many of them were neigh-borhood doctors; some were municipal hospitals. As described in Chapter 8, a patient often visits a doctor accompanied by a close family member or a friend, who is usually allowed to go into the examination room. This custom provided the best field technique for me. As we will see in Chapters 8 and 9, care of the sick is relegated to women in Japanese society, which means that middle-aged women like myself are most often involved in patient care. These visits to the clinics and hospitals thus presented a natural setting for observation.

Everywhere I went, I initiated conversation with people on the subject of illness in order to find the range of variation in patterns of thought and behavior in regard to health and illness. These natural encounters were indeed very suc-cessful; informants did not feel the pressure of formal interviews, and a wealth of information was often eagerly offered.

Intensive case studies are vital to most ethnographic research. Among friends, relatives, long-time acquaintances, and people I met in public places, I was able to locate and follow up on a number of the case studies presented in this book.

Numerous other sources of information went into this book; indeed, too many to list. Since the Japanese are exceedingly conscious of health, information on health and illness was abundant wherever I went. Even while sitting in a station waiting for a train, I was always busy noting the advertisements by clinics, hospitals, drugstores, and pharmaceutical companies that cover almost every inch of public places, including the inside walls of public transportation. Temples and shrines are not far behind in advertising, although these religious institutions are often advertised by transportation companies promoting tours of these places.

In 1979 I spent four months in the field, but decided not to use the remaining two months that had been funded by the Japan Foundation. As will be noted in the next section, the "foreign" behavioral patterns of the Japanese soon started to become familiar, and I felt that I again needed distance from them. After sorting out the data collected in 1979 and reformulating the directions of my research, I returned in 1980 to complete the project. Six months of fieldwork by a native anthropologist, however, is not at all comparable to six months by a nonnative fieldworker. The reservoir of knowledge that native anthropologists possess about their own cultures defies quantitative assessment.

Additional fieldwork was also was carried out in Madison, Wisconsin, during the spring semester of 1979–80, supported by the Research Committee of the Graduate School at the University of Wisconsin. I interviewed a number of Japanese researchers and students and their families about their experiences in the American health care system. I had become more aware myself of the patterning by Japanese culture of my own concepts of cleanliness and other health-related thoughts and behavior when I encountered those of Americans, and experienced the differences. Therefore, I interviewed the Japanese on our campus to examine their reactions to the same situation. This method proved to be one of the best ways to identify Japanese patterns. Hygienic notions and practices are so basic to our daily lives, and are so deeply ingrained, that we usually react very strongly when we encounter different practices – we are shocked when we notice the ''dirty'' customs of another people. Data from these interviews are presented throughout the book, but especially in Chapter 2. My interviews with the Japanese in Madison also gave me opportunities to check the patterns I had found in the Keihanshin area against those from elsewhere in Japan, although I had already done so in Japan.

My generalizations about ''urban Japanese'' are indeed broad, and even bold. Although I frequently use the term ''Japanese'' rather than ''urban Japanese,'' the book is about contemporary urban Japanese health care. More specifically, it is about the urban Japanese of the Keihanshin area. I should further specify that it is about ''middle class'' urban Japanese, although this qualification is somewhat meaningless, since the middle class includes most Japanese. As with all generalizations and any overview, if one wishes to find exceptions, one can find many. One caution here is that the patterns and structures presented in this book are abstractions; they are not isomorphic with behavior itself. Structure generates behavior with infinite variations, none of which is an exact replica of the structure itself.

Native anthropologists

Anthropological study of one's own culture: A contemporary trend

One of the hallmarks of anthropology has been that it is a study of other cultures; this emphasis distinguishes it from sociology, which in the main studies its own culture and society. In recent years, however, sociology, as well as history, political science, geography, and many other disciplines, has in fact been expanded to include the study of other societies. Similarly, an increasing number of anthropologists are engaging in research in their own cultures.[1]

My own decision to study Japanese culture and society was based primarily on my eagerness to test whether or not anthropological methods and theories can be used in studying a complex modern society. With technologically simple societies and their so-called traditional cultures disappearing rapidly, I felt compelled to explore the use of anthropology in studying complex societies – especially in training graduate students, whom I can no longer urge to study hunting-gathering societies. If anthropologists cannot make a contribution to the understanding of complex societies, then we must face the same destiny as our disappearing "folk" or "premodern" cultures.

I chose Japanese culture to test the applicability of anthropology to complex societies, since I felt I had gained considerable perspective on my own culture, having systematically studied the Ainu for sixteen years and having lived in the United States for about two decades. Personally, too, I felt I was ready; having previously gone through a long period of quiet rebellion against my own culture, I found myself psychologically more objective in my reaction to Japanese culture and society.

Studying one's own culture is indeed very different from studying a foreign culture and has profound theoretical and even epistemological implications. In the following section, I explore these implications. For reasons of space, the discussion is confined to major problems that are directly relevant, theoretically and methodologically, to the research presented in this book.

Anthropological fieldwork: Some theoretical problems

Anthropologists used to assume, somewhat naively, that ethnographic data were waiting in their host cultures, like grasses in the field, for them to collect. Very early, anthropologists such as Whorf did point out that anthropologists do not

---

[1] Of North American anthropologists, M. Mead is perhaps the best known for her studies of American culture. Even when she engaged in the study of Samoan society, her basic questions were related to problems at home – the role of adolescents in American society. Among British social anthropologists, those affiliated with the so-called Manchester School have often turned to their own culture in order to study a complex society, as exemplified in Frankenberg (1957). (For a discussion of the Manchester School and their works on their own society, see Frankenberg 1981.) Other British anthropologists, such as Leach and Douglas, have turned to the analysis of the Old Testament. Barthes (1981) has studied his native French culture, despite the skepticism of Lévi-Strauss about the applicability of anthropology to the analysis of complex societies.

In addition to these anthropologists, many of whom spent many years studying other cultures before they turned to their own, in the United States there has been a sudden increase in the number of studies on American culture. Increasing numbers of Third World anthropologists study their own cultures now that anthropology has a longer history as a discipline, both in Western and non-Western countries.

objectively collect and interpret ethnographic data, and that even the process of basic data collection is heavily influenced by the native culture of the anthropologist. Whorf (1952:5) warned: ''The categories and types that we isolate from the world of phenomena we do not find there because they stare every observer in the face; on the contrary, the world is presented in a kaleidoscopic flux of impressions which is to be organized by our mind.....'' We organize these impressions primarily according to the framework of our own cultural categories and meanings. R. Needham (1963) illustrates this point with the analogy of a person born blind and anthropologists who are culturally blind in the society they attempt to understand. Upon gaining sight, a person who used to be blind must find order and sense in a painful chaos of forms, colors, and sounds, just as anthropologists must do in their host societies (see Ohnuki-Tierney [1981a: 3–4] for further discussion of this topic). Nevertheless, for a long time we anthropologists have engaged in ''scientific'' endeavor.

Now that the objectivity of even the natural sciences has been increasingly questioned (Kuhn 1962), anthropologists are even more eager to reexamine basic assumptions about fieldwork and anthropological research in general. One very recent direction in the reexamination of research comes from those interested in the notion of ''self'' and ''reflexivity.'' Their main premise is that by studying another culture, we become reflexive about our own collective self, our own culture, through a study of the ''other,'' another culture. In order to be reflexive, rather than simply reflective about the collective self, one must achieve ''the sense of distancing from self'' (Fernandez 1980:28,36). Reflexivity, then, is the capacity of the self ''to become an object to itself''; that is, to objectify the self (Babcock 1980:2; see also Fernandez 1980:35). Therefore, whereas reflectiveness simply involves ''isolated attentiveness toward oneself,'' reflexiveness ''pulls one toward the Other'' and away from oneself (see Myerhoff and Ruby 1982:5). In the phraseology of semiotics, in the reflexive process, the self becomes a sign (Babcock, 1980:1).

Crapanzano (1980) cautions against a tacit assumption by anthropologists that we do get to know our informants and their culture. He questions the nature of our ethnographic description, which he views not as the reality of another culture, but as ''the negotiated reality'' created during the ethnographic encounter between the anthropologist and the informant(s). This reality is neither that of an anthropologist nor that of the informants, since the presence of the anthropologist and his or her interest in their culture encourage the informants to be reflexive about their culture (Schechner 1982:80). The anthropologist's presence, therefore, encourages the informants to ''perform''; that is, to tell their own stories about themselves.[2]

---

[2] Perhaps the most frequently quoted phrase in this connection is one by Geertz (1973:448): ''a story they tell themselves about themselves,'' which is his interpretation of the meaning of the

Native anthropologists: theoretical considerations
and methodological implications for fieldwork

Some of the important issues that are directly relevant to fieldwork by native anthropologists include the problem of "detachment" in the interpretation of a culture, and the problem of the impact of the anthropologist's presence and the resulting "negotiated reality."

First, the problem of detachment. If studying cultures other than our own presents a journey out from and back to our collective self, our own culture, and if "distancing" is critical for this endeavor, then it follows that native anthropologists face an even more difficult task in creating enough distance between themselves and their own cultures. Therefore, despite the current trend toward studying one's own culture, forced in part by cuts in funding, in most cases it is vital for anthropologists first to distance themselves from their own culture. This distancing is best achieved by studying another culture before undertaking a study of one's own culture.

I encountered the difficulty of distancing from Japanese culture although I had been away from Japanese society, both physically and psychologically, for two decades. Not only had I been living in the United States since 1958, but I had been absorbed in Ainu culture for many years. I went back to Japan frequently, but I went directly to the Ainu people in Hokkaido and did not pay serious attention to the Japanese. When I returned in 1979 to do my first anthropological work among my own people in Kobe, they seemed strange, with intriguing behavioral patterns and thought processes. Everywhere I went, I observed incessantly and took notes. Astonishingly, however, my vivid reactions became increasingly milder after only a month and a half, and I found myself becoming more and more like "them." Their behavioral patterns were no longer as pronounced, and after about four months I felt the need to pull back to regain my perspective; hence my return to the United States. This turned out to be a good strategy, in that I was able to regain my perspective and refine the focus of my research before I resumed fieldwork in 1980.

Native anthropologists therefore share a problem with their informants: We take our own customs and behavior for granted, and so patterns and structures become difficult to perceive. As anthropologists, we must *abstract* patterns and structures from our ethnographic observations. As Lévi-Strauss (1967:273–4)

Balinese cockfight. Anthropologists such as Geertz, Turner, Myerhoff, and Babcock agree that during a ritual people engage in the reflexive act of telling stories about themselves (that is, the collective self), and that during the ritual the collective self is constructed as well as reconstructed. Although I have discussed only the collective self, reflexivity can be individual or collective (see Babcock 1980:10; Myerhoff and Ruby 1982:2–3; Rappaport 1980). For sensitive evaluations of fieldwork and the nature of anthropological data using this line of interpretation, see Rabinow (1977), Dumont (1978).

points out, people are rarely conscious of any real structure; when they have conscious models, they often are inaccurate and become a screen that hides models which are based upon data from the culture but are anthropological abstractions. Perhaps the best example of the difficulty natives and native anthropologists have in abstracting patterns is that of "Japanese germs" discussed in Chapter 2. When Japanese come inside the house from outside, they wash their hands. This practice stems from the notion that the outside is categorically dirty. The accepted Japanese explanation for this behavior is the germ theory – that there are many germs outside. However, there are germs inside too. Thus, the germ theory, as Lévi-Strauss notes, becomes a screen to hide the real model – that is, the symbolic equation of outside with pollution and inside with purity.[3]

In regard to the problem of "negotiated reality," the impact of the presence of an anthropologist differs greatly between native and nonnative anthropologists. For fieldwork in Japan, foreign anthropologists initially have a tremendous advantage. All foreigners, especially Westerners, usually receive the red-carpet treatment from the Japanese, who go out of their way to accommodate them. To some extent, this happens (or used to happen) for Western anthropologists in many Third World countries. Unfortunately, the drawback of this favorable treatment is that the host people "perform" for them; the anthropologist's presence becomes an important factor in the way that the host people act and react. Thus, as Crapanzano notes, the ethnographic observation tends to become the "negotiated reality" between the informants and the anthropologist, at least until the anthropologist's presence becomes less conspicuous.[4]

---

[3] Even though detachment and distance is vital for anthropologists who work in their own cultures, I suspect that most anthropologists find this task easier than would other members of the society. This is because many anthropologists are in some way "marginals" – not quite bona fide members of the society. Being a member of a minority group, or being a woman, may sometimes lead to feeling not fully accepted by our society, and in turn cause us to start questioning the majority culture. Myerhoff (Myerhoff and Ruby 1982) attributes her own reflexive tendency in childhood to her identity as a Jew.

[4] Seen from this perspective, the concept of "participant observation," the traditional and much-heralded field method of anthropologists, is a naive and misleading assumption. At a simple level, the concept means simply that anthropologists participate in many activities, whether hunting expeditions or rituals, in order to gain inside knowledge and a feel for the culture. I did so among the Ainu; I was delighted to go fishing with the men and plant-gathering with the women, and they in turn were pleased with my willingness to do anything the Ainu way.

However, the participant observation approach is quite naive if it gives the illusion that the anthropologist either becomes a member of the society or immediately gains the inside "feel" of the culture. Stories about being adopted by the host people do convey the anthropologists' enthusiasm, and provide good classroom technique for producing future anthropologists. Such stories, however, must be seen as akin to those told by "Man, the Hunter" to women and children after a glorious expedition of big-game hunting. I think it is presumptuous, or even condescending, to think that the natives consider anthropologists, who may stay only a year or two, members of their own society. In fact, my Ainu friends delighted in discussing how their way differed from both the Japanese way and the American way; they knew I was Japanese but came from the United States.

Native anthropologists have a definite advantage in being part of the society from the start, unless they are working in a segment of society radically different from their own. When I visited doctors with relatives and friends, or when I observed at clinics and hospitals, I fit in well enough that people seldom reacted strongly, even though I explained the reason for my presence.

Although there are several other advantages in studying one's own culture, perhaps the most important one is that native anthropologists have intimate knowledge of daily routines that are exceedingly difficult for outsiders to observe. Details such as when people wash their hands, how they treat and feel about the body and its physiological functions, and how they cook everyday food, rather than special food cooked only on festive occasions, are not readily evident to the outsider.

Anthropologists are increasingly turning their attention to daily life and secular rituals, rather than the spectacular rituals that may occur only once every year or even every twenty years. To understand the culture of a people, we must understand their day-to-day life. If native anthropologists can gain enough distance between their personal selves and their collective selves – that is, their cultures – they can make an important contribution to anthropology because of their access to intimate knowledge of their own culture. In short, both native and nonnative anthropologists have advantages and disadvantages, and they can indeed play complementary roles in enhancing our understanding of the cultures of the world.

Part I

Basic concepts and attitudes toward health and illness

2   Japanese germs

Daily hygienic practices are based on one of the most fundamental concepts in any culture: what is clean and what is dirty. In so-called modern societies, where the knowledge of biomedicine has been widely disseminated to the public, we often assume that all hygienic concepts are based on the germ theory. This chapter challenges that assumption by examining the hygienic practices of contemporary urban Japanese.

Lack of detailed description of daily hygiene is common in publications on Japanese culture and society. There are numerous publications, many in Japanese and some in English, describing Japanese concepts of purity and impurity. However, they discuss these concepts primarily within the framework of religious notions in Shinto and Buddhism. Furthermore, these concepts are often seen as remnants of the past, and are not viewed as a part of the health-seeking behavior of contemporary Japanese.

Daily hygiene in contemporary Japan

Daily hygiene and classification of space

Some of the most important early socialization training for Japanese children is to take their shoes off and wash their hands, and, in some families gargle, when they come into the house from outside. The Japanese explain this custom by stating that one gets dirty from germs outside; one takes off one's shoes so that unclean dirt from outside does not get tracked into the clean inside. Similarly, one must wash one's hands and gargle to get rid of germs on the hands and in the throat. The Japanese explain these customs in terms of germs (*baikin* – a term of recent origin, after the introduction of the germ theory from the West); some even have a visual image of enlarged bacteria, often shown to school-children in films. However, a prominent feature behind these hygienic practices is the association of the spatial "outside" with dirt – dirt, expressed as "germs," is the omnipresent "outside." To keep oneself clean and healthy "inside," in one's own living quarters, one must get rid of this dirt through cleansing. The symbolic equation here is of the inside with purity and the outside with impurity.

But the "outside" where germs are located is not somewhere removed from human habitation; rather *soto* (outside) refers to streets, streetcars, stores, and the like. The concept is most succinctly expressed in the Japanese word *hitogomi* (*hito* = people; *gomi* = trash, dirt), a term referring to crowds. The germs are contracted in crowds, or in locations where other people have been, contrasting them with one's clean self. Outside is equated with dirt and germs because that is where the dirt of others is seen to be most concentrated. Ultimately, dirt consists of the excretion of others. Spatially, outside is therefore still within the society, or the cultural sphere, rather than in nature. For convenience in what follows, I use the term "the outside" to mean "the outer margin" where the dirt and germs are located; it should be differentiated from the area that lies beyond the boundary of the society.

To clarify this interpretation, I will first elaborate on the hygienic practices of contemporary urban Japanese. Intensive modernization and industrialization have changed much of Japanese culture and society. Architectural styles have also changed a great deal. At present, in many Japanese homes and apartments, some sections have Western-style architecture, with wooden floors, tables, and chairs. Yet even the tiniest of modern apartments has *genkan*, a square or rectangular space at the entrance where people take their shoes off. At the entrance there are often one or two *ashifuki zōkin*. A *zōkin* is made from pieces of cloth sewn together into a square or rectangular shape like a quilt, and is used to wipe the floor; an *ashifuki zōkin* is a *zōkin* used specifically to wipe one's feet if they are excessively dirty. In the case of children returning from the outside after play, the mother often comes to the entrance with a bucket of water and washes their feet (see Caudill's observation [1976a:174]). The custom of taking off one's shoes is so important in Japan that Japanese children who come to the United States often continue the practice not only in their own homes, where their parents also observe the custom, but also when visiting other people's homes.

The transformation of Western-style shoes after their introduction to Japan also illustrates the importance of the custom. Western-style shoes were introduced around the turn of the century, and today the majority of Japanese wear shoes, instead of traditional footgear such as *zōri* (sandals made of leather or straw) and *geta* (wooden clogs). Many of the shoes in Japan, however, are made like slippers, so that one can easily put them on and take them off. In the case of athletic shoes for children, the transformation is especially telling; tennis shoes are made without laces, but with a strip of elastic in the center to facilitate putting them on and removing them (note the two pairs of children's tennis shoes in Photo 1; two pairs of shoes at the left front belong to a foreign visitor).

This feature is helpful, because children must take their shoes off when they

1. *Genkan*, the entranceway to a Japanese house where footgear must be taken off.

sit on the seat in buses and trains in order to look out the window. If a child violates this rule, adults sitting nearby will express their disapproval in no uncertain terms to those accompanying the child. They do so either by their facial expressions or by literally pushing away the feet of the child with shoes on, if they happen to have the bad luck to sit next to the offender. At other times, a conductor or ticket puncher will rush to the scene to reprimand the accompanying adult, as happened to me when traveling with my uncivilized boys during their first visit to Japan (I had been away too long).

This rule about shoes is enforced in buses and trains because these interiors are like the insides of houses. It is for this reason that in these vehicles, including the bullet trains, seats and backs are often adorned with starched white covers. Some cars are equipped with a feather duster. "The inside," as in one's own house, is vulnerable to dirt because of its exposure to "the outside." Many car owners take their cars to a shrine or temple on New Year's Day to have it purified. Far from being the equivalent of a car wash in the United States, the New Year's Day rite symbolically eliminates the accumulated dirt from the previous year and guarantees ritual purity during the coming year. The Japanese also feel uneasy when a student in the United States casually puts his or her shod feet on a school desk, where others eat their lunch.

Needless to say, if this rule is enforced for humans, its violation is certainly not tolerated for animals. Dogs belong to the outside and cats to the inside. Most Japanese would find the American custom of permitting the family dog on the living room couch or on beds most uncomfortable. After reading a draft of this book, Professor David Plath at the University of Illinois wrote to me, recalling: "Some of my Japanese friends keep two dogs, one for outside and one for inside – the inside dog usually being carried when let out at all, the outside dog rarely being allowed inside but if so having his paws meticulously wiped first." Indeed, you can see Japanese taking their "inside dog" for a walk by carrying it in their arms.

The Japanese word *dosoku* (*do* = ground, dirt; *soku* = feet) means feet with footgear. In shrines, temples, castles, and many other public places there is a sign *Dosoku Genkin* (people [literally, feet] with shoes strictly forbidden). Such public places usually have attendants at the entrance who provide visitors with a pair of slippers in exchange for their footgear. *Dosoku de hairu* (entering with footgear on) is a phrase referring to the utmost in bad manners. It is also used metaphorically, as when someone commits an outrageous invasion of privacy. In other words, despite the rapid modernization that has brought about many drastic changes in contemporary Japanese life, the custom of taking off one's shoes before one enters "the inside" has remained a cardinal rule, whether it is a private home, a public place, a private car, or a vehicle for public transportation.

This custom of taking off one's shoes reveals more than the Japanese perception of the outside as dirty. The Japanese are particularly concerned with the feet and the floor, even after taking their shoes off. The feet are by definition unclean and require extra washing, as we will see below. The floor also requires extra care. In fact, the major emphasis of daily cleaning is on the sweeping of the *tatami* (straw-mat floor), and the sweeping and wiping of the wooden hallways. This emphasis is certainly not due to the presence of visible dirt. The cultural emphasis on the floor, coupled with the architectural feature of nonwashable walls in traditional Japanese houses, results in people being little concerned with the walls of Western-style buildings, such as public offices and hospitals, which often remain visibly soiled. Conversely, even so-called meticulous Japanese housewives who live in the United States leave walls unattended until they learn Americans' concern for clean walls and start cleaning them.

In addition to the entrance, other architectural features of Japanese houses illustrate the relationship between daily hygiene and the spatial classification of inside and outside. Although the architectural designs of Japanese houses vary greatly, a common feature of many homes is a wall, usually made of wood, stone, or clay, that shuts off the residence and its yard from the outside. This type of enclosed residence presents a marked contrast to the typical residence in the United States, where the lawn and the house are much more accessible to and visible from the outside.

The treatment of the demarcating wall reflects the Japanese attitude toward in and out. The exterior side of the wall is often a target for urination, by both men and dogs; newspaper editorials and the Japanese government directed the former to be more "civilized" at the time of the Sapporo Olympics, but with only partial success. The owner of the house, who treats the interior side of the wall as part of the yard, rock garden, and so on, does not seem to mind the stranger's misuse of the exterior; it is, after all, part of the outside, which is by definition dirty. A similar attitude is revealed in a widely circulated anecdote, whose origin I no longer remember, which tells of a highly cultured man who finds a dead mouse in his beautiful rock garden and simply tosses it over his wall. This story is often repeated to point out Japanese negligence in public manners – a topic that has drawn much attention from the Japanese themselves in recent years.

Built into the wall are one or two gates. If there are two, the smaller one leads to the entranceway, where family members take off their shoes. The larger gate leads to the *genkan*, a room for the formal reception of guests. Although the origin of the *genkan* dates back only to the Edo period, and started as an architectural design for the residences of members of the warrior class (Kenmochi 1980:60; Oshima 1980:26), it has become an important feature in houses of the middle and upper classes in contemporary Japan. For socially prescribed visits (and business or other nonsocial visits), guests will not go any farther into the house. The family head, who represents the family to the outside world, goes to work using the *genkan* and the larger outer gate; other family members use it only on formal occasions. The area between the gate and the *genkan* is a circumscribed space where the "inside" meets the "outside." As such, it requires special care: in the morning, the gate, the *genkan*, and the area between them must be swept and watered.

It is at one of these gates that people returning from a funeral must be purified in order to get rid of the pollution contracted by association with death. Upon their return home, a family member brings salt to sprinkle over them. Perhaps reflecting changing family composition, or the fact that some families may no longer have someone at home at all times, some funerals now provide a packet of salt to those in attendance as a part of the return gift for *kōden* (money placed in a special envelope and given to the family by those who attend the funeral). One then can sprinkle salt over oneself on returning from the funeral.

Because the outside is regarded as dirty, most Japanese used, and some continue to use, a face mask when they go outside, especially in winter. The white mask is roughly similar to a surgical mask in the United States. The "scientific" rationale given is that the mask prevents the wearer from breathing in germs from the outside air. Others explain that a mask protects the sensitive membranes of their nostrils and throat from exposure to cold air. Since people may forget to carry one when they go out, masks are often sold at newspaper stands at railroad stations. At one time after World War II, a newspaper article printed an argument that a mask might have a negative effect on one's health, in that one might inhale one's own germs back again. Its use continues, however, and in a recent health section in the *Asahi*, the newspaper with the widest circulation in Japan, a better type of mask was advocated (*Asahi* December 10, 1978). The new type features material whose threads are glued together, as it were, rather than woven material, which lets germs go through more easily. The article includes a lengthy description of scientific experiments testing the impenetrability of the masks to germs.

In 1968, a Japanese visiting professor at the University of Wisconsin, who was an internationally known scientist, asked me why Americans looked at him with surprise whenever he wore his mask. My observation in the United States has been that face masks are used by surgeons and others in operating rooms and by patients with contagious diseases, although some older people use it for pollen, dust, or cold. The difference between Japanese and American uses of the mask relates to its purpose. The Japanese use it to prevent themselves from inhaling someone else's germs, whereas American surgeons and patients use it to avoid transmitting their own germs to others. Above all, the Japanese use reflects the notion that "cultural germs," or "people-dirt," is located outside.

Testimony for the Japanese association of the outside with dirt comes from the socialization of Japanese children. One basic and important vocabulary word in the baby language is *bacchi* (dirty), or its local variant, which is taught to small children by repeatedly pointing out things, such as shoes, that are dirty and hence are not to be touched. Children are also told not to sit on the ground outside, on the street, or on the floor of a store, station, streetcar, or bus. Small children realize the extreme sensitivity of adults on this point and often cleverly exploit it. A fairly common scene is a small child begging its mother or any adult to carry him or her; when the adult does not yield to the request, the child starts to sit down. Needless to say, the adult immediately gives in and rescues the child from getting "dirty."

In her work on the concept of "dirt" among small children in Japan, Tomosada (1976) records a scene observed in a hospital. A mother with a small girl about two years old was visiting a relative in a hospital. As the mother was talking with the patient, the girl started to explore the patient's slippers, which were underneath his bed, with her hands. As the mother realized what the child was doing, she immediately snatched the slippers from the child's hands with a look of horror on her face, while excitedly reprimanding her in a high-pitched voice, "Dirty, dirty." As Tomosada explains, a hospital, where the dirt of others is concentrated, is one of the dirtiest places. Some Japanese doctors take off their clothes and change to white gowns which they make a point of not taking home; they are washed at the hospital so that "germs" are not brought home. A doctor who was hospitalized told me he did not allow his children to visit him because a hospital is very dirty. Clearly, then, three symbols of dirt are represented in this incident: footgear, floor, and hospital. What can be dirtier than footgear that has touched the floor of a hospital? To most Japanese in the United States, then, an infant crawling on the floor of a clinic or hospital waiting room is an uncomfortable scene indeed.

To summarize thus far, daily hygiene behavior is closely correlated with Japanese spatial classification. The outside, or more specifically, outside one's home but still within the cultural sphere, and the below, as represented by footgear, feet, floor, and ground, are dirty. "Outside and below" are where germs and pollution, especially "people dirt," are located.

Daily hygiene and classification of time

The daily hygiene of the contemporary Japanese is related not only to their spatial classification of the universe, but also to their classification of time. Washing one's face and brushing one's teeth are customs too widespread to discuss, and do not particularly distinguish the Japanese from other peoples. However, these commonplace customs are only part of a more complex series of activities that the Japanese carry out in the morning, and that function to mark the transition from night to day. For most Japanese, the first item on the morning agenda is to fold the mattress (*futon*) and put it away in the closet or dry it outside to get rid of the moisture it collects from the body of the sleeper and the straw mat (*tatami*) on which it is placed. *Mannen doko* (a *futon* laid out for ten thousand years) is a phrase used to describe a lazy person. In most families, someone, usually the woman of the house, cleans the entire or at least most of the house every morning.

Just as the morning cleaning marks the transition from nighttime to daytime, the transition from daytime to nighttime is also well marked by bathing. Although there is little need to point out the famous Japanese custom of nightly bathing, it should be noted that, except during the summer, the bath is almost always taken just before one gets into bed. Some Japanese insist that if one does not go directly to bed after bathing, one catches *yuzame*, a chill after bathing, with which they do not have to be concerned in warm weather. In short, Japanese bathing has the function of cleansing the person for the night. It contrasts with the contemporary custom of showering or bathing in the United States, which places more stress on cleaning before going out or when the need is felt, regardless of the time of day. Japanese bedding by definition remains clean, irrespective of how frequently it is washed. It is uncomfortable for many Japanese in the United States to see someone casually putting a pair of shoes on the bed; shoes and bedding never come in contact in Japan.

The daily routine of bathing, however, must be discontinued once a person becomes ill, especially with any of the respiratory illnesses the Japanese refer to as a cold or *kaze*. This rule is enforced very strictly, even for a very mild cold. At home, it is usually the mother who decides when the sick can resume bathing, often several days after the last trace of the illness has disappeared. A setback in recovery is often blamed on the premature resumption of bathing. In a doctor's office, a patient often asks the doctor such questions as: "Is it all right to take a bath?" or "When can I resume bathing?" The doctor, in turn, often volunteers directions about bathing as a part of the medical instructions given to the patients. Instructions about bathing thus become a means by which the doctor indirectly communicates to the patient the nature and degree of illness. A doctor may tell a patient to continue bathing, instead of spelling out that his or her respiratory illness is not serious. Permission to resume bathing is a symbolic way of declaring to patients that they have recovered. Patients then bathe to cleanse themselves of the state of illness and mark their entry into the state of health.

In addition to times of illness, women also abstain from bathing and washing their hair during menstruation; the resumption of bathing after menstruation then marks the return to the "clean and normal" state, just as in the case of sickness. Even today, there are beauticians who make sure their customers are not menstruating before they will agree to wash their hair.

Daily hygiene and body parts

The discussion so far has emphasized how patterns of daily hygiene are aligned with the spatial classification of "inside" and "outside," and the temporal classification of "day" and "night" or "illness" and "health." One additional distinctive feature of Japanese daily hygiene is the emphasis not just on washing per se, which exists in most cultures, but the emphasis on washing certain body parts – the hands and feet, and sometimes the throat. They are the parts of the body that are the passages to outside or where the body is in contact with the outside; the hands touch outside objects, the feet touch the ground, and the throat is where outside air goes into the body. I have already discussed cleansing practices for the feet and throat, and noted that the Japanese wash their hands after returning from outside. The hands are also washed before any form of eating takes place.

Yet the Japanese still do not trust hands, even after washing, since they by definition are vulnerable to dirt – virtually no food is eaten with the fingers (although prepared by washed hands). Eating food and using chopsticks are inseparable; chopsticks are culturally defined as clean. This contrasts with American customs, which also emphasize the use of silverware in eating, but at the same time decree that certain foods should be eaten with the fingers. Whereas an American shudders at the thought of digging into roast beef or steak with fingers, fried chicken is "finger-lickin' good," and most sandwiches are eaten without silverware. Sandwiches were introduced to Japan some time ago, but they are often cut into small pieces, with a toothpick in each piece so that people do not have to touch them with their dirty hands.

Many Japanese find it very uncomfortable to eat sandwiches in American cafeterias, since they must eat them not only with "dirty" hands, but with hands even dirtier than usual; they just handled money to pay for the sandwiches. The Japanese consider money extremely unclean, since, they say, bills and coins are handled by anybody's dirty hands. Furthermore, money represents spiritual dirt; it symbolizes worldly concerns that are impure in at least the ideal Japanese value system. (During the feudal period, the merchant class was at the bottom of the four-caste system, with the rationale that merchants were concerned with money and therefore deserved the lowly status.)

Not only do the Japanese insist on using chopsticks rather than hands, but they also serve an *oshibori* (a hot or cold towel) at meals with which to wipe one's hands. These towels have become well known elsewhere because of their use on the Japanese airlines. In recent years, as carry-out food has become more prevalent, the Japanese have adopted the American disposable towel.

An additional feature regarding the Japanese use of chopsticks is the insistence on the use of common chopsticks; that is, chopsticks provided with a dish shared at the table. A common dish is served with a pair of chopsticks (*otoribashi*) so that one can transfer a portion of the dish to one's own plate without contaminating the common dish. In the absence of common chopsticks, "anyone who knows the manners" must use the other end of one's chopsticks, the ends that do not go into one's mouth. Common chopsticks are required especially when there are guests; the more formal the occasion, the more important their use. Conversely, the Japanese sometimes break this custom to emphasize social intimacy. Thus, a host or a hostess may encourage a guest to use his or her chopsticks, since "we" all belong to the *uchiwa* (inner circle); that is, "family" or equivalent in terms of social intimacy. Even the Japanese, then, are no exception to the rule that germ-sharing is an index of social intimacy in most societies.

The concern over common chopsticks is illustrated by an article that appeared in *Kurashi no Techō* (Notes on Daily Life), a leading home magazine. It reported the results of an experiment regarding the use of common chopsticks. The researchers measured the time for *tsukudani* (cooked seaweeds, fish, and so on served as a relish) to become contaminated by bacteria. One batch of *tsukudani*, a standard item on the table, was served with common chopsticks and the other batch without them. This experiment produced the expected results, which were reported in the magazine. The study illustrates the commonly observed Japanese concern about "people-dirt," including saliva on chopsticks, that is now expressed as "germs." The Japanese use of common chopsticks contrasts with the customs of the Chinese, who do not use them.

The concern over keeping the hands clean shows in other activities as well. White gloves are worn by bus and taxi drivers, train conductors, ticket punchers on buses and at railroad stations, door attendants at banks and hotels, elevator operators, and young women who greet customers at the foot of escalators in department stores. These people work primarily with their hands, touching such "dirty" objects as door handles and money. The gloves, which are washed frequently, protect their hands from getting dirty. And the clean white gloves symbolize the purity of the place, an important factor in appealing to customers. Thus, the young woman at the foot of an escalator in a department store does not touch the railing, which is "dirty" because everyone touches it. Her white gloves, however, become a testimony to the cleanliness of the place. A similar impression is given by the men wearing white gloves who greet and open the door for customers at banks and other businesses.

In a public library in 1979, I noticed a sticker with five reminders on the inside cover of all the books. The first two read: "Before and after reading, wash your hands well"; "Do not lick your finger to turn pages." In Japanese thinking, by licking your finger, you may swallow germs and you may at the same time contaminate the pages for other readers. At the National Institute for Cancer Research, all the books returned by patients are wiped with alcohol before others can use them (Kazuko Inoue 1981), so that germs are not transmitted from one patient to another. This is done even though cancer is not considered contagious. The same concern makes the Japanese very hesitant to use second-hand objects. Some Japanese leave secondhand books outside in the sun for a few hours for the sun's rays to kill the germs before they use the books. They are especially resistant to the use of secondhand clothing, unless it is from a family member or someone they know very well. This contrasts with the cas-ualness with which Americans buy clothes at garage sales and secondhand stores.

Although the hand is seen as a part of the body that should be kept clean although it is always susceptible to contamination, the lower parts of the body remain by definition "dirty," even though they too are frequently washed. The most impure parts of the lower half of the body are the orifices, with urine and excrement epitomizing the "people dirt." Therefore, underwear for the lower half of the body must be washed separately. As we will see in Chapter 9, nurses and aides at the hospitals have low status in Japanese society due to the nature of their job, which includes handling the bodily dirt of the patients.

In the house, the toilet is the most defiled part of the house.[1] Although slippers

---

[1] The structure of the Japanese toilet room has not bsically changed from the time when Morse (1961:228–231) described it in 1885. It used to consist of an outer room or an area in which to

are used in the hallways of Japanese households, there is always a separate pair of slippers or footgear for the toilet room. This is the case not only in private homes, but also at public places, including clinics. Hand towels used in the toilet room must be washed separately, just as dish towels are; the former because they are dirty, and the latter because they are clean and should be kept clean. In the Japanese logic of purity and impurity, then, the contemporary Western arrangement of having the toilet in the bathroom is the utmost contradiction – the juxtaposition of the most defiled place with the place for purification.

Japanese hygienic practices stem from the basic Japanese symbolic structure, which may be expressed as: inside : outside :: above : below :: purity : impurity. Put more precisely, they represent a symbolic correlation between two sets of spatial categories: inside : outside :: above : below, whose meaning is purity : impurity. When returning from outside, one must be cleansed. The gate in the wall of a house and the house entrance are vulnerable areas of spatial transition from inside to outside, and must be cleansed by sweeping and watering. Although the hands are seen as vulnerable to contagion and must be constantly kept clean by washing, it is the lower parts of the body, including the feet, that are seen to be most defiling. Therefore, things representing that area – footgear, floor, and ground – are all dirty, and require either no contact or immediate cleansing. Daily bathing for the Japanese marks the temporal transition from day to night and night to day, as well as from illness to health. Bathing for the Japanese is more than simple cleansing of the body; it has the function of symbolic purification. Most important, dirt to the Japanese is "people dirt" (*hitogomi*). It is the bodily dirt of others, perceived and expressed as "germs," that the Japanese avoid inhaling by wearing a mask and avoid contacting by wearing white gloves. "People dirt" is located outside the home among the crowd and not in the clear-cut outside – in nature.

Illness etiology and the source of healing power

Although an exhaustive examination of illness etiology and healing power cannot be undertaken here, a brief discussion of these topics is presented to further elucidate the differential meanings assigned to the outside and the outer margin.

---

wash hands, and an inner room where the toilet, a rectangular wooden frame in the floor, is located directly over a hole dug in the ground. Today an shallow oval porcelain receptor replaces the bottomless wooden frame and is connected to the plumbing mechanism. The reluctance of the Japanese in adopting the Western-style ilet, even in modern office buildings, is directly related to their dislike of "people dirt" on the toilet seat, which is shared by some Westerners who apply paper coverings for individual use. The Japanese, being used to the squatting position, prefer to avoid "people dirt"; hence the continued use of the Japanese-style toilet, especially in public places.

Technically, *pathogenesis* refers to "the agent or mechanism that produces or aggravates an illness," whereas *etiology* refers to "the circumstances that lead a particular patient to contract an illness" (Frake 1961:125). Most Japanese today are well informed about biomedical pathogens and etiologies of disease. They also have another, more fundamental, etiology that involves climatic conditions. A category of illness referred to as *kaze* illustrates this basic etiology.

Although it translates literally as "wind," *kaze* actually signifies external air with any type of movement. It can mean simply air, a breeze, or a strong wind. Written with the same ideograph, it is also a label for a category of respiratory illnesses that include a number of biomedically distinguishable diseases, such as colds, flu, and strep throat. There is another term, *ryūkōsei kambō*, a more technical term whose literal meaning is a "spreading cold." To most Japanese, *ryūkōsei kambō* is synonymous with *kaze* – both are contagious, and therefore the difference is a matter of degree. Of all the biomedically distinguishable diseases called *kaze*, the least recognized is strep, the initial stage of infection caused by streptococcus. In contrast to the sensitivity that even ordinary people now demonstrate in the United States with regard to strep, neither Japanese doctors nor ordinary people recognize strep as such; hence, there is no common label for it. (Scarlet fever, however, does occur in Japan, and the Japanese are very aware of it.) The ultimate etiology for all these forms of illness is *kaze* itself, or all types of air current. More specifically, it is the chilling effect of wind, rain, and other climatic conditions that produces the humoral imbalance in the body that is considered to be etiological.

In order to avoid these external elements that adversely affect the body, Japanese construction workers and others whose job requires them to be outside are always heavily clothed, even during the summer. They wear a wool sash over their stomachs, a straw hat on their heads, and are well-clothed in general. This is true of both men and women workers; out of necessity, many Japanese women have always done construction work and other heavy labor.

Internal imbalance can be produced by other external factors. Thus, many Japanese stay away from ice cream, ice candy, cold drinks, and various other foods and drinks that are cold in terms of temperature or in terms of humoral valence, and drink hot tea or hot water even during the summer. This explains why hot milk is a standard item at most restaurants. However, due to the intensive Westernization of Japanese diets in the past ten years, together with the introduction of McDonald's, A & W, Kentucky Fried Chicken, and massive amounts of soft drinks, Japanese young people are now consuming much greater amounts of cold drinks.

Humoral imbalance as illness etiology also explains the Japanese belief that the periods between the seasons are dangerous to a person's health. During these transitional periods, drastic changes in climate are more likely to take place, causing imbalance in a person's body. The customary ending of a letter written during these periods, "Please take good care of yourself since this is the change in seasons," stems from this belief. In particular, the *konome doki* (bud time; the time when leaves are budding in early spring) is the transitional time from the cold to the warm season and the time when people are considered susceptible to sickness; sick people and old people must be particularly careful. It is also the time when chronic illnesses recur.

In short, climatic conditions are merely factors that induce humoral imbalance, which then becomes an etiological factor for the occurrence of illness. Humoral imbalance is not a pathogen, like germs in biomedicine. Imbalance is a concept inherent in a system of correspondence that is fundamentally different from a system of thought which uses the concept of causation (Porkert 1974). Not being causal agents, the same climatic conditions may also be used as sources of preventive and curative power, as long as they are utilized in a concentrated form, and in a culturally prescribed way. Thus, the Japanese deliberately expose themselves to the very climatic conditions that are considered to be etiological factors for illness. *Kangeiko* (sports and physical exercises done in midwinter), *reisuimasatsu* (rubbing of the skin with a cold wet towel), and *reisuiyoku* (cold bath) are a few examples. Some pour a few buckets of cold water over the body after a hot bath. All these techniques "to build up the body" are contrary to the usual practices for avoiding illness. Although one ordinarily is not supposed to expose oneself to chill or wind after bathing, one pours cold water over the body. The proverb *kodomo wa kazenoko* (children are offspring of the wind) is based on the same principle, which is similar to the principle involved in immunization or in homeopathy.

What we see is an apparent contradiction: The Japanese meticulously avoid the climatic and extreme humoral elements, but they also use the same elements for preventive and healing purposes. The difference is that when used for preventive and healing purposes, these elements are used in a culturally construed, concentrated form; rather than being passively subjected to potentially harmful natural elements, people instead actively manipulate them for specific purposes. Most important, these elements located clearly outside of human societies are assigned a dual character, constructive and destructive, or good and evil. This contrasts sharply with the outer margin, whose meaning is impurity or dirt.

This discussion poses a curious question: What then is held responsible for the occurrence of illness? Strange as it may sound, I think that the dirt at the outer margin is an omnipresent threat to health, and that the negative power or quality attributed to the outside is held responsible for the occurrence of illness, especially serious illness. As we will see later, in the past calamities and epidemics were believed to come from outside, and often to be brought by strangers and foreigners. Therefore, it would be essential culturally to control any outside force, lest it exercise the negative power. We will continue our discussion of purity and impurity among contemporary Japanese by examining them against the broader background of world views and ethos.

Purity and impurity in the contemporary Japanese world view and ethos

The following statement by Hiroko Nakamura,[2] considered the best young pianist in Japan, succinctly reveals that the concepts of purity and impurity not only govern daily hygienic beliefs and practices, but are also translated into moral values. As such, these sentiments constitute an important part of the contemporary Japanese ethos. Reminiscing about her days as a student of Rosina Lhevinne at the Juilliard School in New York City, she describes her feeling just before her solo performance in Carnegie Hall in 1982:

I was in love with Mme. Lhevinne....She was wonderful. She didn't say much, but when I played for her I felt as though I had *had a nice hot bath*. Everything felt *clean* and marvelous. She was an inspirational teacher. She was so nice to me. She would call me every day to find out how I was making out and to talk with me, encourage me....[After finishing fourth in the Chopin Competition in Warsaw, three years later] I was depressed. I stopped playing for a year or so and thought things out in Tokyo. In New York and in Poland I did not know what I was. I had not found myself. New York has a big *poison*, and if you are not very strong you are destroyed. I was too young to handle it....I am not afraid of *poisons* any more. I have grown up. (Schonberg 1982; italics mine)

Her elated feeling is expressed as being analogous to the cleansing effect of a hot bath, and the word "clean" is explicitly used to describe the "marvelous" feeling. It is noteworthy that the statement was not made by someone in rural Japan or someone leading a traditional Japanese life. Instead, it was made by a Japanese whose life is open to the entire world through her superb musical ability.

This clean feeling is not only personally most desirable and satisfying, as Nakamura notes, it is one of the most cherished moral values in contemporary Japan. As in this statement, the same expressions are used to describe cleanliness in the hygienic as well as the moral sense. Thus, adjectives such as *seiketsu na*, *junna*, and *sappari shita* are all essentially synonymous, expressing the pure or clean feeling that is used to describe both a hygienically and a morally clean state. Conversely, adjectives such as *fuketsu na* and *kitanai* refer both to an unclean body and to a morally unclean person.

The junior and senior high school for girls that I attended in the early fifties had four mottos that were recited every day and were written on podia, school-

---

[2] I was first alerted to this article by Professor Willy De Craemer, Department of Sociology, University of Pennsylvania.

books, and virtually everywhere. The mottos were: Be pure, just, gentle, and strong. It is significant that purity came before justice. Although it was a finishing school for girls and these mottos were echoes from the traditional past, rather than representing the contemporary Japanese ethos, it should be pointed out that the catechism recited at a bank where anthropologist Thomas Rohlen did field-work in 1968–9 contains nine mottos (Rohlen 1974:36–7). One motto is *seiketsu*, the adjective listed above, and it means "cleanliness," either of body or mind. Rohlen translates the word as "purity" and explains the motto as "noble char-acter and proper behavior." Included among the nine bank mottos is *kenkō*, which means "health." Therefore, in the bank catechism we see again the close association between cleanliness of the body and that of the moral character.

There is no need to dwell on the importance of purity as a moral value in Japanese society, both in the past and the present, since many authors have discussed this topic (see Benedict 1967; Lebra 1976; Nakamura 1978). My emphasis is on the close association between the notion of purity as it applies to the body and the general health of the Japanese, and that of moral purity. Judgment as to pure or impure or clean or dirty can remain a cognitive exercise, an intellectual identification of the state of the body or any other phenomenon. However, as in many other cultures, the state of cleanliness and dirtiness produces strong psychological reactions – positive toward the former and negative toward the latter.

It is yet another step when the concepts of purity and impurity enter the realm of ethics, when purity receives the value of goodness and impurity the value of evil. What we see then is that purity and impurity notions constitute not only a significant principle providing order to the world view of the Japanese, but also an important part of their ethos, to which Japanese relate and react with the strongest of emotions. As Geertz (1973:126-7) eloquently put it, *world view*, which refers to the cognitive, existential aspects of a culture, is made "emo-tionally acceptable" by *ethos*, the evaluative (moral and esthetic) elements of the culture. Ethos, in turn, is made intellectually reasonable by world view. The dialectic process between world view and ethos has accorded the notions of purity and impurity a central place in Japanese culture, thereby endowing these notions with intense psychological content. I turn now to the historical trans-formations of these notions, beginning with a brief discussion of purity and impurity in the early Japanese world view and ethos, followed by a description of the dual nature of early Japanese deities.

The early Japanese world view and ethos

The opposition of purity and impurity

In two of the earliest records of Japanese history, the *Kojiki* and the *Norito*, there is clear evidence that the opposition of purity and impurity provided the basic structure of the world view at that time. *Kojiki* (The Chronicle of Ancient Matters), dated to A.D. 712, is the earliest known collection of Japanese myths, legends, historical records, and genealogies centered around the imperial house. In this record, the most important deities are described as born out of purification rites, performed by their father (Izanagi-no-Mikoto), who was defiled by seeing the corpse of his deceased wife (Izanami-no-Mikoto) covered with maggots in the underworld of the dead. According to the theogony, when he washed his left eye, Amaterasu-Omikami, the founding ancestress of the royal family, was born; her brother, Susano-o-no-Mikoto, was born when the father washed his nose (Philippi, transl. 1969:62–70). In other words, the major deities of Japan were born out of the dialectic between the two opposing principles of purity and impurity, which are correlated with life and death. These oppositions in turn are correlated with the spatial classification of the universe into this world and the underworld. Thus, the world of the *Kojiki* revolves around three oppositions: purity : impurity :: life : death :: above : below.

Equally revealing is the *Norito* (legal regulations of A.D. 927). "Sins" are explicitly spelled out in this record (Philippi, transl. 1959:46–7), and among them impurity is the gravest sin of all (see Umehara 1967). Listed among the sins of impurity are these: "cutting living flesh; cutting dead flesh; white leprosy; skin excrescences" (Philippi, transl. 1959:46). In other words, killing, handling corpses, and illnesses were considered sins of impurity. Also of interest is the manner in which these sins are purged. The sins are taken to the great ocean by a goddess, who dwells "in the rapids of the rapid-running rivers." The sins are "swallowed with a gulp" by another goddess who dwells "in the wild brine in the ocean." They are then blown away by a god into the underworld, where a goddess wanders off with them and loses them (Philippi, transl. 1959:47–9). In other words, purification of sin or impurity is accomplished through the use of water, brine, and wind, which are located in nature; that is, outside beyond the margin. These are normal elements of nature, but they are described in this instance in concentrated forms: "the rapids of the rapid-running rivers"; "the wild brine, the myriad currents of the brine, in the myriad meeting-places of the brine of the many briny currents"; and the wind created by a blow that is capable of sending all the sins into the underworld (*Norito* in Philippi 1959:48).

We see, then, distinct parallels between the concept of impurity and purification in ancient Japan and the contemporary notion of hygiene, illness etiology, and healing power. First, impurity in ancient Japan was located in corpses covered with maggots or resulted from killing or handling corpses or diseased bodies, especially those that are accompanied by bodily discharges such as pus. In other words, ancient impurity came from people, just as contemporary dirt is "people dirt." A stronger and more direct connection between impurity and the dead is found in ancient Japan than in contemporary Japan. Second, both in the *Kojiki* and the *Norito*, impurity is located in the underworld; that is, below this world.

In contemporary Japan, "below" receives the value of impurity. Third, both in ancient and contemporary Japan, elements of nature, such as water, brine (salt), and wind, are assigned a positive power, that of purging impurity and promoting health in general. In both cases, these elements are concentrated, thereby making them potentially dangerous; torrents can be destructive, or winds can cause illness. Fourth, nature assigned a positive power is definitely located outside the human society in both ancient and contemporary Japan. Fifth, these elements of nature, used for purification in ancient Japan, continue to be used for purification by contemporary Japanese; they wash their hands with water, and bathing marks the return from illness to health. We have also noted earlier that contemporary Japanese use salt to erase the defilement resulting from contact with death at funerals, just as ancient Japanese considered brine to have purifying power. Sixth, as in contemporary Japanese culture, the purity-impurity opposition in ancient Japan has intellectual as well as moral dimensions. In *Norito*, impurity is clearly defined as a grave sin, thereby receiving a moral value. In short, the equations of purity : impurity :: life : death (illness) :: above : below, as well as the dual power of the clear-cut outside, are present in ancient culture, as described in the *Kojiki* and the *Norito*, and in contemporary Japanese culture.

The Japanese concepts of purity and impurity are usually labeled as Shinto concepts. However, since the early historical records included oral traditions, it appears that Shinto simply gave an official stamp to already well-established values by officially declaring the flesh of animals as unclean, as well as displeasing to the deities. Likewise, the so-called Buddhistic prohibition of the killing of animals and the eating of meat also seems to derive from the indigenous notion of impurity described in the early oral tradition, which reflects the world view of the people at that time.

Numerous Japanese sources attest to the continuity of the concept of purity and impurity throughout Japanese history. For example, in an excellent ethnography of the Chūsei (the Middle Period, A.D. 794–1603), Yokoi (1975) described the notion of purity and impurity during this period in detail. Death continued to be the ultimate impurity, although birth, menstruation, miscarriage, pregnancy, meat-eating, and several other categories of phenomena are also considered impure. He (1975:esp. 267–94) points to numerous documented cases in which female servants were thrown out of the house, often into a river, before death in order not to defile the master's house; the death of a woman was doubly polluting.[3] In a brilliant work, Umehara (1976) traces the notion of purity from the very beginning of Japanese history through the Meiji period.

In contemporary Japan, even in rural areas, the degree of impurity associated with death and reproductive events is much less intense than it was in the past (see Norbeck 1952). The concept of purity and impurity, however, does exist

---

[3] Yokoi (1975:12–13) finds the ultimate source of purity/impurity in the yin-yang philosophy, which formed the basis of divination during this period.

in contemporary Japan in various other forms, including hygienic practices. Therefore, we can agree with Umehara that the purity-impurity principle has not only been with Japanese culture from its earliest times, but it has been one of, if not the most, fundamental principles governing the Japanese world view and ethos. In addition, there appears to be historical continuity in the correlation of the three oppositions, although more extensive work must be done on the various periods before this historical continuity is established as a fact. The presence of historical continuity means that the principles governing the categories of thought have been stable; however, the specific forms of their expression have undergone various transformations.

The dual nature of deities

In order to further explain the dual nature of the outside, I must briefly introduce Japanese deities. A predominant interpretation among Japanese scholars today is that from the earliest times Japanese deities have been characterized by a dual nature and/or power – they are both good and evil, creative and destructive.

The concept of *marebito*, originally discussed in detail by Origuchi (1965a:79–82; 1965b:33–5; 1966:303–17), succinctly expresses this notion. According to Origuchi, the *marebito* was a god in ancient Japan who periodically visited the villages from the world located on the other side of the sea, where no aging and death were known. The god visited the villagers in order to bring good luck, although he was also potentially dangerous.

The prototype of the Japanese god with its dual nature is found in Susano-o-no Mikoto, the brother of the Sun Goddess, Amaterasu, described in the *Kojiki*.[4] Its continuity to the present day is attested to by the deities appearing in contemporary folk festivals, as persuasively analyzed by Higo (1942) and Matsudaira (1977). Ouwehand (1958–59:155) summarizes this view of Japanese gods:

The attitude of the god towards man is ambiguous; it is either of a benevolent or of an evil character. Both possibilities are comprised in one and the same god. They can be abstracted as *nigimitama* (peaceful spirit) and *aramitama* (rough spirit).[5]

Yamaguchi's (1977) synthesis of the parallel in the traditional village between spatial classification and the classification of beings in the universe is illuminating. According to his analysis, until about a hundred years ago each Japanese village had a clear line of demarcation separating the "inside" of the village from the outside. The space beyond the boundary was associated with forces

---

[4] This interpretation is advanced by many contemporary scholars, such as Higo 1942, Matsudaira 1977, Ouwehand 1958–59, and Yamaguchi 1977.

[5] Ouwehand's (1958–59:156–8) own interpretation moves further into an elegant analysis of double ambivalence (both *nigitama* and *aramitama* consisting of the dual aspects) comprising the basically tripartite division (the opposition of the two aspects comprised in the totality of the god).

that could threaten the order of the village society. These forces took the form of masked spirits, gods, epidemics, bandits, and itinerant merchants and priests (see also Embree 1958:246–8). Yamaguchi emphasizes that these forces had the dual quality (*ryōgisei*) and therefore could become either positive or negative, just as Susano-o-no-Mikoto in the *Kojiki* was the cause as well as the remedy for all disasters and disorders, and symbolized creation after destruction. Thus, gods (*marebito*), who were thought to come from outside into the village, could be either beneficial or destructive (see also Suzuki 1974, 1979; T. Yoshida 1981).[6]

Yamaguchi sees ritual as the determinant in this matter; that is, only during ritual can the benevolent power be generated. He states (1977:153–4):

The Japanese have always believed that the gods should visit each village community only at a certain seasonal time. If god's visit is at the proper season, then he can act in a benevolent way. However, if he visits the village at an unexpected period, he is thought to be out of place and a source of evil.

The identity of the *marebito* as an outsider and its dual power constitute the basic characterization of Japanese deities in general, and have remained an integral part of folk religion throughout history. Ebisu and many other deities, who continue to enjoy popularity in contemporary Japan, are direct descendants of *marebito* (see Yoshida 1981).

Early deities, then, can be equated with nature, which in both ancient and contemporary Japan is endowed with dual powers – those of destruction and of creation by purifying and healing. Both the *marebito* and nature are clearly located outside the human society. Their positive power is not in a permanent state. It hangs in tension, ready to turn negative; only through ritual can people harness their benevolent power.

The inside : outside opposition and the classification of people

We have examined the day-to-day behavior of contemporary Japanese and their notions of daily hygiene, on the one hand, and the highly abstract concepts of world view and ethos, on the other, and demonstrated that the oppositions and correlations of purity : impurity :: inside : outside :: above : below are at work in both. Additionally, in contemporary as well as in ancient Japan, the clear-

---

[6] Many of these scholars link *marebito* to the concept of "stranger" in anthropological and sociological literature. Simply put, the "stranger" is in a position to exercise considerable power in the community where he or she is a stranger by the very fact that the stranger possesses the dual quality: Simultaneously he or she is both far and near, or belongs to and does not belong to the community (for the concept of "stranger," see Berger and Luckmann 1967:122, 156, etc.; Schutz 1971:91–105; Simmel 1950:402–8; Turner 1975b:esp. 231–71; van Gennep 1961:26, 27 etc.; Yamaguchi 1978a; for use of the concept in ethnographic analysis, see Frankenberg 1957; Myerhoff 1980).

cut outside – that is, nature, which lies outside human society – is seen as having dual power. Its positive power is secured only through proper rituals, which include secular hygienic rituals in contemporary Japan. We turn now to a brief discussion of yet another area – the classification of people – in order to see if these principles of classification are operative in the organizational framework of the society.

The classification of people in contemporary Japan

In terms of the day-to-day life of contemporary Japanese, one important in-side : outside classification is between *miuchi* and *tanin*. *Miuchi* (*mi* = body; *uchi* = in; within one's body) is a term that refers to the group of individuals most closely related to a person, with the parent-child relationship forming the nucleus of the group (see Doi 1978:33–43; Nakane 1970:3–7). The term *tanin* (*ta* = the other; *nin* = person) refers to those outside the *miuchi*. The distinction often extends to the public domain, where the Japanese distinguish between people within one's own organization and outsiders.

According to Doi (1978:33–43), *amae* (psychological dependence that assumes the alter's indulgence on oneself) characterizes the relationship within the *miuchi* (Doi 1978:35–6). Scholars who espouse the group model in interpreting Japanese society emphasize loyalty based on *amae* as the psychobehavioral principle that provides the bond between the members of an organization, and that renders the group goal of utmost importance. The concepts of *amae* and the group model are subjects of intense controversy. I am hesitant to assume that *amae* is always a personality trait of individual Japanese. It may be a socially patterned behavior and expectation, since the Japanese emphasize mutual reliance and reciprocity in their social transactions. However, one can safely say that the Japanese make a fairly clear-cut distinction between the *miuchi* and the other immediate social groups to which one belongs, and those outside these groups, at least in everyday behavior.

The inside:outside classificatory principle also operates at the broadest sphere of social interaction, distinguishing between acquaintances and strangers. The Japanese attitude toward strangers is easily seen by the neglect or disregard of strangers in public places, such as on the bus. People seldom even exchange smiles or short greetings. Some actually become offended if a stranger tries to initiate conversation, unless it is a request for directions or has some definite purpose. Kimura (1978) reports that it took him some time to be able promptly to return a smile or a "hello" from a total stranger when he traveled in the United States and England. The following remarks by an eight-year-old Japanese boy in a Japanese language school in Paris are also revealing (Omori 1981:614):

French children start talking to you even when they don't know you. I just can't take it. I became very cautious in dealing with these French children. Often at parties, they talk freely and like adults even though they met me for the first time; it makes me feel very uncomfortable.

In this connection, distributing name cards, a well-known Japanese custom, has a definite but somewhat nonformalized function. Let me illustrate this point by describing an experience. I once asked for a letter of official introduction from my sponsoring research institute addressed to the head of a hospital where I planned to carry out fieldwork. I wanted to observe doctor-patient interaction and other activities at the hospital. I had already met the head of the hospital, who thought it would be a good idea to obtain such a letter. After agreeing to produce the letter, an official at the research institute kept stalling for quite some time. After a month-long delay, I again visited his office, and during our conversation happened to mention that I already had the doctor's name card. The official suddenly looked relieved, and told me: "I didn't know that you already had his name card." The letter I had requested was produced on the same day. Obviously, he was hesitant to write such a letter to a doctor whom nobody at the institute knew personally and whom he thought I did not know – that is, know well enough to have his name card. The name card, especially if impressed with the seal of the person, has a well-delineated function in Japanese social interaction. It also serves an important function in the process of referrals from a doctor to another doctor, as we will see in Chapters 8 and 9.

The inside:outside principle used to classify people is also reflected in linguistic usage. In Japanese, one must choose an appropriate level of speech according to the relative difference in social status between the speaker and the listener. Within the household, one must use an honorific form in talking to parents and older siblings, just as one would to superiors in a company. However, if one speaks about a parent to an outsider, the humble form is used, because one's parent is a member of one's own (inside) group. Likewise, an employee would use a humble form when talking about a company superior to customers and others outside the company. Although some say that the use of humble forms when talking to outsiders about superiors is diminishing in importance, I have observed the pattern still in practice, especially among employees of well-established organizations. (For details of speech levels in Japanese, see H. Kindaichi 1966; K. Kindaichi 1967; Kokuritsu Gengo Kenkyūjo 1957; Martin 1964; Ohnuki-Tierney 1971.)

This pattern of classification of individuals in contemporary Japan is relatively simple. However, the we:they distinction is not unconnected with inside and outside; outside is the location of "they," namely, "others" who are the source of dirt. Although Japanese are reserved toward Japanese strangers, their attitude toward Westerners is clearly dual in nature. On the negative side, Westerners can be enemies, as they have been in the past. The long closing of the country (about 250 years) to the outside during the feudal period indicates how Westerners were seen to be a real threat. They were often thought to be the source of epidemics. During the cholera epidemic in 1879, the Japanese government's policy of isolating cholera victims in hospitals led some Japanese to believe that the reason for this was to take out the victims' livers in order to sell them to Westerners (Ono 1968:113).

On the positive side, in ordinary circumstances the Japanese have been very friendly toward Westerners and Western civilizations. Since the opening of the country in 1854, the Japanese have eagerly adopted and adapted most aspects of Western civilization, with the exception of psychoanalysis. Western visitors to Japan usually receive extraordinary hospitality from individual Japanese. An important point, however, is that the Japanese demonstrate this favorable attitude so long as the Westerners can be kept at a distance. Foreigners are seldom allowed to become bona fide members of Japanese society, and receive both personal and legal discouragement from doing so. For example, not until 1982 were foreign nationals able to hold regular positions at national universities; their status must still be reexamined every ten years, and no foreign nationals may hold teaching positions at lower levels.

One of the themes Caudill lists as the major psychobehavioral characteristic of the Japanese is the "we" versus "they" distinction, or in my terminology, the "in" versus "out" distinction. He writes (1976b:27):

A *sense of "we" versus "they"*. This is very pronounced within Japanese society in terms of "our group" versus the stranger or the outsider, and is equally strong when it is applied in terms of "we Japanese" versus the people of any other country. (Italics in the original)

He then refers to a passage from Hearn, who after fourteen years of living in Japan around the turn of the century, wrote about the impenetrable wall that excludes any foreigner who wishes more than lasting and kindly esteem: A foreigner in this situation is like an Antarctic explorer who seeks in vain some inlet through endless cliffs of everlasting ice. I have heard similar complaints from contemporary foreigners who have tried in vain to become permanent members of Japanese society. In short, Westerners are like *marebito*, who are clearly outsiders with both positive and negative power. They can turn into enemies, but they can also bring positive elements as long as they are brought into Japanese society only under controlled conditions.

The same logic applies to the Japanese eagerness for tourism. Foreign countries, like foreign persons, may be enjoyed under prescribed circumstances, and tourism provides the ritual occasion (Graburn 1977). This eagerness for tourism, which has been noted throughout history (Tsurumi 1972), contrasts sharply with the reluctance to reside permanently in a foreign country. Unlike the Chinese,

Koreans, and even the British, most Japanese, including Japanese students in the United States, return to Japan; foreign countries remain foreign to Japanese more so than to other peoples.

There are "marginal outsiders," however, toward whom the Japanese feel ambivalent or downright negative. Non-Japanese Asians belong to this type of outsider. They are not distinctly different, yet they are not Japanese. Japanese prejudice against them may stem from their symbolic marginality. Another example is the *han-japa* (half-Japanese; *japa* from English "Japanese"), who are the children of Japanese parents whose work required the children to be reared in a foreign country. Although these children are Japanese, their behavior differs from that of children raised in Japan, and therefore they are singled out and discriminated against by other Japanese children. A similar discrimination is also exercised against overseas Japanese. Conceptually, these people occupy a position "betwixt and between" – they are neither Japanese nor foreigners.

The burakumin

A brief discussion of the *burakumin*, former outcastes, and their history is presented here to suggest that the notion of impurity which is used as the basis for prejudice even today (Donohue 1966: 138) and the notion of impurity which is found in daily hygiene are closely related.

At present, *burakumin* are a minority group in Japan. The number of the *burakumin* is said to be 3 million, localized in 6,000 communities; more accurate figures are hard to come by. The government census is probably inaccurate; its 1973 figure, 1,048,566 (Ueda 1978a:3–6), for example, seems much too low. *Burakumin* communities are found primarily in western Japan, with the highest concentration in the Kinki district. They have been called "Japan's invisible race" (the title of DeVos and Wagatsuma 1966), because no physical characteristics distinguish them from other Japanese (the use of the term "race" is open to question; see Dumont 1970). The history of the formation of the *burakumin* as a category of people is not clear. What is certain, however, is that so-called outcastes in different historical periods consisted of various types of people; they have not been a monolithic group. There is no clear-cut linear descent link between an outcaste group from one historical period to another (Harada 1978a, 1978b; Noguchi 1978; Ueda 1978a, 1978b).

Without any physical characteristics to distinguish them from non-*burakumin*, their occupations have been the markers of the *burakumin*. Although a variety of occupations have been assigned to the *burakumin* (see Ninomiya 1933: 74–6; Noguchi 1978: 91), they may be grouped into two major categories, each receiving its own cultural meaning and valuation. The two merged as the feudal society became established toward the end of the sixteenth century. The first includes artists, artisans, and entertainers, who visited the village as itinerant priests, minstrels, monkey performers, and so on. In an agrarian society in which farmers formed permanent settlements, they were stranger-outsiders, at least from the perspective of the farming population, although they may have had a permanent residence elsewhere. They performed a vital function for the agrarian population, however, in that they served as culture brokers and brought entertainment, thereby breaking the monotonous cycle of farming life. They were the diviners, healers, and priests who were in charge of the fate of the people, who cured their illnesses, and who became the mediators between humans and supernaturals. Although they had the capacity to function positively toward the agrarian population, they could also turn off their power and cause calamities.

We see in this category of *burakumin* the symbolic equivalent of the ancient deities of the *marebito*, deity-strangers with positive and negative power who were introduced to the community through seasonal rituals. Their symbolic equivalents in contemporary Japan are the natural elements and Westerners. The natural elements can cause illness and yet possess the power to heal, as long as they are introduced into health care practice in a culturally controlled manner, as in the case of using cold water after a hot bath. Westerners can be enemies or bring in epidemics, but they also introduce technology and medicine. These *burakumin*, the ancient *marebito*, the elements of nature in contemporary health care, and Westerners all share the following characteristics: possession of both positive and negative power, an identity as conceptual outsiders to the society or culture, and an introduction of their positive power to the members of the society in a culturally prescribed manner.[7]

The second category of occupations is involved with death and dirt, with pollution as defined in Japanese culture. Many of the *burakumin* occupations deal with the death of both animals and humans – butchers, tanners, makers of leather goods, undertakers, and caretakers of tombs. Execution of criminals too

---

[7] According to K. Inoue (1967), the emperor and the *burakumin* constitute polar opposites in terms of symbolic valuation in Japanese culture. Yamaguchi (1977; also Yamaguchi in H. Inoue et al. 1978) draws on Inoue's interpretation to advance a highly provocative hypothesis which states that both the Japanese emperor and the *burakumin* are symbolic descendants of the *marebito*, the deity-strangers with dual powers. According to Yamaguchi, the emperor is a deity-stranger who became settled, whereas deity-strangers who never settled became *burakumin* (Yamaguchi in H. Inoue et al. 1978:154).

Although these Japanese scholars do not refer to Dumont's proposition about the symbolic opposition between the Brahmans and the untouchables in India, comparability of a whole class of Brahmans with the emperor, even at a symbolic level, is questionable. There is more comparability between the untouchables of India and the *burakumin* of Japan, and the Kshatriyas (warriors) of India and the samurai, including feudal lords, of Japan. In this context, it should be noted that the connection between the outcastes to art, architecture, and other genres in esthetics is also found in India. As Kailasapathy (1968:95) documents, the minstrels (the Pāṇar) were one of the four noble clans and were held in high esteem until medieval times, when the caste system was formed and the word *pāṇar* came to mean a lower caste.

seems to have been primarily the occupation of *burakumin;* as we will see in Chapter 8, the first dissection of the human body was performed in 1754 on a criminal by an executioner, under the direction of doctors who could not touch the corpse for fear of pollution but who eagerly wrote down their observations of the inside of the human body. Falconers also deal with death in that falcons kill animals. As we saw earlier, death is the utmost impurity in the ancient Japanese world view. Both footgear and *tatami* for the floor represent the impure ''below.'' It should be noted here that when leather shoes were introduced from the West, the manufacture of leather shoes was seen to deal both with dirt (since shoes represent the polluted below) and with death (leather is a result of animal deaths). Similarly, cleaning of temples and shrines, an occupation for *burakumin* during the Chūsei, deals with dirt, although it involves its removal. In short, all these occupations, relegated to *burakumin*, deal with impurity as it is defined in Japanese culture. *Burakumin*, then, are specialists in impurity (Dumont 1970:48), who spare others from dealing with the inevitable problems of pollution and dirt. In the process, they became identified with impurity itself, despite the fact that their jobs were to remove impurity and thereby restore purity in society. In short, at the symbolic level, they became the ''cultural germs.''

Although the *burakumin* in the artists and artisans category were temporary visitors to farming communities, I think the *burakumin* of the second type were permanent members of settled villages. Historical records suggest that they often were located at the margin of the community, such as on the river bank, under a bridge, near a slope, or in other places away from the central or main part of the settlement. The term *kawaramono*, which means ''people of the river banks,'' is indicative of this residential marginality. This designation was applied during the Chūsei to those who resided at marginal places such as river banks and were not assessed a tax (Yokoi 1975:335–9). Another term, *sansho*, is also thought to have been applied to the outcastes or the places they occupied. People in these *sansho* locations did not hold land and thus no land tax was levied on them, and they engaged in occupations dealing with death and dirt (Noguchi 1978: 89). The term *sansho* literally means ''the scattered place,'' and it contrasts with the term *honsho*, which means either central or real place (Yokoi 1975: 337–9), although Hayashiya (1980: 130–1) maintains that the term *san* means ''nontaxable.'' Whichever interpretation we follow, we see that the term *sansho* expresses spatial marginality, which in turn symbolizes the social marginality of the occupations.[8]

The symbolic parallel between the *burakumin* of the second category and cultural

---

[8] There is a scholarly controversy in regard to the residence pattern of the *burakumin*. Many scholars claim that the *burakumin* did not have permanent settlements, but traveled from village to village. However, Ochiai (1972:66–7), citing Yanagita, emphatically states that many *burakumin* were not outsiders, but were members of a community. My interpretation relates to the recognition of two categories of occupations.

germs involves the spatial dimension as well; both are located at the margin of society. The *burakumin* resided at marginal parts of the community, just as cultural germs are seen to be located not out in nature, but at marginal areas of society. The spatial location of impurity in the Japanese thought structure, therefore, has always been at the margins.

Although the two types of *burakumin* during early times were very different types of people and represented contrasting symbolic meanings, their common denominator was that they were not farmers and did not have the right to own land. Later in history, the occupations of artists and artisans also began to be devalued, and the distinction between the two types of *burakumin* became lost. This process was completed with the establishment of the feudal society. Significant for this process is the policy promulgated by Hideyoshi, who in 1582 recognized the land tenure of all types of outcastes and at the same time registered them as *kawata* – a designation chosen to label and legally define basically all those who did not belong to the four castes (warriors, farmers, manufacturers, and merchants) (Ueda 1978c:100–1).[9] After that time, numerous well-defined rules placed the outcastes under the strict control of the military government (Ueda 1978c).

The symbolic equation of the *burakumin* and cultural germs may sound crude and even prejudicial. However, I believe that one must understand the symbolic nature of the prejudice against them and realize that legal and economic equality does not automatically establish social equality.[10] (See Ohnuki-Tierney 1984 for details of the historical records on which these interpretations are based.)

Further interpretations

The Japanese thought structure

The description presented in this chapter provides at least partial evidence for the historical continuity of a conceptual structure that has been central to Japanese

[9] *Kawata* included both *hinin* ("non-humans"; beggars, criminals, orphans, etc.) and *eta* (the term used for outcastes until recently). But the *eta* alone were legally assigned a permanent, hereditary status. Beggars, criminals, orphans, and poor priests have been differentiated at times as *hinin*, in contrast to *eta*, the term most often used, until recently, to refer to outcastes. However, the distinction between the two groups has often been vague, especially before the sixteenth century. For a discussion of the origin of the term *eta* and its relationship to *hinin*, see Noguchi 1978:88–9; Ueda 1978c:102–3; Price 1966; Yokoi in Inoue et al. 1978:226.

[10] In his interpretation of the Indian caste system, Dumont (1970) advocates the absolute superordinance of the symbolic principle over the praxis principle. Although the task of scholars of modernization is no longer one of siding with either the materialist or the idealist position, the view that modernization gives the praxis principle increasing power may indeed reflect a bias of Western culture in which the autonomous or "objective" existence of the praxis is assumed. As Sahlins explicates at length in his 1976 publication, "in Western culture the economy is the main site of symbolic production" (Sahlins 1976:211). The task of those interested in the modernization process and its relation to changes in a given culture is to examine how the conceptual structure in a given culture provides meaning to the praxis and how the politico-economic changes in turn influence the system of meaning.

culture from earliest time to the present. This conceptual structure is characterized by a dominant system of meaning, purity:impurity, whose concrete manifestations are expressed in the spatial idioms of in : out :: above : below. In addition, there are two kinds of "outside" – the clear-cut outside, which is the opposite of the inside, and the outer margin. In terms of meaning, the former is assigned dual power, beneficial and destructive, whereas the latter is designated as impure. The expressions of the conceptual structure may not have been identical throughout history, but the structure itself has remained intact.[11]

The "concrete" manifestations, however, should not be taken to mean that the structure itself is found at the empirical level. This set of principles, then, is what Lévi-Strauss refers to as the "structure."[12] He explains its nonempirical nature (1960:53):

> If the structure can be seen, it will not be at the earlier, empirical level, but at a deeper one, previously neglected; that of those unconscious categories which we may hope to reach, by bringing together domains which, at first sight, appear disconnected to the observer. . . .

As Lévi-Strauss maintains, the entirety of the structure is never consciously recognized by the people themselves. Only its partial expressions are found in objects, behaviors, and phenomena (see also Lévi-Strauss 1967:273–5).

Although an exhaustive treatment of the classificatory system in Japanese culture is beyond the scope of this chapter, this discussion at least suggests that the structure or the principle underlying the categories of such abstract areas of culture as time and space are also found in more concrete areas, such as the classification of body parts, people, and occupations. They are also the principles guiding the daily behavior related to hygiene.[13] Although a full-scale analysis of symbolic values assigned to the two types of "outside" will detract from the

---

[11] Throughout this chapter, in order to adhere to the main arguments, I refrain from further delineation of the Japanese concepts of "inside" and "outside." It should be kept in mind that these concepts, not only as spatial units but also as metaphors, are extremely dynamic. Thus, the "inside" is freely created in the "outside," like an area with an invisible wall surrounding it; this practice relates to the traditional Japanese method of marking a sacred place by simply placing a rope around the area. Thus, in the "outside," or what we call "public space" in English, the Japanese create a private sphere when, for example, talking to family members and using verbal and nonverbal behavioral patterns peculiar to the private or inside sphere. They may also create the "outside" within the public sphere when they meet nonstrangers, people whom they know but who are not *miuchi* ("inside" people). Basically, the concept of "public place" as conceived in the United States is little developed in Japan.

[12] A similar concept is expressed by Horton and Finnegan (1973) as "modes of thought" and by Peacock (1975) as a "system of consciousness."

[13] Although this chapter examined the classification of people in the past and at present, I did not seek a model of the Japanese classificatory system in the social structure, just as I do not interpret the mode of production to determine the conceptual structure. Instead, I have placed the classification of people on the same plane as the classification of time, space, etc., all of which are governed by the basic conceptual structure. This is a departure from Durkheim and Mauss, the founders of symbolic classification in anthropology. They (Durkheim and Mauss 1963) maintained that social order and the classification of people provided a model for classification in other

main concerns of this book, a brief discussion will further elucidate the cultural notion of impurity – the central theme of this chapter (for a detailed discussion of anthropological theories on this topic, see Ohnuki-Tierney 1981a).

Concrete expressions of the clear-cut outside are the elements of nature that heal and prevent illness, as well as the ancient *marebito* deities, Westerners, and the *burakumin* who were artists, artisans, and entertainers. If we look at these phenomena and people as "symbols," the common characteristic is the "lack of identity." The elements of nature such as wind and water are formless. The rest are all characterized by lack of membership identity in a community. The *marebito* deities, artists, artisans, and entertainers are outsiders to the community, lacking permanent residence and membership in a settled community in an agrarian society whose social units are settled farming communities. Westerners are clearly outside the entire society and lack any identity in it.

The outside being nothing and nobody means that it can be assigned any meaning or any power. It is therefore especially important that the culture prescribe the manner in which it introduces these elements into its own realm. A prescription of ritual is vital in introducing the beneficial power of the *marebito*. Artisans and entertainers too bring limitless possibilities for creativity, but they do so at certain times of the year, especially after the harvest or any other convenient time in the agricultural cycle.

The symbols of the outer margin are germs, illness, and death. In the domain of people, it includes the *burakumin*, whose occupations deal with death and dirt. A common characteristic may be described as "betwixt and between" – a well-known phrase used by Turner (1967; see also van Gennep 1961) referring to the state of limbo or a state between two well-delineated categories. Death expresses most succinctly this notion of betwixt and between. At the time of death, the dead are neither living nor dead, in that "the freshly dead" have not become "really dead," or ancestors. At the most abstract level of analysis, the recently dead stand between nature and culture; they no longer represent human life, which sustains culture, but they have not yet returned to soil – that is, nature.

Although death is almost universally regarded as a liminal period, and the fear of pollution from corpses is also widespread, Japanese culture is peculiar in this respect because it designates death as the foremost sin. As Umehara (1967) points out, in Japanese culture impure acts become morally evil acts, and not vice versa. Smith's study of Japanese ancestor worship (1974:11–12) explains

domains of the same culture. Among contemporary scholars, Douglas is increasingly emphatic on this point and argues that social systems "generate" classification systems in the thought world. Her revision (Douglas 1975) of her earlier interpretation (1966) of Leviticus is most indicative in this regard. In her revision, she sought the model of conceptual anomaly in Leviticus in the social structure of the ancient Israelites.

that funeral and memorial services, which continue to be carefully observed, are "a means of overcoming the ultimately polluting condition of death." Similarly, dirt and germs, which the Japanese abhor, are those elements they can acquire through contact with *hitogomi* (people dirt). It is the other people's "germs" that one tries not to inhale by using a mask. It is the dirt left by other people on money and in public places that is unclean. Like corpses, or other body wastes (for example, excrement, urine, menstrual blood), Japanese germs are matter that has left the human body but has not yet become compost, or returned to nature. As Douglas (1966) explains, dirt represents a process whereby an item such as a piece of paper is losing its categorical identity; that is, its membership in the class of things.

Note also that the animals *burakumin* encounter in their occupations are all domesticated or tamed animals – cows, horses, monkeys, falcons. Although monkeys and falcons might be considered wild beasts, monkeys that entertain people and falcons that hunt for people are no longer truly wild animals, but instead are "tamed" or partially culturalized. These animals exist between nature and culture. Most of the derogatory names given to *burakumin*, such as *yotsu* and *hinin*, also denote the state between nature and culture. *Yotsu* (four) means four-legged animals, but it is also a homonym for the word "death" (both the character for the number 4 and the character for death may be pronounced *shi*). In this play on words, we see the symbolic equation in Japanese culture between death and animals; both are neither culture nor nature. (The word *hinin* means "nonhuman humans.")

To use the framework of reflexivity discussed in Chapter 1, the outside or nature is "the other" of the inside, which is culture and the collective "self." The boundary for this important distinction is marked by impurity, which renders transgression of the boundary line without ritual a strong taboo. For clarity of argument, I have presented the opposition of purity and impurity as two static categories. However, this opposition is far from a static one. The state of purity must constantly be replenished with a new supply of energy lest it becomes impure. During premodern Japan, village life was doomed to stagnate if the villagers did not periodically perform the ritual in order to harness the positive power of the deities. The ritual not only enhanced the purity of "the inside," it also controlled "the outside"; it secured the pure and positive power of the outside, which, without the ritual, could turn negative. We see the contemporary versions of the rituals of premodern Japan in hygienic practices. The body, the house, and everything else in "the inside" must be cleansed repeatedly in order to keep them clean and pure. The frequency of these hygienic practices is testimony that the act of cleansing only temporarily cleanses the body and other objects.

Modernization and the conceptual structure

This chapter has dealt with various aspects of Japanese culture. The reason for this apparent meandering is to show that a shortcut approach to contemporary hygienic concepts, which seeks explanations only in terms of a biomedically defined concept of hygiene, cannot provide a full explanation of contemporary notions of hygiene among urban Japanese. Just as social discrimination against the *burakumin* was not erased by rapid industrialization and the introduction of democracy into the law, the introduction and intensive dissemination of biomedical knowledge has not resulted either in the eradication of prejudice against the *burakumin* as impure or in the replacement of "Japanese germs" with biomedically defined microbes. The concepts of cultural germs and the impurity of *burakumin* are part of a structure of meaning that has displayed remarkable tenacity through time.

That concepts of cleanliness and dirt derive from the conceptual structure of a culture is commonly acknowledged. However, most descriptions of this phenomenon have drawn examples from traditional or so-called underdeveloped cultures, with the underlying assumption that these concepts will be replaced in time by "scientific" germ theory. A closely related assumption is that culturally constituted categories of thought become weakened during modernization. Douglas, following Kant, suggests that the distinction between primitive and "scientific" culture is that the former is characterized by a closely integrated world view in which order prevails, whereas the latter is free from the "provisional and artificial character of the categories of thought" (Douglas 1975:57).

Although the concept of "modernization" is still ambiguous in the social sciences, the Japanese case described here challenges the assumption that modernization undermines the symbolic realm of the people; either the anthropological distinction between primitive and modern cultures is incorrect, or Japanese culture is "primitive." My own interpretation is that the notion of the "primitive" vis-à-vis the "modern" in anthropology is based on a comparison between nonmodern Third World cultures and the cultures of Western intellectuals – note Douglas's reference to Kant. Modernization, as viewed by social scientists, is to a large extent "Westernization." Westernization, in turn, is equated with "scientific" and "intellectual" developments in the West. On the one hand, these false assumptions call for a systematic study of the structure of meaning and thought through time, especially in non-Western cultures, and on the other hand, they call for a systematic study of the cultures of ordinary people in contemporary Western societies. My hunch is that in the backyards of Western cultures cultural germs lurk abundantly, although they may have different forms of expression.

3 My very own illness: Illness in a dualistic world view

The concept of *jibyō*

With their persistent emphasis on hygiene, one might expect that the Japanese would perceive themselves as clean and healthy; after all, they try so hard to avoid contamination with cultural germs. But the opposite is actually true: Many Japanese regard themselves as somewhat less than healthy, if not sickly. Conversations and greetings frequently relate to the topic of illness, either of the participants or of mutual acquaintances. During the heyday of culture-and-personality and national character studies, an American anthropologist described this tendency as "hypochondria."

Caudill, an American scholar most sympathetic to Japanese culture, once described his reaction to this pattern (1976a:162):

As my first year [1954] in Japan progressed, I found myself increasingly bewildered and irritated by the number of times research assistants or friends would not carry out work or would miss engagements because they were "suffering from being sick." Subsequently, over the following 17 years, I have come to accept this sensitivity about the body and its minor ailments as part of ordinary Japanese character structure.

Today, one of the most popular borrowed English terms is *daun*, or "down," which means to be sick, usually in bed. A greeting between two acquaintances will frequently go as follows:

A: *Ohisashiburi desu ne* (I haven't seen you for a while).
B: *Gobusata shimashita* (I am sorry for not getting in touch with you for so long). *Jitsuwa chotto daun shitemashite ne* (Well, I have been *daun* for a while).

These conversations are one of the best grassroots channels for the dissemination of information about good doctors, hospitals, medicine, and treatments. Needless to say, the readiness and openness with which the Japanese talk about their illnesses makes fieldwork such as mine quite rewarding.

The frequent description of one's health is characteristic of people of every age, sex, and socioeconomic background. Propensity to sickness in no way mars a "macho" image or an image of dignity or high social standing. A stiff upper lip is not required of Japanese men in this regard. For example, when the director of a prestigious research institute, known for his decisive administrative ability and in many ways the epitome of the successful Japanese male, became ill, his secretary told others that he was "down," describing his illness in detail. The news, including the symptoms, would then spread quickly throughout the institute, where many seemed to know a great deal about his past illness episodes – what he had suffered from and what types of medical care he had sought. As Caudill states (1976a:162), "Indeed, people are often rather proud of having a somewhat weakly body...." In fact, the Japanese term *mushinkei* (no nerves or sensitivity) is applied to a person whose body and mind are not sensitive, and has the connotation of being nonintellectual.

Overshadowed by the image of the "workaholic" Japanese, who labor incessantly for the company and for the nation, this side of the Japanese character is hardly known to any but Japanese scholars. Among Japanese industrial workers, only 23% of the men and 20% of the women take paid vacations; others work during vacation without pay (Lock 1980a). Yet these same workers readily take advantage of their sick leave. Furthermore, neither workers nor companies find the typical hospitalization period, which is the longest in the world (see Chapter 9), unreasonable. Rohlen (1974:74) reports that in a bank where he carried out his fieldwork, for the first six months of illness an employee's salary and bonus, which usually amounts to several months' salary and is paid at the end of the year, continue to be paid. After six months, he or she will be placed on leave of absence, which may last as long as one and a half years, and then gradually the salary and bonuses are terminated.

Needless to say, this type of discourse and behavior among adults has seeds in early childrearing. One commonly observes a Japanese mother, opening a diaper, saying to her baby: *Ii unchi ga takusan dete yokkata nē. Kimochi ga sutto shitadeshō* (It's nice that you had a good big b.m. You must feel good). Or, if grandmother or someone else is around, she may be reporting to her. Thus, although Japanese mothers are much less verbal than American mothers in their interaction with their children (Caudill 1976a:165-8), they use indirect modes of verbal communication. That is, instead of telling her baby "I love you" or "You are gorgeous," a mother uses a statement about her infant's bowel movement as a way of expressing her feelings toward him or her.

In 1980 I rode on a city bus with a number of mothers who had just picked up their kindergartners; in Japan mothers, and sometimes other adults, go to the kindergarten at the end of the school day to take their children home, usually on a bus or a bicycle if their homes are not within walking distance. The mother next to me took the sweater off her daughter and pulled a clean towel from a plastic bag, with which she wiped her daughter's back. She muttered that it was unexpectedly warm and therefore her daughter was perspiring. Many Japanese believe that perspiration left on the skin or clothing will have a chilling effect on the body. She then "consulted" with her daughter whether the daughter should take a bath that night or merely wash her feet, since she was *kazegimi*, a term frequently used to describe a state of having a touch of a cold. This type of mother-child interaction is quite common, and children continue to report the condition of their body and bodily functions to their mothers as they grow up.

Jibyō (my illness)

The concept of *jibyō* clearly reflects this aspect of Japanese attitudes toward health and illness. Written in two characters, the first one meaning "carrying" and the second one "illness," *jibyō* means an illness that a person carries throughout life, and suffers at some times more acutely than at others. People very often attribute their "down" condition to an attack by *jibyō*.

In a survey of housewives in the Keihanshin area (the area that includes Kyoto, Osaka, Kobe, and the surrounding areas), 88.1% of the women questioned described themselves as suffering from some type of illness, and 78.7% said they were suffering from *jibyō*. The types of *jibyō* that afflicted these respondents were shoulder stiffness (*katakori*) (31.8%), constipation (18.0%), low blood pressure (17.7%), headaches (16.6%), hip pain (14.3%), menstrual cramps (12.9%), athlete's foot (11.8%), dizziness (10.7%), hemorrhoids (8.8%), and allergies (8.8%) (*Misumi* No. 149 [March 1979]:4). Individuals often have more than one *jibyō* simultaneously or at different times.

The most common types of *jibyō* reported by my own informants were *ryū-machi* (rheumatism), *ijaku* (weak stomach [ventriculus]), *ikasui* (lowered stomach), *ikeiren* (gastralgia), *isankata* (acid dyspepsia), high blood pressure, and low blood pressure (with less frequency than high blood pressure and predominantly among women). For many of these individual labels for *jibyō*, the character *shō* is used. *Shō* denotes a symptom or a prodrome; the latter means a prior and diagnostically distinct condition or a derivative illness. It contrasts with *byō*, which denotes an actual illness. These two characters form the endings of many labels for illnesses and other conditions of ill health. As in the case of the lowered stomach, which will be explained shortly, some of these illnesses are not biomedically definable. Some *jibyō* do not even fit the culturally defined repertoire of Japanese illnesses. For example, one *jibyō* was characterized primarily by dizziness that a woman scholar in her mid-thirties experienced every year at the beginning of spring. She did not feel alert at this time, and her productivity went down. After many unsuccessful visits to a large biomedical hospital she consulted her family doctor, who told her that she had had the same trouble as a child. She now views the discomfort, which she calls *jibyō*, as a given, and settles for *amma* (massage) during this period of the year.

Common to all these *jibyō* is the fact that they are chronic and incurable. They may occur at regular intervals, often between seasons. As noted earlier, the Japanese consider people to be more susceptible to illness during the transitional periods between seasons, especially the transition from winter to spring. Older or sick people and those with *jibyō* pay extra attention to their health during this time.

Taishitsu (inborn constitution)

The concept of *jibyō* is closely linked with the Japanese notion of *taishitsu* – the nature of the constitution with which one is born. In fact, there is some interchangeability between *jibyō* and *taishitsu*, and the same symptom, for example high blood pressure, may be referred to as *jibyō* or as *taishitsu*, depending on its degree. The most commonly recognized basic *taishitsu* are *jōbu* (healthy), *futsū* (ordinary), *kyojaku* (weak and nonenergetic), *senbyōshitsu* (weak and constitutionally susceptible to TB), *horyūshitsu* (weak), and *shinkeishitsu* (extrasensitive). Fine distinctions are thus made between different types of constitutions.

Kyojaku is a weak constitution in general, but *senbyōshitsu* is a particular kind of weak constitution among infants, characterized by physical features that are considered to indicate susceptibility to tuberculosis. In a standard dictionary (K. Kindaichi, ed. 1953:478), such features as a flat chest and anemia are listed as "the features susceptible to tuberculosis," and people's perceptions are similar in that a person who is *senbyōshitsu* is thought to be thin and pale – two features they envision in a person suffering from tuberculosis. In a home manual for health care written by doctors, *senbyōshitsu* is also connected with tuberculosis, with frequent swelling of the lymphatic glands singled out as the link to tuberculosis (Ikeda Shoten Katei Igaku Henshūbu 1977:339) (see also excess lymph in the system being used to explain sluggish thought and action in the United States [Barnhart 1961:727]). Now that tuberculosis, once the prime killer in Japan, is insignificant, people do not necessarily link *senbyōshitsu* with the disease, but the term is still applied to individuals, usually children, who look thin, pale, and weak.

Shinkeishitsu applies to a person who is ultrasensitive and who reacts strongly to minor external stimuli, such as heat, chill, dirt, events, or interpersonal experiences. This concept has been introduced to the English-speaking world as a form of neurosis for which the Morita therapy, an indigenous Japanese treatment method, is used (for details, see Chapter 4). Japanese use the term loosely, however, and apply it to anyone who reacts easily to external stimuli. For example, a person who sleeps lightly, a child who runs a temperature after an exciting outing to an amusement park, or a person who is particularly concerned with dirt (more than usual, using the Japanese standard!) are all often considered *shinkeishitsu*. The term has no negative connotations, as noted earlier. *Horyūshitsu* is not as commonly used as other labels, but it refers to a person who is fragile and thin, who looks like a willow (the characters for *horyū* mean a willow).

Although these terms refer to the basic constitution of the entire body, many other *taishitsu* refer to somatic characteristics of a particular body part. The most common of these is *hieshō* (chilling disposition), characterized by a lowered body temperature, or a feeling of chill at certain parts of the body, often the hip, hands, legs, and feet (Ariyoshi 1978:789; Ikeda Shoten Igaku Henshūbu 1977:157-8). It is said that half of Japanese women suffer from this "illness" (Ikeda Shoten Katei Igaku Henshūbu 1977:157), which frequently affects those in their late teens and those undergoing menopause. Most Japanese, both men and women, consider *hieshō* an affliction only of women. Although men may show the same symptoms – chills in their extremities – they do not use the term *hieshō;* instead, they use descriptive expressions ("My legs and feet get cold easily"). Other common types of *taishitsu* include *hirōshō* (tendency to get tired easily), *arerugīshō* (allergic constitution), *asekakishō* (tendency toward excessive perspiration), and *noboseshō* (proneness to feeling hot in the head and feet and cold in the face). Several other *taishitsu* are recognized by Japanese medical doctors but not as commonly by ordinary people (see Ikeda Shoten Igaku Henshūbu 1977:337-9).

There are also fads and newcomers to *taishitsu*. For example, two *taishitsu* that have gained popularity recently are the acid and alkaline constitutions, the former of which is more prone to illnesses of the digestive system. These constitutions are somewhat different from the traditional *taishitsu* in that they are more easily acquired as well as changed. Thus, if one eats "acid food" (primarily meat, poultry, fish, and dairy food) one's *taishitsu* will be acid, but the intake of alkaline food (fruits and vegetables) will correct this condition. The most healthy and desirable constitution is slightly alkaline, rather than neutral (details in Chapter 4). Another type of *taishitsu* mentioned frequently today is based on blood types (not, of course, the serological types used in biomedicine): various blood types are defined by a set of somatic and temperamental constitutional features. But although particular *taishitsu* may come and go, they are all based on the same philosophy – that a person is born with certain physical and temperamental characteristics.

Most Japanese are amazingly aware of their own *taishitsu*, and are very open about them. One person may be *futsū* (ordinary) in the basic *taishitsu*, but suffer from both *hieshō* (chilling disposition) and *hirōshō* (tendency to get tired easily). Parents are quite concerned with the *taishitsu* of their children, and use the concept to interpret the children's illnesses or behavior. Thus, parents would not feel too concerned to see their daughter run a temperature after a school trip, if they understood that the girl had *kyojaku* (a weak constitution), or was *shinkeishitsu* (ultrasensitive). Most importantly, the Japanese must understand their *taishitsu* because health is a somewhat ephemeral condition that represents a delicate balance between the *taishitsu* and external stimuli; the weaknesses of the *taishitsu* must be offset with appropriate food and behavior.

As this discussion of *jibyō* and *taishitsu* has indicated, some of these illnesses are culture-specific, in that their identification and definition are specific to Japanese culture, and do not necessarily reflect epidemiological patterns. For example, attention to hypothermia in the United States has recently increased because of lowered house temperatures since energy prices have gone up. However, it does not receive as much attention as *hieshō* (chilling disposition) has in Japan. In other words, the same symptoms may exist in two cultures, but one culture may give them far more significance than the other. *Ikasui* (lowered stomach) is another example. It is characterized by a heavy feeling in the stomach, especially after a meal, although it can also be accompanied by constipation, headaches, and insomnia. *Ikasui* is said to occur most frequently in people who are thin. However, a recent concern has been that riding motorcycles, trucks, and cars right after eating is also conducive to this condition (this widely circulated opinion is also mentioned in a home manual for medicine; see Ikeda Shoten Igaku Henshūbu 1977:228). The defining characteristic is the actual lowering of the stomach, which doctors identify by taking X rays of patients' stomachs. Home medical manuals show either an X ray or a line drawing contrasting the lowered and normal positions of the stomach (Ariyoshi 1978:429; Ikeda Shoten Igaku Henshūbu 1977:228). Doctors and home manuals alike stress that this is not an illness, and prescribe only proper eating and behavior. My informants also realized that this was not an actual illness, yet they all treated it as such – for example, by listing it as a *jibyō*. Other examples of culture-specific illnesses include *katakori* (shoulder stiffness), and *gojūgata* (the fifty-year-old's shoulder), characterized by pain in the shoulder usually in a person between forty and seventy (Ariyoshi 1978:598; Ikeda Shoten Igaku Henshūbu 1977:414).

The body and its parts

In order to understand Japanese concepts of illness, a brief discussion of the concept of the body and its parts is necessary. A prominent feature of Japanese illness description is that people often simply point to a particular body part. When someone says, "It is the stomach," it means the person is suffering from some sort of stomach disorder. When someone says *Mune o yararemashite nē*

(My chest got attacked), it means the person is suffering from tuberculosis. Some anatomical terms are not exact equivalents of those in American English. For example, the Japanese term *ashi* refers to both the foot and leg.

In terms of the meanings given to the various body parts, the Japanese division of the body into upper and lower halves at the waist is important. The upper half is cleaner and more important; the lower half is dirtier. Thus, one should pass by the feet of a sleeping person, rather than by the head. This distinction is carefully maintained even in laundry – clothing for the upper half is never mixed with clothing for the lower half. This regulation is even more important in laundry than sorting by color. Here we see another reflection of the symbolic opposition of purity : impurity : : above : below discussed in Chapter 2.

In terms of illness, the greatest attention by far is given to the abdomen, including the stomach and intestines. The importance given to this part of the body, called *hara* or *ichō* in Japanese, has often been pointed out by those studying Japanese culture. Numerous illnesses of this part of the body are recognized. In terms of specialization, in 1979 12.8% of practices (private practices, clinics, and hospitals) in Kobe listed internal medicine as their primary specialization, and 2.2% specified their specialization as *ichōka* (stomach clinic), rather than more generally as internal medicine. Combined together, medical practices whose primary specialization includes the treatment of the stomach represent 15.1% of the primary specializations (for details of medical specializations, see Chapter 8).[1] Although these figures are for the city of Kobe, they should reflect the general picture throughout Japan. Medicine for stomach disorders is also the most widely used, both in variety and in volume sold.

Epidemiologically, cancer is the number-one killer in Japan for people between thirty and sixty-nine (46,000 deaths from cancer in 1977, or 21.1% of all deaths). Nationwide, stomach cancer is the most common form of cancer among both men and women, although it has shown some decrease in recent years (Kōseishō, ed. 1978:119). In the city of Kobe, for example, 1977 statistics reveal that, of all forms of cancer deaths, stomach cancer accounted for 33.7% among men and 30.5% among women. The remainder for men were lung cancer (14.9%), cancer of the liver (11.7%), cancer of the esophagus (5.5%), cancer of the pancreas (5.2%), and miscellaneous cancers (29.0%). For women, the remainder were cancer of the uterus (11.3%), lung cancer (11.0%), cancer of the liver

---

[1] These figures are based on the 1979 telephone directory for the city of Kobe. In the calculation of the percentage of doctors whose specialization is internal medicine, I excluded dentistry and ear, nose, and throat specializations, since the doctors who specialize in these areas do not add other specializations, whereas doctors whose primary specialization is other than these two often add one or more specializations to the primary specialization; as will be noted in Chapter 8, laws about specialization are very lax in Japan. If dentistry and ear, nose, and throat specialists are included in the calculation, those specialized in internal medicine constitute 9.6% and those who specify their specialization to be the stomach clinic represent 1.7%. The combined figure is 11.3%.

(5.6%), breast cancer (5.1%), and miscellaneous cancers (36.5%) (*Kobe* April 15, 1979). Thus, cancer of organs in the abdominal area constitutes a significant illness for the Japanese.

The Japanese give extra attention to the stomach and use various means to protect it. The use of the *haramaki*, a piece of material wrapped around the abdomen, has a long history and illustrates the importance of this part of the body. During the feudal period, samurai were protected by their armor, but foot soldiers protected their abdomens from attack with *haramaki*. During World War II, as part of the governmental program to heighten morale, women sewed white cotton *haramaki*, each with a thousand red knots made of red string; these cloths were said to be bullet-proof, and were supposedly sent to soldiers on the front line. Today many Japanese, especially children and the elderly, use *haramaki*, which are also used extensively by men and women in construction jobs and other manual labor. Pregnant women also protect their abdomens with a long piece of material (see Chapter 8). People often insert a portable heater to better protect the abdomen from chill.

Scholars of Japanese culture often point out the symbolic significance of the *hara*, or abdomen, in the past. The *hara* used to be considered the seat of the soul; it was the *hara* that the samurai cut open with his sword to commit suicide in defense of his honor (for further details on the traditional concept of *hara*, see Lock 1980a:86–7). In contemporary Japan, the term *hara* may be used to mean either the entire area between the thorax and the pelvis, including the flesh and the internal organs (stomach, intestines, liver), or the lower abdomen, excluding the stomach. A more recent term for the first meaning is *ichō*, written in two characters, one for the stomach (ventrilucus) and the other for the intestines, although *ichō* does not include abdominal flesh.

Many expressions in contemporary Japanese include the term *hara*, some of which are listed below:

> Personality traits or other characteristics:
> *hara guroi:* the abdomen being black (not trustworthy; crafty)
> *hara no ookii:* the abdomen being big (generous)
> *hara gitanai:* the abdomen being dirty (base, evil)
> *hara gei:* stomach performance (an extraordinary ability)
>
> Thoughts and emotions:
> *hara ga tatsu:* the abdomen stands up (get mad)
> *hara o iyasu:* to heal the abdomen (to wreak one's anger on someone)
> *hara no mushi ga osamaranu:* the worm in the abdomen is not satisfied (I am not yet satisfied; I am still angry)
> *hara o watte hanasu:* to cut open the abdomen and talk (to talk frankly without holding anything back)
> *hara o shimeru:* to tighten the abdomen (to be prepared, determined)

hara ni ichimotsu ga aru: there is a thing in the abdomen (to have an ulterior motive)

hara o sueru: to set one's abdomen in position (to be prepared for doing something)

hara o yomu: to read the abdomen (to read someone's thoughts)

hara o miseru: to show one's abdomen (to be frank with; to show one's cards)

There is an androcentric flavor, or male emphasis, in these expressions. First, *hara*, if used alone as a word, belongs to the male lexicon; women use the term *onaka*. In Japanese, certain words and grammatical forms are used exclusively by men and may not be used by women, although some of the so-called women's language may be used by men in formal or polite situations. Second, most of the expressions listed here are used by men or in reference to men. They are used by women in very informal situations or situations that call for an abandonment of culturally prescribed femininity. *Hara ga tatsu* (to get angry) is perhaps the only phrase that is used frequently by women; however, a more common female expression for the same feeling is *mune ga mushakusha suru* (my chest is vexed). The *seppuku* suicide, of course, epitomizes masculinity, and was practiced by warriors to prove their manliness (Ōkuma 1973:esp. 22–3). A woman committing suicide would instead cut into her chest from left to right or into her throat. Both verbal expressions and past modes of suicide indicate that the *hara* has been the important body part primarily for men, and that the counterpart for women may have been the chest. Nevertheless, in the formalized ideology of Japanese culture, both men and women seem to have espoused the symbolic importance of *hara*. In many cultures, the male-oriented ideology and world view constitute the formalized world view for the people as a whole; the female-oriented world view takes a subtler form, expressed through symbols in minor rituals and not consciously recognized by the people (for further details on this topic, see Ohnuki-Tierney 1981a:100–3; 129–32).

Most important, the use of *hara* in these expressions, as well as other related customs, points to the fact that the *hara* is not simply an equivalent to the heart in Western thought, but instead represents a combination of the heart and the brain. It is the seat of both thought and feeling, or intellect and affect. Thus, in the case of *hara o sueru* (to be prepared for doing something), one must be both mentally and psychologically prepared. The particular quality that encompasses both thoughts and emotions and is reflected symbolically in the anatomical part called *hara* is best expressed in the phrase *hara gei*. *Hara gei* (the stomach performance, an extraordinary ability) was first used to describe the ability of an actor to communicate the essence of drama above and beyond what words and bodily movements can ordinarily express. In contemporary Japanese, the term is frequently used to show admiration for the ability of a great person, usually a man, whose conduct reflects profound knowledge, vast experience, and great personality. The *hara* in these contemporary expressions, however, is a metaphor; no contemporary Japanese thinks of the *hara* as the seat of the soul, just as no American believes the anatomical heart to be the locus of love. Nevertheless, the content of the metaphor remains germane, just as the notion of love claims a central place in the contemporary American value system, and is expressed in the icon of the St. Valentine's heart.

The importance of *hara* in contemporary Japan may also be seen in the fact that the central event of a recent best seller, *Shiroi Kyotō* (The Giant White Tower) by Yamazaki (1978–79) is stomach cancer. The book revolves around the struggle for a professorship in a medical school, and the protagonist is a young surgeon who acquires fame for his surgical ability in cancer of the esophageal orifice of the stomach. In the end, he too dies of stomach cancer. The author chose stomach cancer as the central topic because it is convincingly dramatic to a Japanese audience, as proved by the popularity of both the book and the movie and television play based on it. We can dismiss this phenomenon simply by pointing to its high frequency of occurrence. On the other hand, stomach surgery, even for cancer, does not seem to be dramatic enough in American society to be chosen as the specialty of the protagonist-doctor in a novel; brain or heart surgery would be more likely. In the United States, newspapers and magazines regularly report on successful open heart surgery, which symbolizes the triumph, very masculine in tone, of medical science. There seems to be more to these differing emphases in the two cultures than the epidemiological pattern of the high frequency of heart attacks in the United States and the high frequency of stomach diseases in Japan. As noted earlier, the stomach in Japan is symbolically the equivalent of the brain and the heart in the United States.

Attitude toward death: Cancer and suicide

By now it is obvious that the Japanese are greatly concerned with illness and are quite open about their own illnesses. There is another side of the Japanese view of illness, however, that presents a drastic contrast to this attitude: The Japanese dread serious illnesses and do not discuss them openly. Until recently, these dreaded illnesses included tuberculosis, insanity, and leprosy; leprosy was one of the sins of impurity in the tenth-century *Norito*. These illnesses were thought to be incurable, fatal, contagious, and in the case of tuberculosis and insanity, hereditary. In arranged marriages,[2] it was customary for the parents to

---

[2] The method of arranging marriage ranges from an informal approach to a fairly formal procedure. Historically, the prototype started with the warrior class, in which marriages were often the means for alliances. Paradoxically, it diffused to other classes of people and to the rural population after modernization started. The pattern familiar to me starts with a documentary screening process during which an informal matchmaker, such as a kimono dealer, facilitates an exchange of doc-

check on the health of the prospective mate's family before betrothal, and they were particularly concerned about these "dreaded illnesses" (see Beardsley, Hall, and Ward 1969:317).

Leprosy disappeared some time ago, and the introduction of streptomycin eliminated much of the fear surrounding tuberculosis, but the Japanese continue to fear insanity. Cancer, on the other hand, is new to the scene. It is extremely feared and people do not discuss it, not because it is contagious, but because it is considered to be synonymous with the death sentence. The Japanese attitude toward tuberculosis and cancer shows striking resemblances to the attitude of Western peoples as described by Sontag (1979). In particular, the wet-dry symbolic opposition correlated with the views of tuberculosis and cancer, respectively, is also present in the Japanese attitude.

Tuberculosis

As in nineteenth-century Europe, until recently tuberculosis was a dreaded illness in Japan. Before World War II it was the leading cause of death, taking an especially heavy toll on people around twenty years of age. After World War II it declined dramatically, and in 1951 it ranked as the second most common cause of death. Cerebrovascular disease had moved to the top rank. In 1953 tuberculosis fell to fifth place, and cancer shot up to second (Kōseishō, ed. 1978:21).

Traditionally, victims of tuberculosis and members of their families often hid the fact from others (see Dore 1973:66). Its contagious nature was suspected as early as the mid-seventeenth century (Tatsukawa 1976:118–23), although until recently the fear of tuberculosis was based in part on the belief that constitutional susceptibility – and not the disease itself – was inherited. As we noted earlier, the *senbyōshitsu* constitution was considered to be susceptible to tuberculosis.

"Wetness," which is attributed to tuberculosis, is a dominant feature in the Japanese image of the illness. In fact, the purpose of airing the *futon* mattress in the sun, which some people do on every sunny day, is to kill "germs," especially those of tuberculosis. However, just as in the case of some Western peoples (Sontag 1979), there is a romantic flavor to the symbolic image of tuberculosis or its victims. As noted earlier, a weak constitution is associated with tuberculosis, but it is also associated with intellectual ability and esthetic

uments between two families. The document consists of a photo and the life history not only of the prospective mate but of all family members, including their educations and occupations. It even lists the prospective mate's hobbies. If there is a mutual interest, the two families meet. If the meeting is successful, "dating" begins with varying degrees of formality. Before a formal engagement, family backgrounds are checked, including a search for the "dreaded illnesses." In some instances, fathers travel long distances to check on the families of prospective in-laws.

quality. "Perfect health," on the other hand, is associated with a lack of sensitivity and intellect. Class differences are probably reflected in these images. The "wet" and negative image of tuberculosis appears when its victims are of a low socioeconomic class; the romantic, esthetic image is associated with sufferers from a well-to-do background, especially when they are young. The two types of association, however, are not unique to the image of tuberculosis. In most societies, people from the bottom rungs are seldom associated with intellectual-esthetic activities. Thus, the protagonists of some Japanese novels, who pursue intellectual-esthetic quests, are also tuberculosis victims. An example of the Western counterpart is the protagonist in Thomas Mann's *The Magic Mountain*, or the young artist in O'Neill's *Long Day's Journey into Night*.

Cancer

Cancer, also a dry illness in Japan, is the most dreaded disease in contemporary Japan. As noted earlier, it is the primary killer of Japanese between the ages of thirty and sixty-nine. For the total population, it is second only to cerebrovascular disease as the cause of death. In 1977, cancer caused 21.1% (145,772) of all deaths; cerebrovascular disease, 24.6% (170,029); cardiac disease occupied third place with 15% (103,564) (Kōseishō, ed. 1978:16).

Although medical science itself still has many questions about the causes of cancer, for some Japanese, the disease has definite causes. For example, a survey was recently made about knowledge of stomach cancer among 156 people in a rural village in Gifu Prefecture, which has a total population of 14,000. When questioned about the cause of stomach cancer, 22.2% pointed to the type of food (spicy food, hot food), 20.8% to the manner of food intake (especially excessive intake of food and drink), and 16.2% to drinking (wine or liquor) and smoking (cigarets). Only 14.2% pointed to the hereditary constitution (*taishitsu*), 10.1% to weakening of the body, 6.4% to medicine, and the rest to miscellaneous causes (Ogawa and Aoki 1978). So the fear of cancer in Japan seems quite straightforward, stemming from the fear of death. A further look at the fear and treatment of cancer within the wider context of Japanese culture and society provides some insights into the overall attitude toward life, illness, and death.

The major feature in the Japanese treatment of cancer is that doctors do not tell the patient the "verdict." Although there are exceptions, of course, this attitude is generally held by family members and doctors, as well as by the patients themselves. Since the subject matter is taboo to cancer patients, I have never discussed the topic with them. However, using the practice of informing patients in the United States as an example, I discussed the topic with a number of people in all walks of life, including doctors, nurses, and other health care specialists, as well as ordinary people of varying educational and socioeconomic backgrounds. When asked whether they would like to be told if they were victims, they responded almost unanimously that they would prefer not to be told. The sole exception among some 40 people questioned was a young man of twenty-four, a college graduate working in a large firm; he was an exceptionally well-read individual who thought he would be "able to handle it." Those interviewed also stated they would not consider it good practice to tell cancer patients, although some said it would depend on the patient and circumstances.

An examination of actual cases, however, reveals more complexity in attitude as well as some changes that are currently taking place. The first case illustrates the caution with which the doctor treats the patient from the very beginning. While I was observing doctor-patient interactions one day at a major university hospital in the Keihanshin area, a woman of forty-four came into the examination room of a *naika* (internal medicine) clinic, where the chief physician, a visiting American physician from the staff of a university hospital in the United States, seven medical students, and I were situated. She had a small lump on her throat that was visible but not large. It was her second visit to the doctor.

The process was started by a medical student, who reported on her general condition. His report, given in a mixture of Japanese, German, and English, included such phrases as "well-developed and well-nourished but not obese" body structure, "consciousness clear," and "vital signs." After briefly checking her eyes, the chief physician asked the woman to take off her clothes, which she did without hesitation in front of everyone. He examined the throat area externally and told her that it would take three weeks to finish the examination and diagnosis of the lump at the internal medicine clinic, but that then she would most likely be referred to the surgical clinic (*geka*) for an operation. He told her that at that time a surgeon would explain the operation. She asked whether the operation was indeed necessary, and if so, why. He explained that the operation was highly recommended because the lump might grow in size and would be unappealing in appearance. After she left the examination room, the doctor immediately proceeded to draw a flow chart in English on the blackboard, explaining the diagnostic possibilities. At this time he stressed, in Japanese but using English medical terms, that if the thyroid nodule was a nodular hypothyroid, it could be a carcinoma. Afterward, when I asked the doctor about his omission of the cancer possibility in his discussion with the patient, he confirmed that he had done so purposely. He added that only in the case of cancer of the uterus, which has a very high success rate, would some doctors tell a family member to inform the patient.

This situation contrasts drastically with my own experience in the United States. When I was examined for a lump in my throat, the first thing the doctor said was that I would have to have an operation because there was a danger of thyroid cancer. He also explained that if one has to have cancer, one should feel lucky to have thyroid cancer, since it is the most "benignly malignant" form – more people die from traffic accidents than from thyroid cancer. After the operation, the first announcement I received on awakening from the anesthetic was that it was indeed cancer, but that it had been successfully removed. When I related this incident to people in Japan, both nonprofessionals and doctors reacted with shock and embarrassment, as though I had told them something they should not have heard. Some commented that I must have been told only because the cancer was completely removed; this situation sometimes occurs in Japan, especially after surgical removal of the affected area is obvious, as in the case of breast cancer.

A second example was related to me by a young doctor at the National Center for Circulatory Diseases, also in the Keihanshin area. When he was still a medical student several years earlier, a professor in his medical school developed cancer and was hospitalized in the same university hospital where he taught. When a colleague and some students came to see the professor on their daily rounds, the colleague, in a slip of the tongue, mentioned his "cancer." The professor himself was absolutely certain that he did not have cancer and chided his colleague, saying: "Even you make such a careless mistake." Concealment of cancer even to medical colleagues is the norm, as illustrated in Yamazaki (1978–79).

A third example was told to me by a head nurse at a major university hospital, who had toured hospitals in the United States and was intrigued by the American custom of informing patients. Some three years earlier, she witnessed in the hospital where she now works a case involving a man prominent in the city where the hospital was located. He was admitted to the hospital with stomach cancer. Since he was a well-educated man who could read both German and English, the two languages most commonly used in writing patients' records, everyone made certain that his record was not left in the room for him to see. One day, however, a student nurse came to check on him and mentioned his stomach cancer. He became visibly upset, and his condition began to deteriorate rapidly. When others found out what had happened, the doctor in charge was enraged at the student. The doctor, the head of the surgery department, and the head of internal medicine all came to apologize to the patient for the conduct of the student nurse. Nevertheless, his condition kept getting worse and he died shortly thereafter. Among the doctors I interviewed, a most frequently cited reason for not informing their patients of their cancer was that the patients would give up hope and their condition would then deteriorate rapidly.

Even at the National Center for Cancer Research in Tokyo, established in 1962, and at nine other regional centers for cancer (Kōseishō, ed. 1978:27), the same attitude about disclosure of the cancer verdict prevails. A doctor at the National Center for Circulatory Diseases told me that patients believe that, whereas all other people there may be cancer patients, "I am somehow an exception." The same information was given to me by several other doctors in various clinics in Kobe. Long and Long also report this attitude at cancer centers: The patients are "expected to believe that their tumor is benign, or that the Institute surgeons were successful in removing all the cancer" (Long and Long 1980:12).

A roundtable discussion (Kurihara et al. 1979) among people who have had cancer confirms the general tendency that only when the success rate is very high are patients told of the diagnosis (one was a case of uterus cancer and the other an early discovery of stomach cancer). A woman who participated in this discussion found her breast missing when she saw herself reflected in the window when a nurse came to change her dressing the day after her operation; before the operation, her doctor had reassured her that it was not cancer.

A brief mention of two other cases, however, explains the complexity involved in the actual situations. When I was observing the doctor-patient interaction in an obstetric-gynecology clinic, a woman in her thirties came to hear the results of a test; she had myoma in the uterus. She asked the doctor whether she had cancer and also asked that her mother not be told because of her age. The doctor told her the test was negative and there was no reason to fear cancer. He added that her aunt and mother had come earlier to inquire about the diagnosis.

Another case was related to me by Kazuko Inoue, who had spent several months at the National Center for Cancer Research in Tokyo. The patient was her husband, a highly educated man who had asked her to tell him the diagnosis even if it was cancer. After he learned of the diagnosis from her, he frequently discussed his condition with his doctor. Before his death, he wrote a letter to the doctor mentioning how it helped him in his final days to know of his real condition and to be able to prepare for death. (Japanese rarely express their innermost thoughts in spoken words, but do express them in writing or through nonverbal modes of communication.) The doctor told his wife that he was indeed relieved after receiving the letter, since he was never sure that he had done the right thing.

One reason is almost always given for the current practice: Many people cite the immediate deterioration of patients who are accidentally told of the diagnosis, and claim that most humans are not strong enough to live with the notion of impending death. If a family member or friend is stricken, they would like to let the victim die in peace (*yasurakani*), without making them go through the agony of knowing their condition. Although the nondisclosure policy still prevails in Japan today, the practice has been frequently debated (*Asahi* March 2, 1979; April 19, 1979). Chiba (1981), a journalist who had a breast cancer operation, made a frontal attack on the practice in a recent publication. She explains that one of the reasons for concealment is related to the lifetime employment system in Japan; someone with cancer, if revealed, might be taken out of the normal career development path. Not only the general public, but doctors too are now debating the issue. There was a session on this problem at the annual meeting of the medical association in 1979 (*Asahi* April 19, 1979), and an increasing number of doctors are reported to agree to the idea of telling the patients "under certain circumstances" (*Asahi* August 21, 1981).

Suicide

The attitude toward cancer among the Japanese is especially intriguing because of their well-known bravery in facing other forms of death, as evidenced by the *kamikaze* pilots, who made the suicidal plunge into American battleships during the final phase of World War II. It is said that every single member of the 201st Air Group stationed in the Philippines volunteered for the *kamikaze* units (Morris 1975: 281–97).

An ideological system in Japan idealizes certain types of suicide, although actual suicides are based on many different motivations, attitudes, and circumstances, and even culturally sanctioned suicides may not be carried out with an idealized attitude on the part of the individuals involved (see Ohara and Reynolds 1970). Indeed, few other cultures sanction – and even extol – the "beauty" of voluntary death to the extent to which Japanese culture does. One can actually classify the types of suicide that are condoned and even romanticized in Japan. A few examples will suffice for illustration.

Seppuku, mentioned above, was considered the only way a *samurai* (warrior during the feudal period) could end his life in honor, under certain circumstances. It entails stabbing across his own lower abdomen, while the person closest to him beheads him in order to hasten the process of dying (for details, see Okuma 1973). *Shinjū*, written in characters that mean "the inside of the heart," is a term used for double suicide, committed primarily by lovers who could not marry because of legal or social disapproval. For example, during the feudal period, the law prohibited marriage between members of different castes. Two individuals from different castes who fell in love then chose the route of double suicide – a recurrent theme in the traditional Kabuki and Bunraku theater. Contemporary versions of these two categories of suicide also abound. The *kamikaze* units toward the end of World War II represent collective *seppuku* by contemporary warriors. During the same period, soldiers also committed *gyokusai*, which is written with characters that mean "to scatter like a crystal ball"; this was also collective suicide, committed by Japanese soldiers who killed themselves rather than endure the shame of surrendering to the enemy.

This notion of suicide is reinforced in contemporary Japan through such cultural institutions as theater, television, and novels, which present romanticized views of suicide to the Japanese public. In addition, Japanese young people frequently go on school trips to various historic sites and scenic spots, where a guide might point out to them a certain pine tree where such and such lovers committed suicide, or a volcano that is known for the lovers who have jumped into it. Although young people may not take to the idea of suicide itself, the romantic air surrounding the act is impressed upon them. The Japanese attitude toward suicide is quite alien to Americans, among whom suicide is often, but not always, considered proof that the individual was suffering from mental illness. In fact, suicide is so taboo in the United States that when the cause of death is not included in an obituary, people suspect suicide.

Discussion

So far, we have seen three conflicting attitudes among the Japanese toward illness and death: first, "my own illnesses," represented by elaboration of minor illnesses; second, an extreme fear of serious illness and an avoidance of accepting death, including even an obvious cancer verdict; and third, a cultural sanction of suicide, which is elevated to the level of an esthetic experience.

The careful concealment of the cancer verdict in Japan involves several factors. Despite the modernization and Westernization of contemporary Japanese society, the decision-making pattern is quite different from that, for example, in the United States. Decisions in Japan are often made collectively; sometimes even family members and close friends make major decisions for individual adults. This pattern results from the notion of "personhood" or "self" in Japanese society, which is basically different from that of "the individual" in some Western societies, even though in the recent past the notion has been changing somewhat under the impact of Western ideas. The individual in some Western societies, such as the United States, is an autonomous, elementary person, whereas in Japanese society a person is structurally defined in relation to others (for an incisive discussion on this topic, see Dumont 1970:8–11). In Japanese society, then, a diagnosis can be given to the family, which then takes the responsibility for the patient. The role of doctors in Japan is much greater than it is in the United States. At least ideally, doctors take full responsibility on behalf of ailing individuals and are expected to make decisions for patients, including decisions about their psychological well-being, without formally consulting them. Legal aspects of health care, such as malpractice suits, are also factors in this difference; American doctors are required to tell a patient the diagnosis.

A social dimension is also an important factor in the Japanese nurturing of *jibyō*, minor chronic illnesses. The Japanese use these illnesses as a means of nonverbal communication, as we will see in subsequent chapters, and illness episodes thus function to test and strengthen human relationships. For the sake of organization, I will relegate these important social dimensions of Japanese attitudes toward *jibyō* and cancer to later chapters; here I will address only their ideological dimensions.

At the risk of oversimplification, I speculate that the explanation for the conflicting attitudes toward illness and death lies in the basic orientation of the Japanese toward the present life, rather than the life after death, and the fact that the present life is seen as a dualistic one in constant flux between health and illness, and between good and evil.

Official Buddhist doctrines stress such concepts as *karma* and reincarnation. Because these phrases are used in daily Japanese discourse, we have often interpreted their use to mean that Japanese hold a cyclical notion of the universe, involving successive lives, each life predestined by behavior during the *zense* (previous life), and the behavior of this life influencing the person's lot in the next. Some people even use the term *zense no innen* (*karma* from a previous life) as a way to account for illness and other misfortune. However, scholars specializing in contemporary Japanese belief systems repeatedly stress the vagueness with which the Japanese think of such concepts as the previous world, life after death, heaven, and hell. Dore (1973:363) studied this aspect of the contemporary Japanese world view intensively during his 1951 fieldwork in a ward in Tokyo, and concluded: "...fatalistic determinism emphasizing the necessity of resigned acceptance of one's lot...would appear not to be very marked among the people of Shitayama-cho today." Dore also comments on the fact that the new religious sects which appeared in Japan after World War II "promise happiness in this life, relief from illness and from suffering" (Dore 1973:356). Smith (1974:51) likewise observes:

It is difficult to find much evidence that the Japanese think of their ancestors as ever being in hell – or in paradise either, for that matter. Perhaps it is that they simply have never been deeply concerned about the worlds beyond this one, and that *only this world and the society in which they live are "really real to them."* (Kitagawa 1965:330; italics mine)

Dore (1973:363) believes that the Buddhist notion of fatalistic determinism was evident in popular literature during the Tokugawa period (1603–1868), whereas Smith (1974) contends that the notion has never taken root in the minds of the Japanese. Referring to the Buddhist notions of *karma* and the cycle of re-birth, Smith (1974:54) emphasizes: "I am firmly convinced that the Japanese never fully assimilated these central concepts of Buddhism." On this point, Miyata's (1975:1954–5) distinction is useful. He holds that *shūmatsukan* (belief that the end of the world is here) characterized Buddhism as interpreted by aristocrats toward the end of the Heian period (A.D. 794–1185). However, this was not a part of the belief of most people at that time. Ordinary people focused on explanations for natural disasters, such as floods, earthquakes, and tidal waves.

The search for such explanations gave birth to many folktales about "speaking fish," which either warned about the catastrophes, explained them, or at times even brought a utopia after the destruction of the present world. The basic tone of the explanations found in these folktales is much different from the *shūmatsukan* of the aristrocrats (for details, see Miyata 1975:156–68; see also "the catfish tale" in Ohnuki-Tierney 1981b; and Ouwehand 1964).

In regard to contemporary Japanese, Minami, a social psychologist, points to the pragmatism (*gōrishugi*) of the Japanese (*Minami* 1961:142–55), and at the same time to their fatalistic thinking, which he labels *higōrishugi* (nonpragmatic or nonrational attitude) (115–42). Fatalism, however, is always highly pragmatic. As Plath (1966) argues, fatalism in general is not a belief in predestination or in the inability of humans to control their lives; rather, it is a way to explain and allocate responsibility for what happens in everyday life. In other words, *karma* and other similar notions may explain some misfortunes, such as illness and untimely death, but they do not reflect a belief in any sort of fatalistic determinism.

It follows, then, that the Japanese are pragmatically fatalistic in turning away from serious illnesses which are beyond their control. These illnesses are eliminated from their universe, which admits only ordinary illnesses. After admitting ordinary illnesses, the Japanese aggressively manipulate their lots in life. This attitude explains the overwhelming prevalence of what I call "urban magic" in contemporary Japanese cities. As we will see in Chapters 6 and 7, Japanese of all walks of life, and with all types of socioeconomic and educational backgrounds, use charms, amulets, geomancy, and other forms of magic. A major feature of magic, in contrast to religion, is its manipulative aspect: A person using magic "negotiates" the outcome of the event. It is an aggressive act for an individual to tamper with reality, rather than to wait for fate to decide the results. This aggressive attitude of magic contrasts with the passivity of religion, in which humans humbly ask for a deity to protect the general welfare.

In this context, the meaning the Japanese assign to suicide also makes sense. Culturally sanctioned modes of suicide constitute an act in which the individual is in control of his or her own life, rather than letting fate decide. These individuals write their own life stories to the very end. At the most abstract level of analysis, these suicides constitute a process whereby a natural death is transformed into a cultural institution – a triumph of culture over nature.

The Japanese attitude toward cancer is directly related to the philosophy of control over life. In contrast to suicide, death from cancer denies the individual an active role; the central role is taken by fate, with little chance for the victim to negotiate. Patients are unable to write their own stories, and instead must wait passively until fate determines life's end, beyond which there are few expectations. Most Japanese would prefer to live in an illusion rather than face such a death. A similar attitude is taken toward uncontrollable serious illnesses; the Japanese expel them from their lives as taboo, rather than dealing with them.

In cancer death we see a condensed expression of the Japanese fears surrounding all forms of natural death. Although fears of death are shared by all peoples, it is the "freshly dead" that the Japanese have regarded as the greatest source of pollution and even sin since ancient times. "The freshly dead" hover at the margin of culture and nature, the point at which the latter threatens the former. "The freshly dead" are therefore cultural germs in a concentrated form: They are at the borderline between nature and culture, between the world of the ancestors and the world of the living, just as cultural germs are found at the marginal space that marks the borderline between culture and nature. Japanese culture is rich in its elaboration of this liminal period of death; there are several stages through which the freshly dead become the truly dead, as an excellent study of contemporary ancestor worship in Japan by Smith (1974) demonstrates.

Once the dead become truly dead, Japanese culture reintroduces them into the cultural universe. Although giving little thought to how they "live" after death, the Japanese collectively transform all the dead, infants and patriarchs alike, into ancestors and then reintroduce them through an elaborate process. They enshrine them in the family ancestral altar and make offerings of food, tea, and water every day (Smith 1974). Furthermore, once a year they perform a series of rituals called *bon*. Now held usually on August 13 to 15, *bon* is the time when the living arrange the return of the ancestral spirits to their homes. Almost all Buddhist rituals deal with the dead, especially the "freshly dead," and therefore are solemn in tone; *bon*, however, is an exception in its festive atmosphere.

The beginning of the *bon* festival is marked in some regions of Japan by the star festival (*tanabata*), in which people dress in *yukata* (summer kimono) and decorate bamboo branches with pieces of colored paper on which poems are written. *Tanabata* celebrates the annual romantic encounter of a male and a female star across the Milky Way. The *bon* festival itself includes such activities as cleaning graves, pouring water over them, and clearing the pathway for use by the ancestors. Other features of the festival include special care of and offerings at ancestral altars and the kindling of a welcoming fire at the entrance to the house to guide and welcome the spirits home. There is also dancing held on a communal basis, and both men and women, young and old, participate in a joyous folk dance. As a corollary to the disappearance in recent years of tightly knit communities and the sense of membership in one's community, the *bon* dance, once the major feature of the festival, is on the decline (Smith 1974:100–1). (For details of *bon*, see Yanagita, ed. 1951:529–31; Smith 1974:99–104).

By accommodating the ancestors in their daily lives and welcoming them back during *bon*, the Japanese symbolically create a dualistic universe that includes death, illness, and pollution; these negative elements in the universe are symbolically acknowledged as an ever-present part of daily existence. Such a universe exhibits a constant dialectic tension beween good and evil, in contrast to a universe of pure good from which evil is expunged and annihilated.

In the domain of illness, the acknowledgment of constantly present illnesses (*jibyō*) and inborn weaknesses of constitution (*taishitsu*) stems, I think, from the basically dualistic world view of the Japanese. Health to the Japanese is an ephemeral phenomenon, temporarily achieved in a constant struggle to keep the balance between, on the one hand, chronic illnesses and the inborn constitution, and on the other hand, the numerous methods of healing. In short, the philosophical basis of both *jibyō* and *taishitsu* is this dualism, which has long characterized Japanese culture.

Besides these illness-related concepts, there are many other concrete contemporary expressions of this dualism. Many of these practices derive from geomancy and other associated beliefs, primarily Taoistic tenets originally introduced from China (Durkheim and Mauss 1963 and Freedman 1969 provide an excellent symbolic analysis of these Chinese belief systems). Although the original Chinese principle was the classical yin and yang symbolic opposition, in contemporary Japan this principle expresses itself most conspicuously as the opposition between good and evil, each existing in varying degrees. It works as a classificatory principle governing important domains of contemporary Japanese culture, such as time and space. *Yakudoshi* (calamitous years) are certain designated years in one's life that are considered to be imbued with potential dangers. For men, *yakudoshi* years are 25, 42, and 61; for women, they are 19, 33, and 37. The years 42 for men and 33 for women are considered *dai-yaku* (the greatest calamity) (Yanagita, ed. 1951:629-30). As Norbeck's (1955) detailed description of *yakudoshi* and associated practices and beliefs reports, the Japanese take various precautionary measures to minimize and circumvent the dangers lurking in these years.

Another example comes from the notion of *hinoe-uma*, the year when the signs of the fire and the horse are in conjunction, which marks the beginning of a cycle of the old lunar-solar calendar. This conjunction occurs every sixty years, and girls born in such a year are believed to be harsh in temperament and to invite misfortune. Thus, if at all possible, the Japanese avoid registering female births during this year by falsifying birth dates, by restricting female births by abortion, and by other means. The most recent *hinoe-uma* year was 1966, when the crude birth rate showed only 13.7 live births per 1,000 population, as compared to 18.6 in 1965 and 19.4 in 1967 (Azumi 1968; Caudill 1976a:159–60; 1976b:22–3). In 1906, the beginning of the previous cycle, female births numbered 668,140, as opposed to 716,822 in 1905 and 798,682 in 1907. Female births dropped by 6.79% from 1905 to 1906, and increased by 19.54% between

1906 and 1907. Comparison of female births in December and January of these three years indicates the effort to juggle the birth dates: 71,511 (December 1905); 66,730 (January 1906); 55,182 (December 1906); 94,763 (January 1907) (Takenaka 1977:187).

Similarly, the year of the dragon used to be considered prone to calamities (Miyata 1975:168–73). Although this belief is no longer strong in contemporary Japan, various days of the month are still regarded as either inauspicious (dai-kichi) or very lucky (dai-an), and are so designated on calendars. Many contemporary Japanese continue to avoid the former days for any event of significance, and instead schedule it on the latter. In a nationwide survey conducted in 1966 of 2,087 Japanese from various age groups, occupational backgrounds, and religious affiliations, 76.1% replied that they would not perform a marriage ceremony or tatemae ceremony (a ceremony performed when the basic frame of a building is completed) on the day of butsumetsu (the day when the Buddha dies, considered very inauspicious) (Takenaka 1977:190–213).

In the spatial domain, certain directions are inauspicious, and others are auspicious. Many common contemporary practices are based on this belief: One does not sleep with one's head toward the north, or place a bathroom or trash area toward kimon (literally, "goblin gate," the inauspicious direction of the northeast). In the survey by Takenaka, 68.9% of the respondents said they observe the sleeping position taboo, and 70.4%, the taboo on the northeast.

The effort to control both omnipresent danger and fortuitous luck is also expressed in various purification rites the Japanese practice today. For example, on New Year's Day shrines are crowded with car owners who flock there to have their cars purified to get rid of the evil accumulated during the previous year, and receive omamori (amulets) to protect them from an attack of evil, such as traffic accidents (see Chapter 6).

These taboos, still commonly observed in contemporary Japan, are equivalent to chronic illnesses and the inborn constitution in the domain of illness. Individuals learn to live with weaknesses of the body, just as they live their daily lives with the knowledge of ever-present danger and evil. If a taboo represents the institutionalization of evil, then the cultural sanctioning of ill health also represents a collective effort to acknowledge illnesses through their institutionalization (see Tominaga 1977; Yamaguchi 1978b). In this context, it should be pointed out that in the Japanese Morita therapy, the indigenous so-called psychotherapy developed for the treatment of neuroses, the basic premise is that human beings are weak. Therefore, the first step for recovery according to this method is to learn to acknowledge one's weaknesses and live with them (Miura and Usa 1974; Reynolds 1976).

Having acknowledged evil and ill health, culture also provides the means to cope with them. The Japanese have numerous measures to deal with illness and weaknesses of the body. These measures are aimed not at the elimination of pathogens, as in biomedicine, but at the restoration of the balance between opposing forces in the body, as we will see in the next chapter. Similarly, in dealing with inauspicious times and places, the Japanese also act to circumvent misfortune.

Seen in this light, the Japanese hygienic practices described in Chapter 2 also appear to be related to the concept of a dualistic universe. They are the equivalent of the purification rites for cars on New Year's Day. Although the purpose of daily hygiene is to achieve cleanliness and health, the act itself is an admission of the presence of dirt in the universe and of bodily contact with it. The symbolic meaning of Japanese hygienic practices, such as taking off shoes and washing hands, is quite different from the "symbolic meaning" of "scientific steriliza-tion" – if I may juxtapose the seemingly contradictory words "symbolic" and "scientific" here. Scientific sterilization processes do not involve the humans themselves. In a biomedical hospital, a doctor puts on a sterilized gown and gloves and uses sterilized equipment. All these items are sterilized in advance by a machine in another location. Likewise, patients must change to gowns and lie on sheets, all similarly sterilized. Only in the operating room is the scrubbing of hands practiced (for a penetrating analysis of the "ritual" of scrubbing and other activities in operating rooms of American hospitals, see Katz 1981). Sci-entific sterilization is basically dissociated from humans, the self, and the body; the removal of pollution is relegated to machines, which annihilate it. A universe in which dirt is sterilized through a mechanical process is an airtight universe in which only health and good prevail, and from which dirt and evil are expelled. It is a monolithic universe.

Ideologically, a dualistic universe is inherently tolerant. However, its symbolic accommodation of evil often results in the existence of some form of scapegoat in the society. In the case of Japan, the most obvious scapegoat has been the *burakumin*, who has had to carry the stigma of impurity throughout history. The dualistic universe, with its ideological dimension as well as its social conse-quences, is not, of course, unique to Japan. In fact, many so-called primitive worlds share essentially the same characteristics; that is, the coexistence of good and evil, and the presence of scapegoats such as witches. Here we again encounter the definitional problem of modernization: Industrialized and otherwise modern-ized Japan continues to exhibit many features characteristic of primitive worlds.

The interpretation advanced in this chapter must now be related to the inter-pretations presented in Chapter 2. That is, "real" death and serious illnesses, both of which are beyond the control of the Japanese, are placed "outside" the Japanese cultural realm; they represent the negative power of the deities, West-erners, and others. The Japanese attempt to keep the inside clean at all times, and yet by so doing they admit the dual nature of the inside. That is, the self, like the other, is characterized by the dual quality. The difference between the dual nature of inside and that of outside is that the former is tamed, or culturally transformed, whereas the latter is wild, uncontrollable. In short, the flexible "dualism" presented here is basically that of yin and yang. Note that there is a dot of yin in yang and a dot of yang in yin. The importance of these small dots cannot be overstressed. The dualism of yin and yang consists not only of complementary, not antagonistic, principles, but also of each principle inherently containing the quality of the other. A dualism of this type is basically flexible and ambiguous.

I have tried to analyze some of the basic attitudes toward illness among the Japanese. In particular, I have tried to interpret the "peculiar" propensity of the Japanese toward mild illnesses. Although this characteristic has often been noted by observers of the Japanese, it has been explained only as a psychological trait and in terms of its function in interpersonal communication. A prevalent view among scholars of Japan is that Japanese culture encourages psychological dependency on others (*amae*), and that a culturally sanctioned illness episode provides a patient with an opportunity to satisfy his or her dependency need (Lock 1980a:77–9). The interpretation presented here emphasizes the world view, and in particular the symbolic structure of the Japanese. It is an alternative interpretation of contemporary Japanese practices that hitherto have been seen as merely superstitious survivals from the past or as expressions of psychological tenets.

Physiomorphism (somatization): An aspect of the
        Japanese illness etiology

The description of the *hara* (stomach) and the dualistic world view of the Japanese
might have given the impression that the Japanese concept of illness is close to
holism, as it is perceived in "holistic medicine" in the United States. However,
the Japanese concept of illness and holistic medicine in the United States are
very different in their concepts of the causes of illness. My own observations
of doctor-patient interactions, as well as the published literature, point out that
both doctors and patients in Japan pay a great deal of attention to psychobehavioral abnormalities. Patients complain of emotional states such as depression and
irritation (*iraira suru*) and personality traits such as a tendency toward introversion,
as well as excessive sweating or shortness of breath. Emphasis on these symptoms
is especially strong in *kanpō*, the Chinese-derived medicine described in Chapter
5. However, these traits receive attention only as symptoms; causal explanations
are almost never sought in the psychodynamics of the patient.

When the Japanese postulate that *ki* (mind, spirit) is responsible for illness,
they really do not mean psychogenesis. When they say *yamai wa ki kara* (illness
from one's mind), they refer to physical illnesses resulting from worries and
other psychological propensities that have negative effects on the body. When
they use the label *ki no yamai*, they refer to a mild negative psychological state,
such as a mild case of hypochondria. In both expressions, *ki* (mind or spirit)
refers to a psychological state in the simple sense of the word. It does not refer
to either "psychological problems" or "psychodynamics" as these terms are
used in the United States. Even more frequently, the Japanese seek etiological
explanations for ordinary illnesses in: (1) atmospheric factors such as chill or
wind; (2) various physiological factors, such as the inborn constitutions (*taishitsu*), *shinkei* (nerves), and "blood types"; or (3) quasi-physiological agents such
as an aborted fetus. The basic underlying etiology is imbalance created in the
body. If there is a cause in the Japanese concept of illness, it is the imbalance
created by these etiological factors.

Therefore, although Japanese emphasize psychobehavioral symptoms, I think
they pay little attention to emotions in illness causation, and consequently have

little interest in "psychotherapy" (see Bartholomew 1981). Holistic medicine in the United States, in contrast, stresses that "*all* disease is related to personality, with the way you handle your emotions" (Leonard 1976:42; italics in the original).

Physiomorphism: Nonpsychological illness etiology

I describe the nonpsychological nature of the etiology of ordinary illnesses in Japanese medical concepts as physiomorphism, a term used by Lévi-Strauss (1966:221) in reference to magic. I hesitate to use the more common *somatization* for two reasons. First, it implies that the causes should indeed be in the psychodynamics of the patient, but that the Japanese "somatize" them by finding causes in the malfunctions of the body. Since the aim of this discussion is to present the Japanese view, rather than to cast so-called medical judgment on it, I find the possible misunderstanding to be dangerous. Second, somatization implies that the etiological factors lie only in the body. Etiological factors in Japanese medical concepts include not only the body, but also other material and physiological agents in the universe.

Shinkei (nerves) as an etiological agent

A frequent etiology of illnesses with a wide range of self-perceived symptoms is *shinkei*. The term *shinkei* may be translated as "nerves," but the Japanese term refers to nerves in the physiological sense, not in the psychological sense. Therefore, in many cases the Japanese explanation of *shinkei* as the etiology of a certain ailment or illness is further elaborated by whether it is a disorder of the autonomic nervous system or of the peripheral nervous system. The imbalance of the sympathetic and parasympathetic nervous systems is also a frequently cited disorder. Today, the borrowed English terms *baransu* (from balance) and *anbaransu* (unbalance) are used both in conversation and in publications. Although in the United States some of these disorders or their symptoms would be viewed as purely physiological, affecting the nervous systems, many would be interpreted as psychosomatic symptoms. In the case of Japanese diagnosis, they are usually perceived as disorders of *shinkei;* that is, nerves in their physiological sense. As a corollary, prescribed treatments all aim at the restoration of the normal balance in the nervous system through physiological and physical treatments such as bathing, massage, acupuncture, and medicine.

Blood type as an etiological agent

The search for illness etiology in the *shinkei* has a long history; a more recent and current popular somatic explanation for health disorders is blood type. As we will see in the section on *kanpō*, the belief that the nature and various states of the blood can cause malfunctions of the body has an antecedent in *kanpō*, which recognizes a distinct category of illness labeled *chi no byōki* (illness of the blood). Its popular and contemporary versions are many, among which the classification of blood into A, B, O and AB (categories not corresponding to our serological types) is a more popularized version of *kanpō* diagnosis. Popular newsletters from drugstores, paperback books on health, and health magazines are full of discussions of these various blood types, and tell readers how to determine their own types: The criteria are inborn constitutions, personality types, behavioral characteristics, and the propensity toward certain types of illness. The purpose of being aware of one's blood type is to counterbalance by appropriate treatment some of the negative effects of the type on one's health. Much of the current popularity of these blood-type diagnosis methods is due to intense commercialization, with drugstores and pharmaceutical companies pushing certain products, such as equipment for certain physical exercises that are supposed to correct ill health. Commercialization, however, cannot operate in a vacuum; it plays upon a concept that has been with the Japanese for a long time.

A similar type of classification is based on acidity and alkalinity. This classificatory schema is all-pervasive in that it classifies not only blood, but also the inborn constitution. Furthermore, most food and drinks are also classified into these two categories, with the acid group consisting of meat, poultry, fish, butter, cheese, egg yolk, rice, bread, noodles, Japanese *sakè*, beer, and the like. The alkaline foods are vegetables, fruits, egg whites, milk, soybeans, mushrooms, wine, and so on. It should be noted that although butter and cheese are classified as acid, milk is in the category of alkaline food. Similarly, Japanese *sakè* and beer are acid, whereas wine is alkaline. Foods rich in protein and carbohydrates are found in both categories. The basis of the classification, according to its advocates, is the production of alkali by alkaline food when it is burned and dissolved in water. Although as a classificatory principle the acid-alkaline classification is based on binary opposition, it does not correlate with any of the traditional Japanese classifications of food, such as *amai* (sweet) and *karai* (salty) or hot and cold.

The basic idea behind this classification is that the human body is at its best when it is slightly alkaline, which is described in popular literature as "pH 7.3" or sometimes "pH 7.4," giving a "scientific" flavor to the scheme. An excessive intake of acid food, which has become increasingly common in recent years because of the consumption of larger amounts of meat, is said to turn the constitution and blood more acidic than desirable. An acidic constitution is described as susceptible to "adult diseases," a label used widely in Japan by both biomedical doctors and the public for a group of degenerative and other diseases afflicting primarily adults, such as cancer, diabetes, and ulcers. Therefore, according to the advocates, one should consume a great deal of alkaline food to maintain health.

Although criticisms of the acid-alkaline system are voiced by some doctors (see *Asahi* April 1, 1979), numerous endorsements by medical doctors also appear in popular literature. The system is widely accepted by Japanese of various educational and socioeconomic backgrounds. One Ph.D. in a social science, for example, was an earnest believer in this system and thought that even the sex of a fetus is determined by the acidity of the mother's body. A man, a manager of a small retail store in downtown Kobe, told me that every day he was forced to eat *umeboshi*, pickled plums that are extremely sour, because his wife insisted on neutralizing his body, which tended to be too acid due to his liking for meat. Included on a label for sesame paste, an all-time health food in Japan, is this statement: Sesame is an indispensable health food because it is an alkaloid food.

Another reflection of the current "craze" for the acid-alkaline classification is the sale of an electric container that looks like a coffeepot, but is larger. It converts regular water into alkaline water containing "calcium ions." The water is said to cure various illnesses of the digestive system. But the importance of this somewhat faddish system as a phenomenon is not whether or not it has so-called scientific efficacy or validity. Instead, it is quite significant as a cultural phenomenon, in that it provides a logical framework for the Japanese whereby illnesses are seen to have physiological-chemical causes that can be corrected by proper diet – that is, nonpsychological treatment.

Aborted fetus as an etiological agent

An altogether different example of physiomorphism comes from a sudden increase in the popularity of the age-old practice of *mizuko no kuyō*, the memorial service for an aborted fetus (*mizuko* = water child, or aborted fetus; *kuyō* = memorial service). These services are held primarily by women who have undergone recent abortions and often are suffering from what we call psychosomatic illnesses.

The service can take several forms. For example, one can purchase a tomb for the fetus. Some temples are now setting up special sections of tombs for aborted fetuses, and engage in intensive advertising to sell these tombs. The tomb consists of a stone carved in the figure of a *jizō*, a buddha in charge of children, wearing a red bib, and with flowers and a pinwheel on each side (Photo 2). On the tomb is written a *kaimyō*, a posthumous name given to a deceased person in Buddhism. Many cannot afford to buy a tomb; instead, they acquire a *kaimyō* from a priest, who will write it on a tablet. The tablet is placed in the ancestral alcove of the family, and people observe the regular memorial services as they do for other ancestors.

2. Advertisement display of tombstones for aborted fetuses with *jizō* buddha, wearing a red bib, flowers, and small pinwheels.

Another form of holding a memorial service is the use of *ema*, which the Japanese have used for a long time for various purposes. *Ema* are wooden boards with roof-shaped tops. People write prayers on them, asking, for example, for the cure of particular illnesses, or for a successful passage of the entrance examination to a university. They are then hung at a specified place in temples and shrines (see Yanagita, ed. 1951:70–1). Although *ema* have long been very popular among the Japanese, it is only in the past few years that innumerable *ema* have appeared with prayers for and apologies to aborted fetuses. They are hung most often at temples that are known for the protection of children. The vast majority of *ema* bear a prayer to the fetus, *Yasuraka ni nemutte kudasai* (please sleep peacefully). Many others, however, carry an apology: *Gomen ne* (please forgive me). Most of them are signed by *haha* (mother). Some are signed by both the mother and the father, reflecting the recent trend toward more involvement by young fathers in childbearing and rearing. In a few cases the names and addresses are written, and in even fewer cases, the names of the entire family.

These memorial services in one form or another are observed predominantly by women, although sometimes their husbands also participate. The women all have undergone abortions, usually in the recent past. Many of these women suffer from what we call psychosomatic illnesses, often of a mild nature. They attribute their sufferings to the aborted fetus, to whom they have not given proper treatment – that is, proper funeral procedures – which include the acquisition of a posthumous name. Some women who perform the memorial services do not have a particular illness. One woman in her early seventies, for example, who has been a widow for some fifteen years, believes that an aborted fetus caused the death of her adult son, although the two incidents occurred several years apart. Now, some twenty years later, she has acquired a tablet and a posthumous name for the fetus. In another case, a male novelist, in a brief but candid essay (Genji 1982), tells how his wife twice had an abortion shortly after the end of World War II, without any particular reason except that they thought two children were enough. At the time, he did not give abortion much thought. But now, after over thirty years, he and his wife feel acutely sorry for the fetuses as they see their children and grandchildren in good health. So the couple obtained a figure of *mizuko jizō* (a buddha for aborted fetuses) from a temple and pray to it every morning.

As noted earlier, the Japanese pay little attention to the details of life after death, but they do take good care of the dead, collectively called *sosen* or ancestors, including children. One of the reasons for this care of the dead is to ask for their protection of the living. Some also say that if the living do not take proper care of the dead, then the dead may harm them. In practice, however, this belief is not very strongly held (Smith 1974:123–5). As T. Yoshida (1978:114) points out, unlike what happens in many other belief systems, ancestors in Japan seldom punish their own relatives; if the souls of the dead do wrong to the living, they do so to those who are not related to them through kinship ties.

In the case of deceased children or aborted fetuses, there has traditionally been a belief that unborn fetuses and children, who never have committed sins, are easily reborn. In the past this belief formed the basis at least in part of the ease with which the Japanese practiced abortion and also of the lack of elaborate funeral treatment (Yanagita 1963:251; 1964:104). The same attitude seems to continue in the present. Since the end of World War II, Japan's birth control has been spectacularly "successful." In 1978, among all married women, including those who are infertile, 36.1% had had at least one abortion. The total number of abortions between 1950 and 1977 reported to the government by doctors was 24,196,016. The figure was at its highest in 1955, with 1,170,000 reported cases, and has been decreasing since that time, with 640,000 cases in 1977. Since these figures include only reported cases, estimates of actual cases may run two to three times higher (Fujita 1978). Sono (1980a and b), a Catholic writer, drew much attention by pointing out that the high abortion rate reveals that the Japanese attitude toward abortion is strikingly carefree in contrast to that of Christians, especially Catholics, among whom abortion has very deep religious significance. Sono (1980a:195) points out that in 1979, the number of abortions was about 100 times greater than the number of traffic deaths.

Mizuko no kuyō, the memorial service for the aborted fetus, reflects an increased incidence of what we might suspect are "psychosomatic" illnesses among Japanese women, or at least the fact that they are more aware of their problems and are trying to cope with them by observing one type or another of memorial service. But the search for an explanation of illness etiology in aborted fetuses poses an apparent contradiction to the Japanese belief system and attitude toward abortion. On the other hand, if we look at the phenomenon as another case of physiomorphism in illness causation, then it fits the pattern of logic in Japanese medical concepts. Although an aborted fetus is quasi-matter, the vital point is that it has never entered the network of human relationships. Ascribing suffering to the aborted fetus therefore avoids the involvement of interpersonal relationships in the sufferings of an individual. The cause of an illness does not lie in a person or the soul of a person who has been involved in interpersonal relationships with the sufferer. Furthermore, this explanation precludes any possibility of seeking causal explanations in the psychological state of the individual. (Further information on the aborted fetus and its interpretation as a multivocal symbol is presented in Chapters 6 and 7, respectively.)

Lack of interest in psychotherapy

As a corollary to the absence of psychological explanations for illness causation, in Japan there is little emphasis on psychotherapy. It has often been pointed out that Freudian psychoanalysis has never been widely accepted, despite the fact that the Japanese have eagerly adopted many Western technological and intellectual innovations. Western psychotherapy continues to be little appreciated, and is even viewed with suspicion (see Bartholomew 1981:198; Caudill and Doi 1963:376). Even most of the members of the Japan Psychoanalytical Association have not received training in psychoanalysis. The membership of this organization was a mere 300 in 1959, and the Japan Psychoanalytical Society, the national chapter of the International Psychoanalytical Association, had only 41 members in 1959 (Caudill and Doi 1963:397).

There are indigenous therapies, but to refer to them as "psychotherapy," as some scholars do, is quite misleading. Morita therapy, for example, focuses on the treatment of severe *shinkeishitsu*. As noted earlier, *shinkeishitsu* is characterized by greater-than-average sensitivity to the social and natural environment. It may be viewed simply as an inborn constitution, but when it is quite severe, some individuals seek therapy. The goal of Morita therapy is for the patient to achieve a state of *aru ga mama*, which means to accept reality as it is. This includes the acceptance of oneself, with all one's weaknesses. It is based on the view that no individual is perfect and that a lack of self-confidence is shared by all. Thus, one must accept oneself as *aru ga mama*, and must learn to work around one's weaknesses. In the therapy, it is therefore important to break the cycle of hypersensitive introspection. The basic philosophy of Morita therapy contrasts sharply with that of psychoanalysis, which emphasizes self-examination and introspection. To break the cycle of *shinkeishitsu*, Morita therapy immerses the patient in constructive activities involving manual labor, after a first stage of therapy that consists of complete bed rest for four to seven days (for details of Morita therapy, see Caudill and Doi 1963; Jacobson and Berenberg 1952; Miura and Usa 1974; Reynolds 1976). Therefore, even though both psychodynamic psychotherapy in the West and Morita therapy deal with individuals with psychological problems, many resulting from interpersonal relationships, Morita therapy neither examines the causes of psychological conflicts nor utilizes such therapeutic techniques as dream analysis and transference. My interpretation is closer to that of Jacobson and Berenberg (1952), who view Morita therapy as essentially different from Western psychodynamic psychotherapy, than to the interpretation of Reynolds (1976), who sees basic similarities between the two with some minor differences.

Naikan therapy, another indigenous treatment, is based on the philosophy that although every human being is fundamentally selfish, he or she usually receives many favors and love from others. The goal of this therapy is to allow an individual to find out through introspection how much he or she has received from others. It attempts to transform feelings of bitterness and mistreatment into feelings of gratitude toward others. The major emphasis of Naikan therapy is self-reflection. The patient must sit in an isolated place for seven successive days from 5:30 A.M. to 9:00 P.M., leaving this position only to go to the bathroom (Murase 1974).

Morita therapy has been practiced for some sixty years and Naikan for the past forty years. Shinryō Naika was started in the early 1960s by Dr. Ikemi, a medical doctor who was influenced by research on psychosomatic illnesses, especially in the United States. The term *shinryō* literally means psychological treatment, and *naika* means internal medicine. As Ikemi stresses in a later publication (1978:1, 43, 51–2), his treatment does not aim at primarily psychological illnesses; his practice is definitely internal medicine, and he is interested in the effect of psychological states on the body in diseases that are basically physiological in nature. He distinguishes psychosomatic illnesses from psychological illnesses in that the former are usually illnesses of a particular organ whose condition may be aggravated by psychological states, whereas the latter are characterized by effects on various organs, especially their functions. His book (1981, originally 1963) became an immediate best seller, and his practice and the University of Kyushu became very popular and well known throughout Japan.

Common to all three indigenous therapies is the absence of any emphasis on a search for psychological explanations of the disorders. These therapies focus on the acceptance of self and one's social environment. This attitude, in my opinion, is pragmatic, giving the person strength to cope with life. Although the acceptance of reality without a fight is a weakness and the sign of a "submissive personality" in many Western societies, to accept reality (*aru ga mama ni*) enables a Japanese to move forward, rather than dwelling on his or her problems. Therefore, the philosophy behind these therapies is like the fatalism discussed earlier, which provides a pragmatic solution to problems in life by assigning responsibility for the outcome of one's endeavors to a neutral party. None, in my opinion, requires the individual to conform passively to the norms and expectations of others, or of the social group. Nor do they imply that individuals who accept reality possess a weak or submissive personality.

Emphasis on physiological treatment

Physiomorphism also explains the dominant methods of treatment for most illnesses in Japan: They all aim at physical or physiological treatment. Bed rest, corrective diet, and medicine are the most frequent methods. Although jogging has become popular in recent years, physical exercise is stressed very little.

Bed rest, called *ansei* (peace and quietness), is recommended for almost all illnesses, including mild colds. The extent to which the Japanese resort to corrective diets, or *shokuji ryōhō*, is demonstrated by the vast number and popularity of publications on the subject, which fill many of the shelves in bookstores. For almost every major illness, there are several kinds of books telling how to treat the illness through diet.

Japanese consumption of medicine is very high. Medicines prescribed by doctors and sold over the counter number well over 100,000 varieties. The proportion of average Japanese income paid for medical care is 4%, which is comparable to expenditures in most industrialized societies with social welfare programs. However, the percentage paid for medicine within an individual's medical expenditures went from 25% in 1961 to 43% in 1971. During the same ten-year period, the production of medicine in Japan also jumped five times. The 1971 figure of 43% reflects in part the Japanese health insurance system, in which doctors, who are reimbursed by the government through a point system, tend to overprescribe medicine to gain points for reimbursement – a phenomenon called *yakugai* (medicine pollution) that is now receiving much criticism. Nevertheless, even taking this factor into account, the figure is very high in comparison with those of other countries, such as 12% in the United States, 12% in Sweden, and 10% in the United Kingdom. (Statistical information on the use of medicine in Japan is from Ikemi 1978:7.)

Discussion

Amid the criticism of "inhuman" biomedical theories and practices in the United States, in which disease is seen as "a biomedical thing" (Fabrega 1975:969), ordinary Americans have sought alternative types of health care. This search has become an important part of the antistructural movement active in the United States since the 1960s. Some people have looked toward so-called primitive medicine, with its shamans and witch doctors. Others have sought salvation in so-called Oriental medicine. Together with Zen, yoga, and other practices, aspects of Asian cultures have been seen as offering tranquillity and harmony to Westerners who no longer trust their own societies and cultures, including their medical systems. Unfortunately, both researchers and the public often seem to have found only their own wishful thinking in their quest, as the equation of the Asian medical system with Western holistic medicine shows.

Physiomorphism in early Chinese and Japanese medicine

Another source of misunderstanding of Japanese medicine, I suspect, originates in a misinterpretation of Chinese medicine, from which Japanese *kanpō* is derived. The causes are twofold. According to J. Needham, ancient Chinese medicine recognized both internal and external causes. However, these terms and concepts are altogether different from "internal" and "external" as used in English. The Chinese "internal" (*nei*, translated by Needham as "inner," "internal," and "inside") means "everything this-worldly, rational, practical, concrete, repeatable, verifiable, in a word, scientific." *Wai* (translated by Needham as "outer," "external," and "outside") means "everything other-worldly, everything to do with gods, spirits, sages and immortals, everything exceptional, miraculous, strange, uncanny, unearthly, extra-mundane and extra-corporeal or incorporeal" (Needham 1970:272). As an addendum to his explanation of the term *wai*, Needham (1970:272) makes an important statement: "it is deeply true to say that in classical Chinese thought there is nothing outside Nature." He therefore points out that the concept of *wai* does not include the notion of the "supernatural." Although Needham himself uses the terms "psychological disease" (1970:267) and "mental health" (1970:286), his more systematic description of classical Chinese medicine, such as the one quoted above, reveals that it did not recognize psychological *causes*. Needham's quotation from the *Huang Ti Nei Ching, Su Wên* (Candid Questions in the Inner Classic of the Yellow Sovereign) is most revealing on this point:

Pneuma (literally, wind, *fêng*) is the beginning of all diseases. If there is purity and calm in the mind, then the flesh and the interstitial tissues bar the doors and resist entry (*ching ching, tsê jou tshou pi chü*). Then though powerful winds and virulent poisons may be at work, they are quite unable to do any harm.

The quotation clearly indicates that there are no psychological causes, even though the person's state of mind can induce or prevent illness. I think much of the misunderstanding of both Chinese and Japanese notions of illness comes from a hasty superimposition of the meaning of the English terms "internal" and "external" on *nei* and *wai*.

The misunderstanding is compounded when the biomedical notions of symptoms and etiology are superimposed on the Chinese explanation. This misinterpretation is quite serious, since, as Jung, Needham, and Porkert have pointed out, the concept of causation as defined in the Western mode of thought is absent in the Chinese mode of thought. The basic principle in Chinese thinking is called "synchronicity" by Jung (1971:505–18) and "correlative thinking" by Needham (1969:279–303). Porkert (1974) explains this "system of correspondence" by "systematic inductive links" among the data; he sees Chinese inductivity as the complement to causality.

Therefore, I am not convinced that the notions of illness pathogenesis and etiology in classical Chinese medicine are similar to those in Western biomedicine. It is perhaps for this reason that the most fundamental and important difference between classical Chinese medicine and Western biomedicine is that the former focuses on the treatment of symptoms, whereas the latter's emphasis is on diagnosis – that is, the identification of illness in terms of causal agents. In the actual delivery of health care, biomedicine is sometimes accused of too much emphasis on diagnosis at the expense of actual treatment. This biomedical bias is reflected, for example, in Glick's (1977:61) statement that "the underlying cause" is "such a central consideration that most diagnoses prove to be statements about causation." He argues that "the third [cause] is always present as a critical consideration and, moreover, is of central importance to comparative studies." We cannot assume a priori the presence of causal notions in every medical system, just because it is the central issue in biomedicine.

In particular, we cannot equate the Chinese notion of "internal" agents with either psychopathology in Western psychiatry or psychological causation of illness in contemporary holistic medicine. Scholars of contemporary Chinese, both on the mainland and on Formosa, emphasize that the Chinese do not postulate psychological causes of illness (Kleinman 1980:146–78; Topley 1976). Contemporary Chinese, according to these scholars, see psychobehavioral abnormalities as symptoms of an illness whose cause lies in the body – the process Kleinman refers to as somatization. Because Japanese *kanpō* derives from Chinese medicine, the misunderstanding is carried over; thus it is often asserted that Japanese notions of illness causation, and those of *kanpō* in particular, see the emotions as causal agents. Bartholomew (1981) is critical of Lock's interpretation of Chinese medicine on this point. The information presented in this chapter also attests to the contrary.

Not only in contemporary Japan, but in every dominant school of medicine in the past, all of which were derived from Chinese medicine, nonpsychological causes have been emphasized. For example, the Goseiha School (sixteenth to nineteenth centuries) postulated intrinsic causes (emotions), extrinsic causes (climatic conditions), and nonintrinsic–nonextrinsic causes (improper behavior of the individual) in their pathogenesis. However, all these causes were seen to bring about the ultimate cause of all diseases – the stagnation of *ch'i* or "air." *Ch'i* is the most important substance in maintaining the universe as well as in maintaining the human body (Ōtsuka 1976). Thus, although emotions were said to be intrinsic "causes," they were not seen as the direct causes of illness; they only result in the stagnation of *ch'i*, the ultimate cause of illness. Treatment consisted of bathing, the use of bear gall, and moxibustion, none of which deal with psychodynamics.

The real significance of physiomorphism, however, is not so much its reflection of a cultural preference for physiological etiologies over psychological ones; instead, it is that it reflects a mode of thought. It represents the logic underlying so-called magical thought. As Lévi-Strauss (1966:221) explains, *magic* consists of "a naturalization of human actions" or "the physiomorphism of man," whereas religion consists of "a humanization of natural laws" or "the anthropomorphism of nature." The mode of thought behind a magical practice, then, is an optimistic one that believes in the capacity of humans to "intervene in natural determinism to complete or modify its course." Physiomorphism, therefore, enables the Japanese to intervene in the process of illness and cure it by means of physiological agents such as diet and medicine.

The magical logic involved in the physiomorphism of illness causation also explains the extensive and intensive use of amulets, talismans, and so on by educated urban Japanese in their everyday life. We will examine urban magic in detail in later chapters, and question a commonly held assumption that the development of science, modernization, and industrialization are incompatible with the presence of magic.

Social dimensions of physiomorphism

To look at physiomorphism only from the perspective of the ideological system, however, falls short of understanding the total picture. Physiomorphism performs a definite social function in eliminating the possibility of blaming another person for misfortune. It falls into the same pattern as the logic behind Morita therapy, which emphasizes that patients must accept their own weaknesses, and that behind Naikan therapy, which directs patients to realize their indebtedness to others, rather than the wrongdoings of others. The logic behind physiomorphism and the Japanese methods of therapy is to displace the cause of misfortune and evil in the universe from other people, especially from those closely related to the patient.

In terms of social function, physiomorphism is the opposite of witchcraft and sorcery, which sees the loci of evil in the universe in certain individuals and their behaviors. Physiomorphism also contrasts with the notion of psychological causation, since any psychological cause inevitably involves other people with whom the patient has experienced events that have contributed to psychological conflicts. Its function for the social group, however, should not overshadow its function for the individual; above all, it enables the individual to get on with his or her life. Physiomorphism is therefore the dominant mode of causal explanation for illnesses. It is consonant with the fact that the causes of more serious illnesses are usually attributed to human and nonhuman agents that are not closely related to the sick person.[1]

Physiomorphism: Metonyms as metaphors for illness causation

Rather than dismissing physiomorphism with a simple description of its presence in the past and present medical concepts of the Chinese and the Japanese, it is necessary to briefly discuss physiomorphism as a mode of thought and a symbolic process. I propose that physiomorphism involves a complex process whereby metonyms, which symbolize causes, become metaphors for the imbalance of bodily forces – the basic cause of illness in Chinese and Japanese medicine.

First, nerves, blood types, and aborted fetuses are metonyms for the causes of illness in that they are or were body parts. They are metonyms because: (1) they operate within the same context, the body; (2) as a corollary, they are a part of the whole; (3) their association with the body is characterized by contiguity; and (4) as etiological factors in illness, they operate on the principle of "cause and effect," allowing a time lag between the cause and its consequence, the occurrence of illness. Some symbolists consider the cause and effect principle as a defining characteristic of metonym (see Fernandez 1974:125; Lévi-Strauss 1966:150). Others (Leach 1976) consider it to characterize "signals," which are altogether different communication events from both metonym and metaphor.

Although nerves, blood types, and aborted fetuses are metonyms for the causes of illness and are therefore linked to the causes through syntagmatic association,

---

[1] Hori (1968:esp. 199–201) explains that the belief in *goryō*, "a belief that the spirits of persons who had died as victims of political strife haunted their living antagonists in their lifetime" (Hori 1968:199), originated at the end of the eighth century and was widely held among aristocrats but later became diffused among the common people. Yoshida's systematic study on possession among contemporary Japanese, however, indicates that in the majority of cases involving possession by human souls, the soul is not personally related to the victim (T. Yoshida 1978:esp. 14 and 114). For an exhaustive treatment of epidemics and their causes, see Miyata (1975). For a particular and somewhat representative case of an epidemic during the tenth century, see Yoneyama (1979).

their relationship to the basic notion of illness causation, the imbalance in bodily forces, is metaphoric. Thus, the association between the imbalance of bodily forces and any one of these physiomorphic factors is paradigmatic and methaphoric. The association rests upon "equivalence of function – the capacity to occupy the same frame in the chain of experience" (Fernandez 1974:126). What we see here in operation, then, is transformation and countertransformation between metaphors and metonyms – the process and mechanism that have received considerable attention from symbolists (see Fernandez 1974:125–6; Lévi-Strauss 1966:150).

Therefore we cannot simply dismiss physiomorphism as an "erroneous" conception of illness causation using the yardstick of so-called empirical science. It is deeply embedded in the cultural logic in addition to having a definite social function. It involves "the positive, persuasive and creative...features of analogical thought and action," as Tambiah (1973:229) explains in his discussion of ritual and magic as performative acts.

Part II

Medical pluralism

5   *Kanpō*: Traditional Japanese medicine of Chinese origin

Of all the medical systems used in Japan today, only *kanpō* and biomedicine exist as formal systems, in that they are institutionalized and their practitioners are professionals. In addition, most people recognize only these two as "medical systems." As the word *kanpō* (*kan* = the Han Dynasty in China, *pō* = the method) indicates, *kanpō* was introduced to Japan from China, probably by the sixth century. Since its introduction, *kanpō* has undergone extensive transformation within the Japanese sociocultural milieu. Even in its basic premises, *kanpō* in contemporary Japan differs significantly from Chinese medicine, both ancient and contemporary (Mori 1977). I will use the term *kanpō* to refer only to the system as it is practiced in contemporary Japan. The primary treatment methods in this system are plant and animal medicine, acupuncture, and moxibustion (burning small cones of dried mugwort on certain parts of the body) (see Photos 3 and 5).

Although the overall history of *kanpō* will not be described here, it is significant to note that the system was legally prohibited at two different times (for the history of *kanpō*, see Ishihara 1978; Leslie 1974; Lock 1980a; Otsuka 1976). In 1868 Japan reopened its doors to the West and began an intense effort to become one of the great world powers. In 1875 the government proclaimed that, in order to practice *kanpō*, a physician must first pass an examination in seven subjects of Western medicine. This was an attempt to suppress the practice of *kanpō* and to Westernize medical practice in Japan. Although this first proclamation was targeted at physicians, the second legal prohibition was aimed at the eradication of both moxibustion and acupuncture, and was issued by the Allied Forces in Japan shortly after the end of World War II. All such "barbaric and unhygienic" practices, including other traditional therapeutic practices such as massage and bone-setting, were prohibited. Despite these legal prohibitions, *kanpō* was never successfully suppressed. In fact, in recent years *kanpō* has made a dramatic comeback, and it is now recognized not only by the government, but also by biomedical establishments.

Perhaps the basic reason *kanpō* has not only survived oppression but has actually gained strength is that throughout its long history in Japan, the basic premises and principles of *kanpō*, as revealed by its diagnosis and treatment methods, have always been very close to the views held by most Japanese. To the Japanese public, *kanpō* does not appear as a distinct or alien system of medicine, but rather as an integral part of their own health maintenance practices. Most Japanese roughly equate *kanpō* with plant and animal medicine, without clearly differentiating between the plant and animal medicines of *kanpō* and those of folk medicine (*minkanyaku*). In the latter category, for example, is the use of lobster (*Panulirus japonicus von Siebold*) for measles. In a meticulous study of its history and diffusion, S. Yoshida (1970) proves that this idea diffused from Korea, where the lobster (*Cambaroides sinilis* Koebel) has been used for measles; the practice, therefore, is not part of *kanpō*. Moxibustion in particular is practiced regularly at home, after a specialist has determined where on the body the dried mugwort cones should be burned. In fact, it is part of the nonverbal communication during which members of a family take turns in caring for each other without verbally expressing their concerns and affection.

Theoretical foundations of *kanpō*: Comparison with biomedicine

As medical systems, *kanpō* and biomedicine differ radically in their basic premises and perspectives. Needless to say, a satisfactory treatment of the theoretical foundation of either system requires an entire monograph. At the risk of oversimplification, I will briefly compare the orthodox versions of *kanpō* and biomedicine as their respective specialists have developed and viewed them, not as individual practitioners carry them out or as ordinary people perceive and use them.

Diagnosis

With its major emphasis on diagnosis, biomedicine has been far more successful (although not as successful as hoped) in diagnosis than it has been in treatment. The identification of disease in biomedicine consists primarily of the identification of causality. Even more specifically, it is the identification of a pathogen, the direct cause of the disease, rather than of etiologies, the circumstances that led to the contraction of the pathogen. It follows, then, that treatment in biomedicine consists of the removal of the pathogen.

This approach contrasts markedly with that of *kanpō*, whose primary emphasis is on the treatment of symptoms. An important term in *kanpō* is *shōkōgun*. Although *shōkōgun* literally means a cluster (*gun*) of symptoms (*shō*) and prodromes (signs forecasting the onset of an illness, *kō*), the concept is quite different from the notion of syndromes in biomedicine. In dictionary definitions, a *syndrome* is "the pattern of symptoms in a disease"; in biomedicine, a syndrome thus defines a disease. *Shōkōgun* includes any number of symptoms, which may or may not define a particular disease. These symptoms include those consciously perceived by the patient as well as those detected by the *kanpō* doctor. The *shōkōgun* concept is clearly revealed in the first ideograph, *shō*, of the term. *Shō* means a departure from the norm but not necessarily a well-defined illness, for which the ideograph *byō* is used. A *shō* is something like the chilling illness (*hieshō*), which is not really an illness but a culturally recognized departure from the norm, or at least a departure from a desirable condition.

The concept of *shōkōgun*, then, results in a diagnosis and treatment procedure basically different from that of biomedicine. The differences are presented schematically in Table 1. Patients consulting a biomedical doctor will describe their symptoms. These self-perceived symptoms, however, are not considered symptoms by the doctor unless they are biomedically relevant. Often, then, only some of these conditions become bona fide symptoms, and their evaluation rests strictly in the hands of the doctor. In fact, the evaluation may rely less upon the doctor than upon the "objective" results of a series of tests and internal examinations, such as blood tests, X rays, and ultrasound pictures. Malfunctions and abnormalities "caught" in these tests, which sometimes are not even apparent to the patient, are considered to be "objective evidence" for the presence of a disease, and often are assigned more importance than the symptoms perceived by either the patient or the doctor.

The orthodox diagnostic procedure of a *kanpō* doctor consists of four types of diagnosis (*shin*). The first is *bōshin* (observation diagnosis), a close examination of the color and texture of the facial complexion, eyes, nose, ears, hair, lips, teeth, and all other external surfaces of the body, as well as excreta. Special emphasis is placed on the observation of the tongue. The second is the listening diagnosis (*bunshin*), which includes examination of the voice, breathing, and coughing. It also includes examination of the smell of excreta and the body odor in general. The third is the questioning diagnosis (*monshin*), in which the doctor asks the patient various questions, including the history of the illness as the patient has experienced it. The doctor also asks about bodily habits, such as the frequency and amount of excretion (including sweating), feelings of thirst, preferences for taste (sweet, salty, hot), and sleeping habits, as well as about inborn constitutions. The fourth is touching diagnosis (*sesshin*). *Sesshin* consists of two parts: reading the pulse, and touching the stomach and other parts of the body in order to determine their condition. Instead of relying on test results and internal examinations, *kanpō* doctors rely heavily on their visual, olfactory, auditory, and tactile senses. Any symptoms a *kanpō* doctor sees as indicative of a bodily

Table 1. *Diagnosis and treatment: biomedicine and kanpō*

	I Patient's presentation of symptoms	II Diagnosis — A	II Diagnosis — B	III Treatment
Biomedicine	a,b,c,d,e	a,c,e → syndrome → x,y,z (symptoms detected by the doctor)	Identification of a disease = identification of a pathogen	Treatment of the disease = removal of a pathogen
Kanpō	a,b,c,d,e	a,b,c,d,e + f,g,h,i (symptoms detected by the doctor) + age / sex / inborn constitution / natural environment →	Determination of the nature of imbalance in the patient's body	Restoration of the balance

imbalance are added to the list of symptoms described by the patient. The sum total is *shōkōgun*, the unique configuration of all the symptoms for that particular patient.

In addition to the concept of *shōkōgun*, another important diagnostic principle of *kanpō* is a set of inherent patient characteristics, mostly physiological but some psychological, that must be understood in order to prescribe the right treatment. These characteristics include sex, age, inborn constitution, and various other conditions. Most important is the distinction between the strong constitution (which tends to express *jisshō*) and the weak constitution (which tends to express *kyoshō*). (For a detailed description of *jisshō* and *kyoshō*, see Shanghai Chūi-gakuin, ed. 1978:197–202.) Often, the configuration of *shōkōgun* is different between the two types of constitutions, as will be shown by examples in the next section. Herbal mixtures good for patients with strong constitutions may even harm those with weak constitutions. Even factors of the natural environment are taken into account. For example, patients with the same *shōkōgun* and the same set of physiological characteristics will be given different treatments depending on whether they live in an arid or a humid environment. The treatment described in Chinese texts for a certain *shōkōgun* cannot be used for a Japanese patient with a similar *shōkōgun* because the climate is so different in the two countries.

The goal of *kanpō* diagnosis, then, is to determine an accurate *shōkōgun* for a patient at the time of diagnosis and also to synthesize it with his or her inherent psychophysiological characteristics and environmental factors. The diagnosis is not intended to identify a particular illness or disease. The identification of illnesses in *kanpō* takes place only at a very basic level. For example, the chilling illness is an illness of the *chi*, or blood – that is, it results from an imbalance in the circulation of the blood. Despite the extensive transformation of *kanpō* in Japan after its initial introduction, the lack of emphasis on illness identification, as well as the importance placed on *shōkōgun* and patients' physiological traits, are both important characteristics of the original Chinese medicine as described in various Chinese medical texts (such as *Shang han lun* [*Shōkanron* in Japanese] by Chang Chung-ching [Chō Shukei in Japanese pronunciation]; see Okazaki 1976:23).

In contrast to the biomedical emphasis on pathogenesis afflicting a specific organ, imbalance of the bodily system is the fundamental ''cause'' of all illnesses in *kanpō* (Nakajima 1978). Specific types of imbalances identified in *kanpō* may be translatable, at least in many cases, into etiological factors in biomedicine that encourage the invasion or development of a pathogen.

Pathogenic causality, however, is not unique to biomedicine. Although this interpretation may sound heretical, in sorcery, as it is practiced in many parts of the world, an illness is seen to be caused by a ''foreign object'' somehow projected into the body of the victim by a sorcerer. The doctor, whether a shaman or a witch doctor, then "sucks" out or somehow removes the "pathogen," just as a biomedical doctor removes a pathogen through surgery or kills it with medication.

Treatment

The basic premises of *kanpō* diagnosis determine its modes of treatment. Thus, it is a logical consequence that there are no specialized drugs for particular pathogens. Only when a specific pathogen is identified, as in biomedicine, can such drugs as antibiotics be incorporated as a logical consequence of the causal notion. Similarly, surgery has no place in *kanpō*. In surgery, pathogen-afflicted tissues are removed. Not only is the idea of an operation logically incompatible with a medical system that attributes illness to a bodily imbalance, but surgery, in fact, is seen as actually aggravating an imbalance through its radical alteration of the bodily system. Any growth, such as a fibroma, is considered to be not an illness in itself, but rather an expression of an imbalance in blood circulation. Instead of removing the growth through surgery, *kanpō* doctors would prescribe herbs to stimulate the blood circulation.

The basic treatment in *kanpō* is the regulation of daily habits, of which diet is considered the most important. In addition to the overall rule to avoid excess, there are specific dietary rules for specific health problems. The more specific treatment methods of *kanpō*, however, consist of animal and plant medicine, acupuncture, and moxibustion. Although used only infrequently, animal medicines are made from a wide variety of creatures, such as musk deer (musk), oyster (shells), chicken (egg yolk, liver), pig (fat), bee (honey), leech, horsefly, and donkey (glue made from the hide). More dramatic examples, such as rhinoceros horn, vipers, or charred monkey heads, are often displayed at so-called *kanpō* stores for advertising purposes; however, they are rarely used.

The majority of *kanpō* medicines are made from dried herbs. A *kanpō* doctor will prescribe a mixture consisting of a great number of herbs selected to treat all the patient's symptoms. There are a considerable number of standardized mixtures. For example, the widely used decoction called *kakkontō* usually is made from the following formula: *kakkon* (*Radix Peurariae*) 8 gm; *maō* (*Herba Ephedrae*) 4 mg; *shōkyō* (*Rhizoma Zingiberis*) 4 gm; *taisō* (*Fructus Zizyphi jujubae*) 4 mg; *keishi* (*Cortex Cinnamoni*) 3 mg; *shakuyaku* (*Radix Paeoniae*) 3 mg; *kanzō* (*Radix Glycyrrhizae*) 2 gm; *kankyō* (ginger) 1 gm. This mixture is brewed in 500 cc of water until it decreases in volume by half (Ishihara 1962:433; see also Okazaki 1976:23). The decoction is then strained, divided into three, and taken three times a day, an hour before each meal. This formula is recommended when a patient demonstrates any number or combination of the following symptoms: stiffness of the neck or the shoulder; feverish and chilled feelings at the same time, without sweating; headache; nasal congestion; diarrhea; rashes; pain at the joints; prominent but hard veins. *Kakkontō* is good only for people with strong constitutions; it is not beneficial for people with weak constitutions, even when they have some of the above symptoms. Most *kanpō* decoctions are fairly bitter in taste, and *kanzō* (*Radix Glycyrrhizae*) is included to add sweetness, as in the formula for *kakkontō*.

Whether used in combination or separately, *kanpō* treatment methods are aimed at the removal of all symptoms. One of the standard *kanpō* herbs with a long history of use is ginseng, which has long been harvested in the United States and exported to Japan, sometimes via Korea, whose government inspects its quality. Called *Kudara Ninjin* (Korean carrots), because the best ginseng grows most abundantly in Korea, the herb is widely used for various kinds of weaknesses, such as those after operations and childbirth, and for heart problems. Although ginseng is often used alone, and many people use it for health maintenance even when they experience no particular symptoms, most herbal prescriptions are mixtures of many herbs, as noted above. The medical competence of a *kanpō* doctor, then, rests heavily on the correct mixing of the herbal formulas. The effectiveness of these formulas depends, in turn, on the doctor's judgment of the "fit" between the unique *shōkōgun* of a particular patient and the medical properties of a number of herbs, each effective for a variety of symptoms.

It is worth presenting my own case to illustrate Dr. I's competence and the medical efficacy of *kanpō*. Before I left for fieldwork in Japan in 1979, I was told by my gynecologist that I had multiple fibroids requiring "immediate" surgery. The doctor reluctantly agreed to delay the operation because of the fieldwork provided that I would have it immediately after my return. In Japan, I decided to be a participant observer and asked Dr. I to prescribe herbs for me, although I was not a believer in *kanpō*. I took his medicine, consisting of twenty herbs, for three months. Upon my return to the United States I surprised my doctor, who found none of the fibroids. Even if we take into account other factors that may have contributed to the disappearance of the growths, it would be hard to deny the real "medical efficacy" of the herbal treatment.

Herbal medicines are basically different from the synthetic drugs used in biomedicine. First, most of them are multipurpose rather than single-purpose like the specialized drugs in biomedicine, each of which is effective for a particular symptom (for example, aspirin for pain). Second, since *kanpō* herbs work on the entire bodily system, which in turn removes the symptoms themselves, most *kanpō* herbs do not produce quick results. Instead, patients must often wait six months to a year or more until their bodies become healthy, at which time the symptoms will disappear. Some *kanpō* drugs, however, are quite potent, and their effects can be seen fairly quickly. Third, since most herbs work gradually,

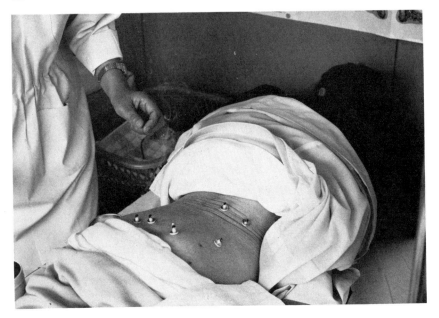

3. In the moxibustion treatment, cones of dried young mugwort leaves are burned on the body.

they do not have the acute side effects of some of the potent synthetic drugs in biomedicine. This factor is one of the reasons for the recent popularity of *kanpō* medicine among the contemporary Japanese, who have experienced their share of the side effects of synthetic drugs. Finally, because herbs have the same stable structure as food, the body can digest and absorb herbs more easily than synthetic drugs, which are more foreign to the body.

In moxibustion, cones made of dried young mugwort leaves (*mogusa* in Japanese) are burned on the body to provide stimulation from the heat (see Photo 3). The process at first leaves blisters on the skin, but after repeated applications the spots form scabs. In acupuncture, various types of needles, from 1 mm in length to those long enough to penetrate through the body (Photo 4), are inserted into the flesh. Although in Japanese-style acupuncture only plain needles are used, in Chinese-style acupuncture the needles are connected to a machine that sends out electrical stimuli at certain intervals. The strength and frequency of the electric stimuli are determined on the basis of the ailment or illness, but they may be adjusted during the course of the treatment, usually from light stimuli at long intervals to stronger stimuli at shorter intervals.

In both moxibustion and acupuncture, the most important step is determining the locations, called *tsubo* in Japanese, where the mugwort cones or needles are

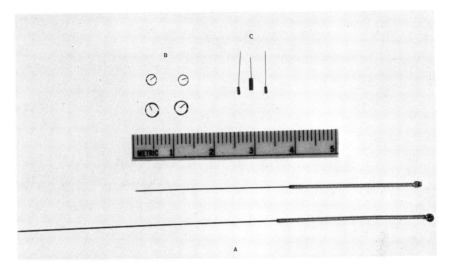

4. Three types of acupuncture needles.

to be placed (for detailed discussion of these points, see Ariyoshi 1978:797–812; Manaka 1972; Mann 1973). Although both moxibustion and acupuncture are used to treat a variety of symptoms, including allergic reactions, they are most effective for the treatment of pain and paralysis. Sometimes the effect is felt almost immediately. An important requirement of both moxibustion and acupuncture is that the patient be relaxed; many Japanese patients immediately fall asleep when treatment starts.

Medical efficacy

Because *kanpō* and biomedicine are based on radically different premises, especially in regard to illness causation, they succeed in treating very different kinds of health problems. Biomedicine has made dramatic progress in the treatment of pathogen-specific and organ-specific diseases, most of which are acute in nature. In contrast, *kanpō* has been more successful in treating chronic and degenerative diseases, including diabetes. Acupuncture and moxibustion, in particular, have also been effective in easing pain and paralysis; *kanpō* has been widely used in treating such ailments as arthritis, neuralgia, headaches, shoulder stiffness and other pains, and excessive chilling. Although useful for chronic and degenerative diseases, whose victims are older people, *kanpō* has also had wide application among infants and young people. Infants suffering from colic, children with bed-wetting habits, sickly youngsters, and young girls with menstrual irregularities often turn to *kanpō*.

Above all, *kanpō* has played a vital role in health maintenance, and by doing so has proved important in preventive medicine. Treatment of all symptoms and minor illnesses undoubtedly contributes to the prevention of major diseases, although this contribution is not easily demonstrated, since negative evidence is the only proof.[1]

Discussion

This description of *kanpō* diagnosis and treatment is too brief to adequately cover its complex body of knowledge. It does illustrate, however, that the *kanpō* approach is closer than biomedicine to the health concepts of people themselves, whether Japanese, American, or of any other society. People in any culture go to the doctor because of symptoms that they observe and that are of concern to them. We feel uncomfortable if a doctor tells us that these symptoms are "all in the mind" or that they are "common complaints of women of your age" – that is, that they are not significant enough to deserve biomedical treatment. In addition, it is apparent that *kanpō* is especially suited to the Japanese, who are concerned with *jibyō* and other minor illnesses as well as with inborn constitutional weaknesses.

The proximity in basic approach to illness between *kanpō* and that of ordinary people may be illustrated through the case of a woman patient at a *kanpō* clinic. As I was interviewing patients in Dr. I's waiting room, a woman in her early forties complained about her previous experiences with doctors, all of whom practiced biomedicine. She had been in a car accident five years earlier. Her husband and another male passenger had recovered fairly quickly from the health problems incurred by the accident, but she had continued to suffer from *muchiuchishō* – a new term for a particular type of condition resulting from traffic accidents. As *muchiuchishō* ('whipping illness'; whiplash syndrome) indicates, the condition is characterized by acute pain, as though one were being whipped. The woman's doctors had told her that she was suffering from this pain because she was a woman: "Women complain more about minor ailments because their nerves are more sensitive." Dr. I was different. He took her complaints seriously and proceeded to treat them. After each treatment her pain disappeared for one day, and her general condition was gradually improving.

The close similarities between *kanpō* and the lay view are also evident in

---

[1] The biomedical efficacy of herbal medicine, acupuncture, and moxibustion has long been under investigation. The first successful finding was the isolation of ephedrine from *Ephedra vulgaris* by Nagayoshi Nagai in 1855. The electrophysiological effects of acupuncture and moxibustion as well as the possible production of morphine by acupuncture have all been under investigation. In recent years, much effort has been made to find new biomedically effective substances in herbs to prevent the growth of cancer cells (see *Asahi* June 5, 1978). (For further details of biomedical efficacy of *kanpō*, see Ishihara 1962:432; Lock 1980a:65; Mann 1973.)

several more specific respects in regard to diagnosis and treatment. Both see illness as an expression of humoral imbalance in the body. Patients feel symptoms such as fever or chill and *kanpō* doctors recognize them, regardless of whether they show up on tests or are necessary diagnostic features defining any particular disease. Just as ordinary people do, *kanpō* doctors use their five senses in diagnosis, looking at the patient's complexion, listening to his or her coughing, and so on. Thus, *kanpō* doctors share a common ground with patients in regard to the diagnostic procedure. The doctors, however, proceed as medical specialists whose expertise lies in their ability to detect and interpret symptoms, to synthesize them and translate them into a particular mode of treatment. The sharing of common ground is often reflected in the transaction between a *kanpō* doctor and his or her patients. Despite individual differences among *kanpō* doctors, they tend to converse with their patients without resorting to medical jargon. For example, a *kanpō* doctor might ask, *Onaka ga goro goro shimasuka?* (Does your lower abdomen make *goro goro* sounds?), or *I ga chabu chabu shimasuka?* (Does your stomach cause *chabu chabu* pain?), using the onomatopoetic terms that are part of daily discourse. *Kanpō* doctors' treatment methods are also not alien to ordinary people. *Kanpō* herbs are like tea, and the emphasis on proper diet as a major factor in health maintenance is a view also held by most people.

Biomedicine, on the other hand, has progressively removed itself in every society from the public, in part because of its theoretical premises. As noted earlier, Fabrega (1975) distinguishes between *disease*, which is a departure from health defined in biomedicine as "an abstract biological 'thing'," and *illness*, which is a sociopsychologically defined departure from health in non-Western societies: "It is interesting indeed that in contemporary society one can have a disease and not feel ill and one can feel ill and be told he does not have a disease" (p. 973). In any contemporary society there is a culture of medical professionals who diagnose and treat *disease*, and a culture of people who experience *illness*. More strongly than Fabrega, Stein (1977:15) attacks the cultural bias reflected in the biomedical concept of disease by stating that "the mechanical-biological, pathogen-specific or organ-specific disease *is* the illness" (italics in the original). The resulting cross-cultural difference or misunderstanding is not between the Americans and the Japanese or any other specific "cultures," in the ordinary sense of the word; instead, it is between the culture of the biomedical specialists of any society and the culture of the people in that society.

Differences between some Western societies, especially the United States, and non-Western societies may be that in the former, the people and the medical professionals share the common "Western culture" out of which biomedical science has grown. As Kuhn (1962) has pointed out, "science" is the product of a certain paradigm in a given place (culture) and time, rather than a culture-free "objective" entity. The causal analysis inherent in biomedicine may be closer to the view of people in the United States, for example, than it is to that of the Japanese. In contrast, the *kanpō* mode of thought comes more naturally to Japanese than to Americans.

Increased recognition of *kanpō*

Although *kanpō* has always been a significant component of Japanese health care, its popularity during the past ten years or so is quite remarkable. Not only has the public become more interested in and aware of medical efficacy, but the Japanese government, which in the past attempted to suppress *kanpō*, has taken the official position of recognizing and encouraging its practice. The factors responsible for this development are numerous and complex. Some are responses to the dissatisfaction with biomedicine that is increasingly recognized the world over; others are sociocultural factors peculiar to Japan.

The first set of factors result from the recent realization among many peoples that biomedicine, which until recently was thought to be a cure-all, has serious shortcomings. One important cause of the dissatisfaction with biomedicine is increased knowledge of the side effects of synthetic drugs. These side effects, called *yakugai* (medicine damage), have been a great threat to the health of contemporary Japanese. *Yakugai* and *kōgai* (public damages = pollution) are classed as two major *gai* (damages) in the lives of people, and are given considerable attention in daily newspapers and other mass media. Although thalidomide victims in Japan numbered over 1,000 (Sunahara 1977:1–19), the so-called Smon disease, with some 11,000 victims (*Asahi* May 17, 1979; the figure is 11,033 according to a 1975 survey, see Sunahara 1977:19–31) has received most attention. Smon is an acronym for the major symptoms of the disease – subacute-myelo-optico-neuropathy (Ariyoshi, ed. 1978:532) – and was adopted before the cause of the disease had been identified. The major symptoms include damage to exteroceptors, especially vision, and lack of control of the lower limbs. In 1972, a committee appointed by the Ministry of Health and Welfare came to the conclusion that the disease was caused by Quinoform (5,7-diiodo-8-hydroxyquinoline), the most effective drug for amoebic dysentery. Prior to this decision, Quinoform had been banned in 1970 (Ariyoshi, ed. 1978:532).[2] Until 1970, it had been a component of a number of medicines used for various intestinal disorders. The medicines had been prescribed by doctors and had also

---

[2] A small number of scientists have questioned whether Quinoform is the cause of the disease, largely because of its epidemiological pattern. It occurred with high frequency in Japan but not elsewhere, and two-thirds of its victims were women. Furthermore, 5% of the "victims" with the same symptoms had not taken any medicine containing Quinoform. However, no new Smon cases have been reported since the ban of Quinoform in 1970 (Sunahara 1977).

been sold over the counter in large amounts. Information about Smon disease has been widely disseminated through the mass media, in part because of the prolonged lawsuits against pharmaceutical companies by the victims.

Although serious side effects from synthetic drugs are not at all unique to Japan, there are several reasons for the severity with which this phenomenon has affected the Japanese public. First, Japanese laws are fairly lax in controlling the sale of drugs, and fewer drugs require prescriptions than, for example, in the United States. Drugs containing Quinoform require a prescription in the United States, which was not the case in Japan (Sunahara 1977:22). The laxity of the law is indeed serious for a people like the Japanese, who tend to be very concerned about their health, and whose consumption of medicines is very high. (Note also that Quinoform was used in medicines for disorders of the stomach, which constitute the most common illness in Japan.)

Another significant factor responsible for the high incidence of "medicine damage" is Japanese health insurance systems and their misuse. Since 1961, practically every Japanese has been covered by some form of insurance provided by the national or municipal government, or by employers (see Kōseishō, ed. 1978:172–3). All the insurance programs provide extensive coverage, so that it costs very little to visit a doctor, or even to be hospitalized. Doctors and other health care specialists and institutions are in turn reimbursed on the so-called point system, which assigns a fixed number of points for each type of medical practice (for its breakdown, see Okuyama 1976:129). A doctor who conducts a certain kind of test is reimbursed on the basis of the points assigned to that test. Because medical practice and drug dispensing have never been separated in Japan, under the current insurance system it is profitable for doctors to prescribe a large number of medicines for their patients, who do not have to pay for them. This practice has resulted in *tōyaku* (throwing of medicine), the overprescription of medicine. Ironically, then, the current insurance system, when misused, can produce a very negative effect on the health of the Japanese because it encourages frequent visits to doctors on the one hand, and tempts doctors to dispense too much medicine on the other. A number of informants told how patients return home from a visit to the doctor with an armful of various medicines; since they cannot take all of them, they often take only a portion of them.

The medical significance of *kanpō* medicines, whose side effects are minimal, have been reevaluated by the Japanese public and by some biomedical doctors and researchers. This has been done against the background of the overuse and misuse of synthetic drugs, and resulting tragedy such as Smon disease. The efficacy of *kanpō* has been highlighted even more dramatically because, ironically, many of the side effects of synthetic drugs are precisely those kinds of symptoms, such as chronic pain and paralysis, for which biomedicine has proved ineffective, and for which *kanpō* has been quite efficacious. In 1979 the Ministry

of Health and Welfare pledged ¥ 100,000,000 ($455,000 in 1979) for research
into the treatment of Smon disease, and earmarked part of the money for research
on the effectiveness of acupuncture and moxibustion in treatment (*Asahi* March
26, 1979). The serious side effects of synthetic drugs also highlighted the com-
partmentalized approach to health problems in biomedicine; these drugs are given
to kill pathogens, regardless of what they might do to the rest of the body. The
kanpō emphasis on the entire body has therefore become more meaningful and
appealing to the Japanese public.

For the Japanese, the shortcomings of biomedicine that are corollaries of its
basic premises are now merged in their mental picture with the increasingly
impersonal way in which biomedicine is delivered in Japan. In contrast to the
United States, family and neighborhood doctors (*machi-isha*, or "town doctors"), who are private practitioners, are the doctors most often visited by the
Japanese, at least for initial visits and ordinary problems. Because these doctors
must rely at least in part on their reputations among their patients, who are also
neighbors or long-term acquaintances, most of them are personable and have at
least a general knowledge of the health of their patients. But in recent years this
pattern has changed considerably. The current impression of biomedical health
care delivery among most Japanese is expressed in the often-cited phrase, "Wait
three hours and see the doctor for three minutes." Some blame the insurance
system, which increases the overall number of patients by encouraging people
who are not seriously ill to visit the doctor, thereby shortchanging the more
seriously ill who deserve more time and attention.

The second set of factors responsible for the increased popularity of *kanpō*
relates to a new epidemiological pattern that Japan shares with all other industrialized societies. In most societies, we now see a greater incidence of degenerative and chronic diseases, as well as new types of disease brought about by
industrial pollution. The success of biomedicine in producing a longer life span
and in the control of acute diseases, as well as changes in our environment due
to industrialization and urbanization, are some of the major factors responsible
for this new epidemiological pattern.

In 1977, Japan became the leading nation in the world in terms of longevity,
with the average life span for men at 72.69 and that for women at 77.95. Japan
thus surpassed Sweden, where the average life span was 72.12 for men and
77.90 for women in 1976 (Kōseishō Hakusho 1978: 8–9). Within the twenty
years after the end of World War II, the population of those over sixty-five in
Japan increased 2.6 times, and was 9,900,000 as of September 1978. This age
group constituted 8.6% of the total population in 1978 (*Asahi* September 15,
1978). The number of victims of industrial pollution and of traffic and industrial
accidents has increased sharply in Japan, as elsewhere. Such terms as *seijinbyō*
("adult" diseases, or degenerative diseases) or *nanbyō* ("difficult" diseases,

including all those for which an effective cure has not been found) are household words in contemporary Japan, indicating the prevalence of these ailments and the general public's awareness of them.

For all these diseases, biomedicine has not been able to provide ready solutions, or has even proved to be unsuccessful. Furthermore, these diseases are often accompanied by chronic pain and paralysis, for which *kanpō* has proved far more effective than synthetic drugs, whose side effects are often too strong for prolonged use. Consequently, the general public in Japan, and biomedical researchers as well, have turned increasingly to *kanpō*. Widely known examples of the efficacy of *kanpō* include acupuncture and moxibustion treatment of Smon disease victims, victims of traffic accidents, and terminal cancer patients.

Another new "health problem" is obesity, which has never been a problem for the Japanese until recently. Thinness was generally considered unattractive, and some people even feared to be thin lest they look like a tuberculosis victim. Even now, one often hears remarks such as these: "You lost weight. Are you all right?" Conversely, such adjectives as *pocha pocha* (onomatopoeia for chubbiness) and *fukuyoka* (plumpness that is thought to reflect the person's satisfaction and happiness) are terms frequently used as a compliment in describing a person. Department stores continue to sell padding for the breasts and the buttocks for women. Recently, however, some Japanese have adopted the American preference for thinness. In addition, extreme cases of obesity have become a medical problem; cases of obesity even among young children are now being reported. And as we will see later, acupuncture and herbal medicine have been found effective in weight reduction at least for some people.

Two additional factors unrelated to those discussed above have contributed to the current popularity of *kanpō*. First, an epoch-making event in the history of *kanpō* took place in 1954 when a pharmaceutical company called Kotaro Kanpō succeeded in making extractions of herbs and converting them into fine granules. The availability of *kanpō* in this form was one of the factors responsible for its dramatic popularity more than a decade later, because *kanpō* for the first time became readily accessible to Japanese with a fast-paced life style. Second, communication with the People's Republic of China has been opening up, and Japanese admiration for Chinese culture, which has a long history, has been revived. The Japanese are eager to learn what has happened in China while the communication between the two countries was closed. Numerous exhibitions depicting Chinese culture and society in the past and the present are now held in Japan, and they include exhibitions of the Chinese medical system from which Japanese *kanpō* is derived. This cultural-historical factor has undoubtedly contributed to the current popularity of *kanpō* in Japan.

The health profession has responded to this rising popularity. The Society for Oriental Medicine, a research organization for the study of *kanpō*, was founded in 1950. Various other research institutes for the study of *kanpō* have been established, especially since the early 1970s (for details, see Ōtsuka 1976:335–7). In 1978 the first three-year junior college for acupuncture and moxibustion was established in Kyoto (*Asahi* February 12, 1979). Before the establishment of this school, the training of acupuncture and moxibustion practitioners had been conducted at special vocational schools. Here they received their training and then had to pass an examination for a license to practice, which was issued by local administrative agencies. The Japanese government has also started to take positive measures to recognize *kanpō* as a medical system. In 1976, it passed a law to cover some herbal prescriptions under the National Health Insurance; by 1979, thirteen herbs were covered by the insurance (Dr. I 1979, personal communication). In addition, about eighty types of extracts from herbs are covered.

Although the insurance system in Japan has made biomedical care extremely inexpensive, *kanpō* has remained quite costly by comparison. A visit to a *kanpō* doctor is covered by the insurance because the doctor is an M.D.; however, most *kanpō* treatments are not covered (with the exception of the herbs mentioned above). In the case of six diseases, including neuralgia and rheumatism, charges for acupuncture and moxibustion may be covered by insurance only after a patient presents evidence of their medical necessity, verified by a doctor (*Asahi* February 12, 1979; K. Inoue, ed. 1979:154).

Because most of the ailments for which these *kanpō* treatments are sought are not biomedically definable diseases, the insurance system discourages patients from pursuing insurance coverage. Most of the patients at a *kanpō* clinic where I did observation paid several thousand yen per week for their herbs. In some cases, the cost can be even more exorbitant. For example, one Buddhist monk paid ￥ 30,000 ($136 in 1979) for 15 bags of *kanpō* herbs. Since he uses one bag every day, the cost amounts to ￥ 2,000 ($10) per day. He had been taking the herbs for several years. Similarly, 300g (30 roots) of first-quality ginseng, which has been grown for four years, was sold in 1979 at ￥ 10,000 ($45). A single session of acupuncture, done at a medical clinic or by a paramedic, costs about ￥ 2,000 ($9). Examples of average monthly income by occupation in 1979 were: office clerk (￥ 161,947 = $736); factory manager (￥ 394,950 = $1,795); electrician (￥ 207,696 = $944); high school teacher (￥ 267,676 = $1,217) (Sōrifu Tōkeikyoku, ed. 1980:414–15). Receiving these treatments on a weekly basis or more frequently, instead of obtaining almost free biomedical care, therefore, is not to be taken lightly; it implies a serious commitment on the part of the patient. The patients at *kanpō* clinics, then, are people who have made a conscious decision to invest in *kanpō* because their health problems have not been satisfactorily remedied by biomedical treatments.

One additional remark is necessary here. In many societies, people often feel

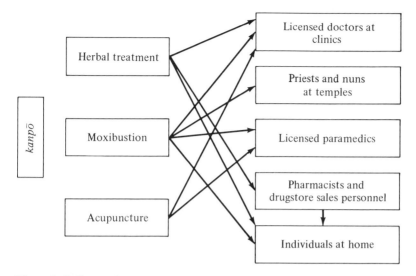

Figure 1. Delivery of *kanpō*: multiple levels.

that if they are paying a high price for goods or services, they are receiving good treatment. The Japanese are known for their eagerness to pay higher prices for brand names (see Chapter 9). However, the high price of *kanpō* does not have the same meaning as the high price of name-brand goods, which enter into social relations either as items of exchange or to impress others. With health care services people are concerned about their health, and not the impression they give to others.

The dissatisfaction with biomedicine and the way it is delivered in Japan has provided a general impetus for the Japanese to seek an alternative health care system. For many, *kanpō* provides an answer not only because it has already been a part of their health care system, but because its strengths complement the weaknesses of biomedicine. Despite high cost, therefore, the Japanese are increasingly turning to *kanpō*, which as a result is being recognized as a major medical system by the government as well as by health professionals. We look next at how this health care system is delivered (see Figure 1).

The delivery of *kanpō*: Multiple levels

Delivery by licensed physicians

As noted earlier, since 1875 in Japan a physician can practice *kanpō* only after completing regular training to become a doctor in biomedicine. Today, there are three kinds of licensed doctors in Japan: those who practice only biomedicine, those who practice *kanpō* exclusively, and those who use both. The great majority belong to the first category. According to Dr. I (personal communication), among the 100,000 physicians in Japan, only 100 to 150 practice *kanpō* exclusively. Although no statistics are available, physicians who use both biomedical and *kanpō* treatments are more numerous.

Physicians who practice kanpō exclusively. Currently, only three physicians in Hyōgo Prefecture practice only *kanpō:* Dr. N in Akashi City, Dr. I in Tarumi City, and Dr. K in Nishinomiya City. Their patients are drawn from a wide area, including many from the city of Kobe, which has by far the largest population in Hyōgo Prefecture, and some even from Kyoto. Dr. N was the first *kanpō* practitioner in the area, although he began in biomedicine. Born in 1898, he is an outgoing, friendly person who radiates warmth toward his patients. He prides himself on his knowledge of the condition of his regular patients and on his ability to detect any changes in their condition. He therefore requests that his patients not tell him their self-perceived symptoms before he has a chance to observe them. This rule is posted in his waiting room and written on paper bags for his herbal medicines. The patients I interviewed were very impressed with his diagnostic ability.

In terms of personality, Dr. I, who was trained under Dr. N, is quite different. He is sensitive and warm, but not outgoing. Dr. I was the head of a medium-sized hospital in Kobe for a number of years. After experiencing several "close calls" from the side effects of synthetic drugs, he left the hospital in January 1972 to open his own clinic to experiment in *kanpō*. For a while, he used both *kanpō* and biomedical diagnostic and treatment procedures, but since 1973 he has relied exclusively on *kanpō*. Dr. I is well known not only among patients, but also among biomedical doctors and medical researchers, especially at university hospitals, and they regularly refer patients to him. His clinic is located in Tarumi City, a relatively small city located on the shore of the Inland Sea.

In appearance, this small clinic is no different from biomedical clinics. Its sign says: I, [his name] Internal Medicine – Research Institute for *Kanpō*. It is meticulously clean, with a small waiting room furnished with one L-shaped bench for patients, as well as a small room used as a receptionist-cashier's room and a pharmacy, an examination room, a bathroom, and an X ray room that is permanently closed. In the examination room are Dr. I's desk, a bed for examinations, and three other beds where patients are given moxibustion and acupuncture. Dr. I's shelves are filled with books on *kanpō*, and there are several wall charts showing pressure points on the body and meridians. Three women are employed at the clinic: a nurse (Photo 5) who administers moxibustion and

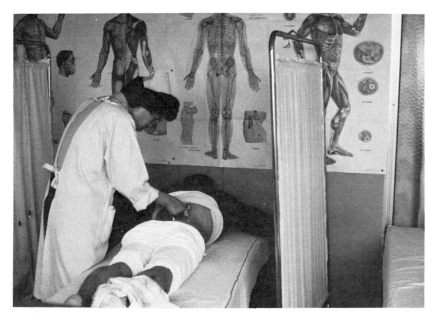

5. A nurse at a *kanpō* clinic determines the pressure points for moxibustion treatment. Background pictures show the pressure points and meridians.

acupuncture, a woman who prepares herbs, and a woman who is a receptionist-cashier. The first two were trained by the doctor.

Dr. I sees patients only in the morning; the intense concentration required in the examination exhausts him by noon. Moreover, he believes that patients seriously in need of his care should be able to adjust their work according to his clinic hours. Although many private practitioners also have afternoon and evening hours, he feels that such hours would simply invite people to visit doctors because of the low cost – one of the posters on the wall of his waiting room advocates the revision of the current National Health Insurance system. Dr. I uses no blood tests, X rays, or internal examinations procedures. Although in general he follows the usual *kanpō* diagnostic procedures, he places particular emphasis on diagnosis through feeling the pulse, tongue examination, and examination of the heart and abdomen, for which he uses both his hands and a stethoscope. Although patients who receive either moxibustion or acupuncture, about 15 per morning, stay about 40 or 50 minutes, the time Dr. I takes for examining each patient is relatively short. Between 9 A.M. and noon, he usually sees 40 to 50 patients – roughly the average number of patients seen in a morning at biomedical clinics I am familiar with. His treatments include herbs, moxibustion, and acupuncture. He is reluctant to recommend surgery because of the overall shock to the body, which increases any imbalance within the body. Even with cancer, Dr. I believes that the chance of the cancer spreading because of an operation often outweighs the positive effects of surgery.

When a patient is called into his examination room, Dr. I gives him or her a brief but penetrating glance. At this time, he says, he often notices changes in the patient's condition by the overall body smell. After listening carefully to the patient's own description of symptoms, he usually pauses to think for a few minutes. He then gives any directions to the woman who administers moxibustion or acupuncture, and to the woman who prepares herbs. Before I began observing his practice, I visited Dr. I as a patient. I was almost frightened when he first looked at me, for he seemed to look right through me. His manner contrasted sharply with that of biomedical doctors both in the United States and Japan, who often concentrate more on studying test results than on looking at the patient.

Most of Dr. I's patients suffer from chronic illnesses for which they had already gone to a number of biomedical clinics and hospitals without success. They come to see him because of his reputation and because he uses only *kanpō*. Dr. I spends little time discussing illness identification with patients. I asked Dr. I about the lack of emphasis on illness identification in *kanpō*, explaining that many of us feel relieved to hear what we are suffering from, even if the prognosis is not good. In reply, he pointed out that many people start feeling sick only after they are told they have a specific disease (this statement may apply especially to Japanese, the majority of whom, for example, would rather not know that they have cancer). He then explained that most of his patients come to him after having been told by biomedical doctors what disease they have. Dr. I personally does not see much significance in biomedical categories and pathogenic causes. Instead, he is a firm believer in multiple etiology. For example, when a young woman expressed concern over her weight loss and asked if there was a possibility of tuberculosis, he pointed out multiple factors that could be responsible for the condition. When a middle-aged woman with a reddish rash around her neck asked him if it was caused by a hormonal imbalance, he simply replied that the causes could not be determined. In each case, he proceeded to ask questions and prescribe treatment without offering a causal explanation for the disorder.

Another case involved a young woman in her late twenties. She lost 6 kg during a ten-day visit from her father-in-law. Her other symptoms included diarrhea, a lethargic feeling, a frequent urge to urinate, as though she had a urinary tract infection, insomnia, hives, and an irritable feeling. She asked Dr. I if these symptoms were caused by a selfish desire not to take care of her father-in-law. He replied gently, "I don't think so. All of us are selfish." He then asked questions, such as whether her legs and feet felt chilly or whether her body felt flushed. He took an extra long time before prescribing herbal medicine for her. He then told her, "Try out the medicine. It's better not to be too concerned" (*Maa kusuri nonde kudasai. Amari shinpai senho ga iiyo*). This case also illustrates physiomorphism in Japanese illness etiology; as noted in Chapter 5, the Japanese are willing to deal with psychological and psychosomatic symptoms, but they do not seek psychological factors in illness causation.

Dr. I does not promise recovery at any specified time. One young couple, for example, came with a three-year-old child who had epilepsy. The child had about two seizures a month except during early spring, when he had two per week. The family had visited the Kyoto University Hospital, but a doctor there referred them to Dr. I. The synthetic drug prescribed by the doctor at the university hospital had been able to control mild seizures but not strong ones; and the doctor could not increase the dosage. Dr. I told the parents to keep using the synthetic drug when strong seizures occurred, but to discontinue using the laxative the other doctor had prescribed. He then prescribed herbal medicine, telling the parents simply to try it and see, without a guarantee of complete recovery.

Most of Dr. I's patients receive instructions about diet and other day-to-day habits, together with herbs that he prescribes; some also receive acupuncture and/or moxibustion treatments. Dr. I asks patients during their first visit if they want to have these treatments, because according to him these methods are ineffective if the patient is not at ease. Most of his patients are very relaxed or even fall asleep during the treatments. When I visited him as a patient, I had told him that I did not mind acupuncture. However, when I saw the woman patient before me with needles stuck between her eyebrows and in the top of her head, I became hesitant. He noticed my hesitation and told me with a smile that acupuncture would do no good if I felt that uneasy about it.

If a patient agrees to receive either acupuncture or moxibustion, Dr. I gives instructions to the nurse on how to administer the treatment. The nurse begins by determining the nature of the imbalance of the body with an electronic instrument. She sometimes uses just the acupuncture needles themselves, but usually she practices so-called Chinese-style acupuncture, in which the needles are connected to an electric current. She adjusts the interval and strength of the current depending on the nature of the illness or pain. Although moxibustion may be administered by itself, the nurse often combines it with acupuncture by placing a large *moxa* cone at the tip of an acupuncture needle and lighting it. This way, the heat of the burning *moxa* can penetrate deeper into the body than it does when burned on the skin. At times, Dr. I instructs her to perform bloodletting, using small rubber suction cups.

Combined kanpō and biomedical treatment. There are at least three ways in which physicians administer both biomedical and *kanpō* treatments to their patients. First, an increasing number of doctors who do not practice *kanpō* themselves regularly refer their patients to *kanpō* doctors such as Dr. I when their own methods fail to produce the desired results. When I interviewed a number of doctors and patients who have had *kanpō* treatment, it became apparent that referrals by biomedical doctors are more common in large hospitals, such as university hospitals, where the doctors keep abreast of recent developments in biomedical research. Among doctors in smaller hospitals, and among *machi-isha* ("town doctors," doctors in private practice), there seems to be a greater tendency not to venture beyond purely biomedical practices.

Second, at some clinics biomedical doctors practice alongside paramedics who perform acupuncture and moxibustion. In 1977, the Hyōgo prefectural government opened a clinic called Tōyō Igaku Kenkyūjo (Research Institute for Oriental Medicine) staffed by four doctors, six paramedics for acupuncture and moxibustion, and one nurse. The clinic specializes in *nanbyō* (difficult diseases), including Smon disease and neuralgia. In one year the staff saw over 28,000 patients, one-third of whom came from outside Hyōgo Prefecture. The clinic was forced to set up an appointment system; as we will see later, the appointment system is rarely used in Japan, and patients at clinics and hospitals simply wait until their turn comes. Because of the clinic's popularity, the prefectural government is now planning to send several doctors to the People's Republic of China each year to learn more about Chinese medicine. Although this clinic is the first of its kind to be financed by government, there are privately operated clinics where both biomedical doctors and *kanpō* paramedics work together.

Third, some doctors practice both forms of medicine themselves. Although no statistics are available, it appears that the number of these doctors is increasing. Dr. I meets with a dozen young physicians every Saturday to engage in research on *kanpō*. The group has formed an organization called the Kobe Chūigaku Kenkyūkai (Kobe Research Institute of Chinese Medicine) and has published a translation of a medical text edited by the Institute of Chinese Medicine in Shanghai (see Shanghai Chūigakuin, ed. 1978). The group members are primarily young doctors in their thirties who work in various medical institutions, hospitals, and rehabilitation centers. All combine biomedicine and *kanpō* in their work. They are dissatisfied with biomedicine; they are also critical of the limitations of *kanpō* as it is understood today in Japan. Their translation and research efforts are intended to improve *kanpō* through knowledge of Chinese medicine, which they regard as more analytical than Japanese *kanpō*.

Acupuncture and moxibustion administered at temples and by paramedics

One reason many Japanese do not associate acupuncture and moxibustion with *kanpō* is that these treatments are often administered separately by specialists.

Traditionally these have been the occupations of the blind, as are other folk therapies such as the *anma* and *shiatsu* techniques of massage. In fact, recent attempts by local and national governments to provide training in these skills to those who are not blind has met with some opposition from the blind, who see it as a threat.

The Japanese make some distinction between acupuncture and moxibustion. Although they feel very comfortable with moxibustion, even to the extent of performing it themselves at home, acupuncture has remained somewhat alien, retaining a ''foreign'' flavor. In addition, the thought of the needles gives many people an uneasy feeling. Thus, many Japanese who are reluctant to receive acupuncture treatment readily accept moxibustion.

There is great variety in both acupuncture and moxibustion treatment methods. Acupuncture needles come in different sizes and shapes (Photo 4) and are made of different metals. They can be inserted as they are, or they can be connected to an electric current – ''Chinese style'' acupuncture. Similarly, there are different techniques of moxibustion, although all use *moxa*, or cones made of dried mugwort. Garlic moxibustion (*ninnikukyū*) is a fairly popular form and can be applied in three different ways: (1) Place a slice of garlic ⅛ inch thick on a pressure point, and then place a *moxa* the size of the tip of a little finger on the garlic and light it. (2) Place a piece of newspaper on a pressure point, sprinkle salt on it, and place a slice of garlic and a *moxa* cone on the newspaper. (3) Prepare a paste of ground garlic and *miso* (soybean paste) and place it on a pressure point before putting a *moxa* cone on it.

Most Japanese who seek acupuncture and moxibustion treatments receive them from licensed paramedics or from nuns and other religious specialists; treatments administered by medical doctors specializing in *kanpō* are numerically quite insignificant. Some temples are known for their moxibustion treatments, which are performed without religious ritual or instructions. Muryōji at Ueroku in Osaka is an example. Its clinic hours are from 7 A.M. to 3 P.M. People come to the temple from a wide area, including Kobe, and by 7 A.M. there are usually seventy to eighty people waiting in line outside the temple. Nuns use large *moxa*, the size of a thumb, with rice paste at the base where the cone touches the skin. Two large *moxa* are placed right above the hip on the back three times. The cost is ¥ 300 ($1.36). The treatments are known to be effective for all types of illness.

A typical one-man clinic is that operated by a paramedic who administers both acupuncture and moxibustion. Mr. Y, who is not blind, is one of the many paramedics found in most areas of Japan. He was a soldier who had lived through the end of World War II in Manchuria, where he had brought his family. His family perished in the turmoil and he was sent to a camp along the Ob River as a prisoner of war, where he served three years of hard labor. For his present job, he spent four years attending night school while making a living at various jobs and supporting his second family. He has licenses to practice not only acupuncture and moxibustion, but also chiropractic. All the certificates are hung on his wall. He believes that the effectiveness of chiropractic lies in straightening and strengthening the bones, and that of moxibustion in applying heat to the surface of the body. In his opinion, acupuncture is the most effective method, because it penetrates into the body and stimulates the nerves; among the three treatment methods, its effect is felt the fastest. He uses his knowledge of chiropractic in determining, for example, which vertebra is causing a backache, as he did when I first visited him as a patient. However, he no longer gives chiropractic treatment.

Mr. Y's small clinic is in a suburb of Kobe, and it consists of a waiting room and an examining room with two beds. He owns a white doctor's gown, as many paramedics now do, but never wears it; it is hung on the wall. He is clean but often unshaven, and appears very easygoing. Mr. Y sees patients officially every day from 9 A.M. to 7:30 P.M., but usually till later, taking off only every Thursday. Unlike at doctors' clinics, where no appointments are made, his patients are seen on the appointment system, as are the patients of most paramedics. He generously spaces patients every hour to hour and a half. He charges ¥ 2,000 ($9) for the first visit, when he must locate the pressure points, and ¥ 1,500 ($6.80) for subsequent visits.

Pointing to the fact that insurance does not cover his fees, Mr. Y emphasizes that his clients are well-off, citing some well-known people and especially their wives; however, most of the patients I interviewed were not exceptionally wealthy. They had chosen him over other paramedics because of recommendations by friends, relatives, and acquaintances. He considers his specialty to be the treatment of various types of pain, such as headache, toothache, shoulder stiffness, backache, menstrual cramps, and pain from neuralgia. However, his patients have other problems as well, such as obesity and menstrual irregularity. There was even one case of a growth in the uterus that Mr. Y says disappeared after his acupuncture treatment. He estimates that the sex ratio of his patients is nine women to one man. Most of the women are over thirty, and many are at the menopausal stage. During the period of my observation, there were also a number of young girls in their teens, most of whom had menstrual irregularities, and two of whom had an obesity problem. Men come with backaches, hip pains, and other types of pain. Men are particularly vulnerable, according to Mr. Y, to *gikkuri goshi*, an acute pain resulting from straining one's muscles while lifting something heavy.

Although needles are available in gold, silver, iron, and stainless steel, Mr. Y prefers stainless steel, since it does not rust or tarnish, even when connected to the electric current. He refutes the claim made by some that gold needles are

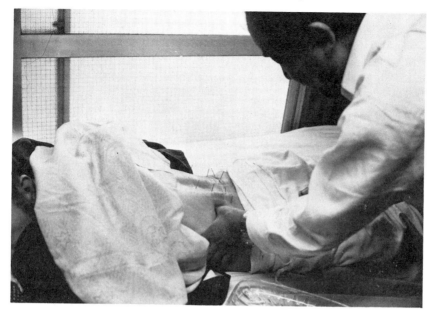

6. A paramedic determines pressure points and inserts acupuncture needles 4 to 8 cm long.

most effective. Although he specializes in Chinese-style acupuncture, in which the needles are connected to an electric current, he does not use the extra-long needles used by the Chinese. Instead, the points of his needles are only about 4 to 8 cm long (Photos 4A and 6). He also uses *embishin* (Photo 4B), originally invented in China. These are very small needles with circular rings around the needle; they come in different sizes, but all are small; the rings are 2 to 4 mm in diameter, and the needles are 2 mm in length. Mr. Y uses *embishin*, especially for cases of weight reduction. He places regular acupuncture needles in pressure points on the ear, which is thought in *kanpō* to represent the entire body, and then replaces them with *embishin* on the pressure points, over which he puts small pieces of adhesive tape. These *embishin* can stay on the patient until the next visit, usually a week later, at which time he repeats the procedure. Through this method, he succeeded in helping a thirty-one-year-old woman lose 8.5 kg between October 3, 1978, and February 20, 1979. He was using the same method on a fifteen-year-old girl weighing 98 kg. Since she had first come to him two months earlier, she had lost only 2 kg. He was not anticipating dramatic results in this case because she did not come regularly.

In the past Mr. Y also used *hinaishin* (Photo 4C), but he discontinued their use. *Hinaishin*, invented by the Japanese, are similar to *embishin* except that

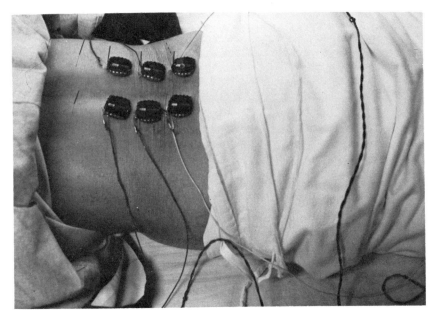

7. An invention by a paramedic. Next to an inserted needle is placed a beer-bottle cap, with a raised metal mesh inside. Lighted incense is placed on the metal mesh so that heat from the incense penetrates the body via the needle.

they do not have a circular ring around the needle, which is 0.3 to 1 cm in length; instead, they have small heads 1 to 3 mm in length. They too are left in the body of the patient for several days at a time.

As the example of using *embishin* for obesity cases illustrates, most paramedics, including Mr. Y, are quite ingenious. With the basic training they receive for their licenses, they try to develop effective methods of their own. Another technique of Mr. Y's invention involves caps from beer bottles. He puts a piece of fine metal mesh over the inside of a cap (Photo 7) and places a lighted piece of incense, 5 mm in diameter and 2 cm in length, on it. He places these caps next to acupuncture needles so that the heat from the incense can penetrate the body through the needle.

Kanpō treatment at drugstores

To a casual observer of Japanese daily life today, perhaps the most conspicuous presence of *kanpō* is at drugstores. Pharmaceutical companies have seized on the revived interest in *kanpō* and have begun to mass produce *kanpō* medicines in pill and other easy-to-use forms. Whereas the traditional method is to select types and amounts of various herbs according to a particular cluster of symptoms, the commercial *kanpō* medicines are standardized mixtures. Some are sold as dried herbs, often more finely minced than those at *kanpō* clinics and packaged like tea bags. Most drugstore *kanpō* medicines are sold as pills, fine granules, and other types of extracts placed in colorful containers. These medicines are advertised all over Japan through television commercials, magazine and newspaper ads, and billboards. It is an overwhelming advertising bombardment. Although far less effective, according to both *kanpō* doctors and my own experiments, these commercial medicines are convenient for the fast-paced life of the contemporary Japanese.

At a prosperous drugstore in the heart of Kobe, synthetic medicine accounted for 60% of sales, although many of the synthetics now contain extracts from *kanpō* herbs. The remaining sales were *kanpō* and folk medicines. Herbs (not their extracts) comprise only 10% of sales. At present, most pharmaceutical companies produce particular types of medicine in both forms. For example, every major pharmaceutical company manufactures medicine for the stomach in two forms – one consisting purely of extracts from *kanpō* and labeled as such, and the other made primarily of synthetic medicine, though often containing extracts from *kanpō* herbs.

Commercial *kanpō* medicines are also geared to the biomedical approach of a particular treatment for a particular disease, rather than to a cluster of *shōkōgun* (symptoms and prodromes). Thus, a particular mixture of herbs made into pills and extracts might be advertised as ''*kanpō* X, effective for illness Y.'' It is not uncommon to find an advertisement in front of a drugstore that reads something like this: ''*Kanpō* for empyema of the nostrils without operation.'' Appealing to the fear of surgery among the Japanese, these ads promote *kanpō* for illnesses that often require surgery in biomedical treatment. Another tactic used is the appeal for *biyō* (beauty), including weight reduction. They also emphasize the weak spots of biomedicine – for example, *kanpō* for diabetes, a disease for which biomedicine has not provided an effective cure.

To promote these pharmaceutical *kanpō* medicines, local drugstores now provide *kanpō sōdan* (*kanpō* consultation). To provide the service, many pharmacists and drugstore employees now take instruction in *kanpō*, and some are quite knowledgeable. In fact, my first informant about specialized knowledge of *kanpō* was the owner of a prosperous old drugstore in the heart of Kobe that had been our family's drugstore for over fifty years. The owner, now semi-retired, had a profound and authentic knowledge of *kanpō* which he was eager to transmit to me.

It should be stressed that to many older druggists, including this man, *kanpō* is not new. Japanese drugstores began as *kanpō* stores long before the introduction of biomedicine, and they continued to sell *kanpō* medicines even during periods of legal repression. This store, established by the present owner's grandfather in 1888, started as a *shōyaku-ya (shōyaku* = herbs; *ya* = store), the label my grandmother continued to use even after it started to sell synthetic drugs. The present owner has been attending a meeting on *kanpō* every Sunday for twenty-five years.

Kanpō consultants at drugstores often ask customers to fill out a questionnaire. The questions and descriptive phrases used in these questionnaires, especially in the better ones, are derived from orthodox *kanpō*, although they inevitably are incomplete in many ways. Medicines are chosen according to the self-perceived physiological characteristics and symptoms customers indicate on the questionnaires. Although the consultants do ask pertinent questions, *kanpō* treatment at drugstores misses the vital step during which *kanpō* doctors examine their patients and use their expertise to read symptoms and synthesize them. Furthermore, prescriptions cannot be fully individualized, since the *kanpō* medicines the drugstores offer are limited to standardized and prepackaged medicines produced by pharmaceutical companies.

An example of these questionnaires is presented in Photo 8. The questionnaire is fairly comprehensive and is presented here in literal translation, which tells us something about Japanese perceptions of their bodies in health and illness. The top portion of this Customer's Card for *Kanpō* is for address, telephone number, height, weight, name, sex, and age. The front and back human figures and the chart between them identify how the numbered items below determine the prescription. The blank column on the right is for recording the main symptoms at the time of the first *kanpō* consultation and the drugs taken by the customer before the consultation. The numbered columns in the lower half of the questionnaire are "basic data and self-perceived symptoms." The first ten columns pertain to the physiological conditions and habits of the individual and the rest relate to symptoms. They read as follows:

12 physical constitutions: muscular; obese, fatty, flabby with water; average; thin.
2 inborn constitutions: sturdy; average; weak (of *senbyōshitsu* type); allergic; tires easily; susceptible to chill; excessive sweating; feeling cold easily; feeling hot easily; weak.
1 personality: strong-willed; short-tempered; easily angered; optimistic; easy-going; weak-willed; cries easily; extrasensitive.
2 entire body: insomnia; restless; feverish; tired feeling; perspiration while sleeping.
6 food preferences: no likes or dislikes; no problem with bitter taste; preference for cold items; hot items; salty items; sweet tooth; hot (temperature) food; oily food; fish; meat; vegetables; fruits; wine/liquor; cigarettes; coffee.
9 facial complexion: reddish-dark; reddish; reddish on cheeks; pale-dark; ordinary; lustrous; yellowish-dark; swollen; white; anemic; no luster; rough.
9 skin: inflamed; rough; secretion (much, little); itchy; peeling; hives; infected.

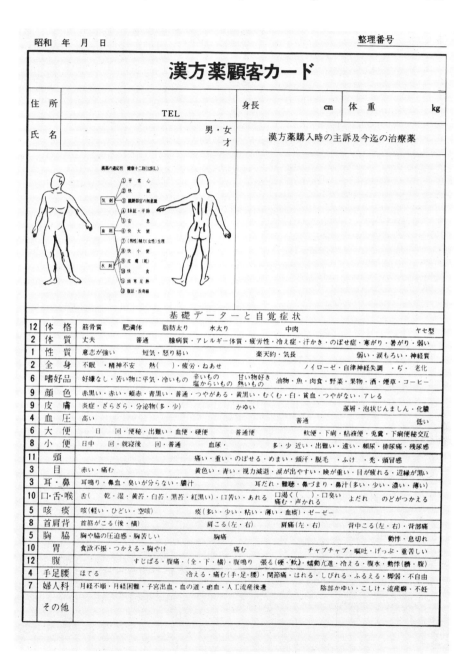

8. A questionnaire to be filled out at drugstores in order for a pharmacist to choose an appropriate *kanpō* medicine.

4 blood pressure: high; average; low.

6 stool: daily frequency (fill in the number); constipation; hard to go; bloody stool; hard stool; average stool; soft stool; diarrhea; stool with slime; "rabbit stool" (in small balls); alternating diarrhea and constipation.

7 urine: daily frequency (fill in the number); frequency after falling asleep; average; bloody urine; great quantity; small quantity; hard to go; infrequent; frequent; urination accompanied by pain; feeling of some urine remaining in the bladder.

11 head: headache; heavy; flushed; dizzy; sweaty head; loss of hair; dandruff; balding; head cold.

3 eyes: reddish; painful; yellowish; greenish; vision weakening; tearful; heavy eyelids; easily tired; presence of dark frame.

3 ears and nose: ear sound; bloody nose; no sense of smell; nasal pus; ear wax; hard of hearing; plugged nose; nasal mucus (much, little, thick, thin).

10 mouth, tongue, and throat: tongue (dry, moist, yellow "moss," white "moss," black "moss," reddish dark); bitter taste in the mouth; hoarseness of the throat; thirst; foul smell; painful; hoarse voice; drool; feel like something stuck in the throat.

5 phlegm: coughing (light, heavy, dry); phlegm (much, little, thick, thin, bloody); cough sounding like zē zē (heavy coughing).

8 neck, shoulder, and back: stiff neck (back, sides); stiff shoulder (left, right); pain in the shoulder (left, right); stiff back (left, right); pain in the back.

5 chest and sides: feeling pressure in the chest and on the sides; heavy feeling in the chest; chest pain; throbbing; out of breath.

10 stomach: no appetite; feeling of food being stuck; heartburn; painful; feeling chabu chabu (water going around); vomiting; burping; heavy feeling.

12 lower abdomen: stiff, painful (entire area, lower part, sides); making noise; bloating (hard, soft); feeling like a worm crawling; chilly; too much liquid in the stomach; palpitation (navel, stomach).

4 hand, arm, foot, leg, and hip: flushed; chilly, painful (hand, arm, foot, leg, hip); painful joints; swollen; numb; trembling; weak legs; no control.

7 gynecological: irregular menstruation; difficult menstruation; vaginal bleeding; dizziness; vitiated blood; after-effect of miscarriage; itchiness; white discharge; tendency for miscarriage; sterility.

Other

The translation of the questionnaire is presented here not just to show the shortcuts in *kanpō* delivered through drugstores; it also serves as ethnographic data to demonstrate a theme I have been stressing in this book – the minutely detailed knowledge the Japanese possess about their physiological condition. Such questionnaires are possible only among people with considerable knowledge of their inborn constitutions and minor illnesses. All the conditions in these columns are familiar to most Japanese. Perspiration during sleep, for example, is a frequently mentioned danger signal. If a mother observes it in her child she is greatly concerned, because it indicates that the child is constitutionally weak or might have a serious illness, such as tuberculosis. The questionnaire also expresses the concept of physiomorphism discussed in Chapter 4: Note how little attention is given to personality compared to physiological characteristics.

Knowledge of the physiological self, then, is the basis that enables *kanpō* specialists, whether doctors or drugstore personnel, to communicate with ordinary people in Japan. And the drugstore phenomenon clearly illustrates how *kanpō* has grown within its sociocultural milieu – the daily discourse of the ordinary people.

Computerized kanpō treatment

Although drugstore *kanpō* without a doctor's examination may be an undesirable shortcut, an even more abbreviated form is *kanpō* by computer. This method is now advocated in popular health magazines, in booklets published by pharmaceutical companies, and sometimes even on streetcorners, as I observed on a busy Kyoto street in 1979. An example of this approach is a booklet that accompanied the March 1979 issue of a popular health magazine called *Watashi no Kenkō* (My Health), published by Shufunotomo. The title of the booklet is *Shinan Konpūtā Hōshiki Taishitsu to Shōjō ni Pittari no Kanpōyaku ga Jibun de Eraberu Hon* (A Book to Tell You How to Choose by Computer the *Kanpō* Just Right for Your Constitution and Symptoms). What is referred to here as a "computer" is actually not much more than a multiple-choice list to be used by the reader-patient to choose a particular kind of *kanpō*.

The juxtaposition of age-old *kanpō* and the computer, symbolic of the mechanical aspect of modern technology, is at least eye-opening, or even, if one chooses not to be "objective," appalling. Anthropologically, however, this phenomenon is yet another example of physiomorphism in the Japanese concepts of illness. The "individualized" delivery of *kanpō* as described in this chapter essentially involves a physiomorphic individualization; the patient is treated as a physiomorphically unique person with an individual configuration of *shōkōgun*, inborn constitutions, and so on. Therefore, the diagnosis can be ascertained, in theory, by a computer.

Overview

An examination of *kanpō* as practiced in Japan reveals that the Japanese view of illness, as described in previous chapters, is almost indistinguishable from the underlying premises of *kanpō*; *kanpō* merely systematizes and institutionalizes people's assumptions. Thus, the Japanese sensitivity to the fine details of health and the tendency toward physiomorphism are systematized in *kanpō* diagnosis and treatment. The sharing of these basic views of health and illness is ultimately responsible for *kanpō*'s strength throughout Japanese history; it not only survived legal oppression and competition from biomedicine, but has surged ahead in popularity in the past decade.

Kanpō obviously is not a folk medicine. Despite its roots in the folk perception of health and illness, it has become a highly developed medical system effectively contributing to the health maintenance of the Japanese. It offers an effective alternative to biomedicine, since the two systems are almost ideally complementary; the weakness of one is the strength of the other.

6   Medical roles of Japanese religions:
A descriptive overview

Anthropologists are now increasingly interested in the pluralistic systems of medicine that characterize many complex societies of the Third World. In studies of medical pluralism, however, primary attention is usually given to narrowly defined "medical" systems, such as Japanese *kanpō* or traditional Chinese medicine in the People's Republic of China. Healing at religious institutions is accorded a separate category, sometimes with the implication that it is a second-class practice whose medical efficacy must be proved before it can be admitted into the ranks of legitimate medical systems. At the other extreme, romanticism on the part of anthropologists has made religious healing the most powerful healing method. In either case, this separate treatment is unfortunate, because people use these various systems of medicine simultaneously.

A tacit assumption behind the neglect of the medical role of religious institutions is that although religion once played a major role in health care, as in medieval Europe, the modernization process, especially scientific development, has separated medicine from magic and religion. In some cases this generalization may be applicable (see Thomas 1971), but the assumption ignores many instances of religion-based medical care in contemporary societies. Catholic priests in the United States, for example, still perform a vital role in health care: They perform special services for the sick and engage in psychological counseling of parishioners. The difference between the situation in medieval Europe and contemporary United States may lie in the fact that in the latter religion has become a nonformalized medical system, to which people no longer consciously assign a medical role, but which nonetheless delivers health care. Likewise, in non-Western societies, including Japan, major religious institutions continue to play a significant role in health maintenance. The Japanese too, however, do not consciously label the services given by temples and shrines as *iryō* (medical treatment).

The discussion of health care provided by various religions here excludes the so-called new religions (*shinkō shūkyō*), shamanism, and ancestor worship. The number of new religions mushroomed in Japan after World War II. Although they have many adherents and often fulfill health-related functions, their role in health care is limited to their memberships. Furthermore, there are many publications on the subject already available in English (for a comprehensive overview, see Norbeck 1970; for a detailed case study of one of these new religions, see Davis 1980). Once a powerful nonformalized religion in Japan, shamanism has played a significant role in the health care of the people. Many of the functions of shamanism have been taken over by the new religions and its strength has waned considerably in the recent past, although it has by no means disappeared. Information on shamanism is also available in English (Blacker 1975; Hori 1968). Although ancestors are said to look after the living, their role in the welfare of the living is a diffused one (see Smith 1974 for an exhaustive treatment of ancestor worship in contemporary Japan). My description focuses on the most important segment of religious health care – that provided at temples and shrines, which are the most frequently used type of religious institutions in the health care system today. Customarily, the term *temple* refers to a building dedicated to the worship of a buddha or buddhas, and the term *shrine* to a place for the worship of a deity or deities in Shintoism, a native religion of Japan (see Chapter 7 for further discussion of these religions).

Temples and shrines in contemporary urban Japan

Without restricting the discussion to the medical domain, the uses of temples and shrines in contemporary Japan are first introduced to provide a general background for two case studies presented later.

The current popularity of temples and shrines in Japan is phenomenal, and in fact has been increasing for some time. Many temples and shrines throughout Japan attract literally thousands of people a year. In all three cities, Kobe, Osaka, and Kyoto, municipal bus companies operate regular tour buses that take people to temples and shrines. The tours are often aimed at older people, many of whom, as we will see later, have now been squeezed out of Japanese society, which until recently had formalized ways of caring for them. So the bus tours emphasize temples and shrines that specialize in illnesses of older people, such as strokes and hemorrhoids.

Medical and other uses of temples and shrines is by no means confined to the aged. For example, I once attended a New Year's gathering of several related families, all with urban, educated backgrounds. A young man of nineteen was late for the New Year's dinner because he was visiting three shrines known to be efficacious in successful passage of the university entrance examination. In fact, Tenmangū in Osaka, which traditionally has been known as a shrine for learning, has been exceedingly popular among students facing entrance examinations, as well as with their families. Similarly, with the strong tradition of school trips (*shūgaku ryokō*) in Japanese schools, one often sees school tours at temples and shrines, with elementary, middle, and high school students flocking to buy amulets, charms, and other souvenirs for themselves and for their families. The youngsters hang the amulets and charms from their knapsacks or pocketbooks.

The great demand for *omamori* (amulets and talismans) is described in Swanger (1981:242–3). He refers to Kōganji in Tokyo, where Toge Nuki Jizō (Splinter-pulling Buddha), noted for its various healing abilities, is enshrined. The temple distributes a small paper image of the *jizō* (a guardian Buddha for children) designed to be swallowed or stuck to the skin over the affected area. Swanger describes the demand for the paper amulets as ''astronomical''; the temple has even received mail orders from overseas Japanese in Los Angeles, San Francisco, Hawaii, and elsewhere. Not infrequently people purchase a great number of them at a time, although when the supply is short, they are asked to restrict their purchases to only two *omamori* per visit. It should be noted here that this temple is located in Tokyo, a city some Japanese consider to be less religious than the Hanshinkan, where the research for this book was conducted. Swanger (1981:240) also reports the presence of factories for manufacturing amulets and talismans; their representatives make the rounds of shrines and temples all over Japan.

One of the most popular uses of shrines and temples in contemporary Japan is for the purification of automobiles on New Year's Day. With the rapid increase in private car ownership, ''my car'' – a term borrowed from English and pro-nounced in Japanese as *mai kā* – is both a popular word and a symbol of a new way of life, as the conscious adoption of the term ''my'' indicates. The use of the English possessive reflects the recent increased emphasis on the individual, at least on the surface, rather than on the person defined within a social network. In addition, the term ''my car'' symbolizes the new emphasis on nuclear families; the image of young parents with a strong conjugal bond is contrary to the traditional family structure, which has emphasized the extended family with consanguineal ties.

Despite the modern image of these ''my car'' owners, who are usually young or middle-aged, all flock to shrines and temples on New Year's Day to have their cars purified. According to a report by the *Asahi* newspaper (April 14, 1980), Hiramaji Temple in Kawasaki City purifies cars, as many as forty at a time, every half-hour beginning at 9 A.M. At a cost of ¥ 2,500 ($11.40 in 1979), the purification service includes a purification rite, a prayer, amulets, and bumper stickers. In 1970, the temple purified 25,000 cars; in 1979, it purified 67,000 cars, bringing in an income of ¥ 167,000,000 ($759,091). The purifi-cation rite for cars is not the exclusive domain of temples. Sōzō Taisha, a shrine in Kyūshū, recently constructed a hall for the dedication of prayers for cars. It accommodates 200 cars at a time for the purification rite; the shrine also has a parking lot that holds 10,000 cars. Income from the purification of cars alone takes care of 80% of the annual maintenance cost for the shrine; in 1979, total maintenance fees were about ¥ 300,000,000 ($1,363,636) (*Asahi* April 14, 1980).

With this cursory sketch of the general picture of both the meaning and functions shrines and temples offer to contemporary Japanese, I turn now to two case studies that illustrate specific roles one shrine and one temple play for a great number of people in the Keihanshin area.

Ishikiri Shrine and its role in surgery

Near the beginning of my fieldwork, I was interviewing a large number of people on the street, on public transportation, at restaurants, and in biomedical hospitals, and I encountered frequent references to the Ishikiri Shrine, situated at the eastern end of Osaka. One of my sources was an elderly couple, both in their sixties, who were vegetable vendors in front of a railroad station in Kobe. During my frequent stops, I engaged in conversation with them whenever they were free of other customers, and the husband described his monthly trip to Ishikiri Shrine, 45 km from his home. He had visited the shrine about ten years earlier, when he had a very painful corn on the sole of his foot. His doctor had told him he had no choice but to have it removed surgically; desperate to avoid surgery, he decided to try Ishikiri Shrine, on the recommendation of relatives and friends. Although the corn was causing almost too much pain for him to walk, he visited Ishikiri and tried *ohyakudo* several times. The corn miraculously disappeared. *Ohyakudo* literally means ''one hundred times,'' and refers to the custom of making one hundred pilgrimages or visits to a shrine or temple in the hope of recovering from an illness. In front of Ishikiri Shrine are two cylindrical stones, roughly 10 m apart. As one of the practices required for healing, visitors, the sick or their relatives and friends, walk rapidly between these two stones one hundred times, touching them each time. Ever since the miraculous disappearance of his corn, the vegetable vendor had been visiting the shrine once a month.

A career woman in her forties, originally from a rural part of Fukuoka in Kyūshū, described her experience at Ishikiri when I joined her at a table in a busy department store lunchroom in Osaka (at most restaurants and other eating places in Japan, one is expected to share a table with anyone who comes along). Six years earlier, when her brother was found to have lung cancer and had to have surgery, she paid her first visit to Ishikiri and gave her brother an amulet from the shrine. The brother's wife later told her that right after the surgery, when he was in great pain, he threw the amulet against the wall of the hospital room, shouting, ''A silly superstition.'' His operation was a success. Two years after the operation, the man's wife came to Osaka and paid a thank-you visit to the shrine. The woman I spoke to said that her brother's recovery from cancer must have had something to do with the healing power of the shrine.

A second couple, whose case will be studied in detail in Chapter 8, provides another example. This couple, both in their forties, are college graduates who lived in a Western country for several years. At the time of the man's operation for an ulcer, his brother went to Ishikiri to obtain an amulet; after his recovery, the man and his wife went to Ishikiri to thank the deities. I met the couple accidentally on a street just as they were returning from Ishikiri. They were somewhat embarrassed about their visit, and told me that they had gone in part out of gratitude to his brother, who would be happy to hear of their thank-you visit, and in part because they had to pay a thank-you visit to his superior at work, who lived not far from Ishikiri.

As I talked to various people, the magnitude of the shrine's "popularity" slowly but steadily emerged, and its importance was confirmed when I visited a university hospital. During a talk with two surgeons and several nurses, our conversation touched upon the use of amulets, which I had noticed hanging from beds as I visited the patients' rooms. The doctors and nurses confirmed that almost all patients have amulets hanging from their beds, the majority of which come from Ishikiri Shrine. They also commented that many patients forgot to take their amulets home; they no longer paid attention to them once their surgery was a success.

I was planning to visit Ishikiri Shrine, but was postponing it in order to concentrate on visiting biomedical and *kanpō* clinics, when I met a middle-aged man in a Chinese restaurant. He did not think much of Ishikiri, but he became quite interested in my work. He volunteered to take me to the shrine in his pickup truck the next day, when he could take off work from his small factory. The next morning I met him at a railroad station near his home, located in the heart of Osaka. During our ride, he described numerous Korean shamans practicing in Osaka whom both Koreans and Japanese visited, and during our visit to the shrine he made many perceptive observations that greatly enhanced my understanding of the meaning of the pilgrimage to Ishikiri.

Before I describe the shrine itself, I must complete the narrative of what happened that day. After we visited the shrine, we decided to look for a shaman (*ogamiya*) in the area, since we had noticed a weather-beaten shingle as we walked along the road that connected the shrine to a nearby railroad station. Demonstrating his marvelous skill as a fieldworker, and using his Osaka dialect, which is close to the local dialect, my companion began inquiring about the whereabouts of shamans in the area. The woman whose name came up most often, with strong recommendations from several people, lived about 9 km away. Those who recommended her stressed her ability to diagnose a client's problem when the name and the age of the client was the only information given. We decided to visit her, although we had to cross a mountain range to get to her place.

As we drove, my companion decided to ask the shaman whether or not neglect in erecting a tomb for his father because of its cost was in some way related to his recent problems in business. I decided to ask about a friend who had been ill off and on for the past several years. We had no difficulty finding her house, which was typical of wealthy farmhouses in the area. Her daughter-in-law explained that the woman was still at a hospital where one of her regular clients was hospitalized, but was to return any minute. She led us into this large and meticulously clean house and told us to wait. The woman, who was about sixty-five, came back shortly, and we began talking. She explained that she became a shaman during the grave illness of one of her daughters. She also described some of her clients, who varied a great deal in terms of socioeconomic and educational background, and the problems for which she was consulted. After we explained the reason for our visit, she prayed to Kōbō Daishi, a famous priest-buddha of Shingon Buddhism; she had worshipped him during her shamanistic career. When she became possessed, my companion's father spoke through her, reassuring him that he would rather see his son take care of his family than erect a tomb. For my case, she diagnosed that my friend's trouble was due to *mizuko* (water child, or aborted fetus), and gave me small pieces of paper on which the name Kōbō Daishi was written. My friend was to swallow the paper with water every morning.

This rewarding day, with its visits to both a shrine and a shaman, convinced me that any investigation into the health care system in contemporary Japan should not ignore the importance of shrines, temples, and other religious institutions such as shamanism.

After this initial visit, I visited Ishikiri by myself three more times, once during the annual spring festival, although the number of visitors was not significantly greater than at other times. The shrine turned out to be an excellent place for fieldwork, since all its visitors had been or were currently experiencing illness, either of themselves or of their family and friends. They were eager to discuss their health problems and their search for cures. The following description of the shrine and its surroundings is a composite of my observations during these four visits.

Ishikiri and its surroundings

Ishikiri Shrine is situated at the eastern end of the greater Osaka region. This region is at the foot of the Ikoma mountain range, which has retained strong religious meaning to the present day. The Ikoma area is full of shrines and temples, most of which are known to have specific types of healing power. It is also in this mountain range that shamans, who are no longer very numerous in the Keihanshin cities, are found in the greatest concentration.

The formal name for Ishikiri is Ishikiri Tsurugiya Jinja, which means "a stone-cutting sword and arrow shrine." This designation derives from the fact that the shrine keeps as the bodies of the deities a sharp sword and an arrow, both "capable of easily cutting even the hardest and largest rock." The two deities enshrined are the grandson and great-grandson of the Sun Goddess (Amaterasu Omikami), who is considered the most important deity in Japanese mythology. According to the literature distributed at the shrine, its origin is related to the time when these deities came to the western foot of the Ikoma mountain range to control the area.

The shrine is known to people in the Keihanshin area for its effectiveness in curing illnesses, especially *dembo*, a term in the Osaka dialect for tumors. The analogy between the surgical knife used in removing tumors and the sword and the arrow enshrined as the bodies of the deities is fairly obvious. In addition, stones traditionally have been assigned multiple symbolic meanings in Japanese culture, and have played an especially important role in healing. A belief in the effectiveness of stones in curing, especially for warts and for excessive discharge from the ears, is found throughout Japan (Yanagita, ed. 1951:22).

It must be pointed out at the beginning that one striking feature, obvious even to a casual observer, is the close, long-standing relationship between the shrine and the most famous *kanpō* distributor in the Keihanshin area, Sakamoto Kanpōten. Various types of advertisement for this distributor are highly visible not only in the shrine proper, but also along the road leading from the railroad station to the shrine. The railroad station is quite a distance from the shrine itself, and the narrow road that connects the two is studded with souvenir stores, vendors, casual eating places, roadside healers, and numerous outfits offering various types of divination.

Next to the station is one healer who spreads a piece of yellow cloth on the roadside (Photo 9). He has a small statue of Kōbō Daishi, a buddha of the Shingon sect, and a scroll on which a picture of Kōbō Daishi is painted. He offers to cure illnesses through the healing power of Kōbō Daishi. Every now and then a person stops out of curiosity, but usually does not consult him. Once, however, a woman in her fifties sat down on the piece of cloth and started to consult him about a pain in her knees. Only a short distance away from this healer is another, a man clad in a white kimono. He has a large white piece of cloth hanging between two poles. Written on the cloth are the names of a number of illnesses, including neuroses (*noirōze*), which he claims to be able to treat. When there is no customer, he talks in a loud voice about how he can cure illnesses to catch the attention of passersby. At one time, another woman in her fifties stopped to consult him. Although the conversation involved interpersonal relationships within her family, she seemed unconcerned and talked in a voice clearly audible to those passing by.

9. Roadside healer.

Farther along the road on the left-hand side, after numerous souvenir stores, is a large advertisement for the memorial service for *mizuko* (water child, or aborted fetus) at a temple called Yōseien Jizōji. The sign in the photo says: "Let us erect *jizō*, which is a familiar figure to us all through television, radio, and newspapers. For the memorial service for *mizuko*, choose Yōseien Jizōji." (*Jizō* is the guardian buddha of children.) The lower half of the advertisement urges readers to stop at the office located near the sign or at the office at Tennōji in Osaka, and lists the telephone numbers. Behind this sign and the small office is a plot with twenty-one tombs, each with a *jizō* with a red bib, a pinwheel, and flowers (Photo 2). In addition, one medium-sized and one larger *jizō* and tombs are placed farther back, in front of a large mural. As I was taking pictures of the place, I heard a woman say: *Osaisen ireru toko ga nai ya sanpuru ya na* [There is no place to put *saisen* (offertory money); they must be samples (*sanpuru* is derived from the English word "sample")]. This woman, in her sixties, was accompanied by her married daughter, who lived elsewhere but who made a point of going out with her mother once a month to various places such as this one. They informed me of various other temples that had recently set up large plots for memorial services for aborted fetuses.

Close to this office is a small shrine specializing in the treatment of ringing ears and excessive discharge of ear wax, as the large signs in front of the shrine

10. Shrine for treatment of ringing ears and excessive discharge of ear wax.

indicate (Photo 10). In front of the shrine, next to the road, are two piles, one of rectangular pieces of board and the other of small stones (Photos 11 and 12). Written on these boards and stones are prayers asking the deity to treat problems, usually problems of the ear, or thanking the deity for effective treatment.

Near this shrine is a large statue of Daibutsu (Great Buddha) erected by the *kanpō* dealer mentioned earlier. In the compound are numerous large stone edifices on which the amounts of the dealer's donations to various civic causes are inscribed (Photo 13). There is also a small roadside shrine where people often stop to pray (Photo 14). The outfits offering divination services include Anshindō (Peace of Mind Store, Photo 15), advertising ''decisive decisions'' to customers in practically all areas of life, such as marriage, entrance examinations, runaways from home, illness, business, and lawsuits. They offer to make decisions for customers, instead of offering consultations. Nearby, on the opposite side of the street, is another diviner who advertises fees of ¥ 3,000 ($13.60) for divination and ¥ 1,000 ($4.50) for palmistry. Another diviner (Photo 16) has a table and a few chairs on the street and advertises Takashima divination – perhaps the most widely used ''school'' of divination in contemporary Japan. People consult these diviners at the time of naming, house-building, marriage, health problems, and so on. Every time I

11. Prayer boards at a shrine for ringing ears and ear wax.

12. Prayer pebbles at a shrine for ringing ears and ear wax.

13. Large stone edifices indicating the amount of donations by a *kanpō* dealer to various civic causes. The business has been closely associated with the Ishikiri Shrine.

14. Roadside shrine near the Ishikiri Shrine.

15. Advertisement by a diviner offering to make ''decisive decisions'' on various matters in life, such as marriage, entrance examinations, runaways from home, illness, business, and lawsuits.

passed, there were customers at this diviner; as the photograph shows, the customers were usually women, both young and old.

Numerous other outfits advertise a variety of divinatory services, including reading personalities through brush strokes (*sumi iro*), divination using cards (*toranpu uranai*), character reading by facial features (*ninsō*) or by the shape of the nose, and reading the fortune of a house through its construction (*kasō*). Reading the house character (*kasō*) through its shape and directions is still widely practiced in contemporary urban Japan; many people consult a diviner before they build or remodel a house. In this case, the advertisement urges customers to consult before putting a new gas pipeline into the house.

All these divinatory practices are still quite widespread in urban Japan, and

16. Roadside diviner.

used not only by older people, but also by college students and other young people. These beliefs and practices are derived from Taoism, originally introduced from China. Although Taoism has never been institutionalized in Japan, it has penetrated deeply into folk belief systems and practices. As we will see in Chapter 7, Kōshin-san, a Taoist god, is assigned numerous healing functions and remains an important deity in Japan today.

In between these places offering divination, the road to the shrine is crowded on both sides with stores and vendors. They sell souvenirs, various kinds of herbs in bundles, and food, particularly local treats such as ricecakes with mugwort leaves in them. People who come with friends and relatives stop to enjoy themselves in the semi-open restaurants. Many purchase souvenirs for family and friends. During one of my trips, I talked with a woman in her early forties who purchased a small porcelain badger to place next to her potted plant. She explained that when she had come to the shrine last time with her teenage children, they had forbidden her to buy a badger because they did not want her to follow a "superstition." However, her sister had one and it had brought her a string of good luck, and so the woman had come alone this time in order to purchase one.

Conspicuous among the souvenirs are porcelain figures of badgers, frogs, monkeys, and other animals that are familiar figures in Japanese folk beliefs.

Called *mayoke danuki* (evil-exorcising badgers), badgers feature prominently in Japanese folk tales and are reproduced as various icons, such as porcelain figurines. Likewise, frogs (*kaeru* in Japanese) are believed to bring good luck to a person, since *hikigaeru*, the Japanese word for toad, includes the term *hiki*, which also means "to draw" (draw good luck). Similarly, the word *kaeru* (frog) is a homonym for the word that means "to return." Thus, *kaeru* signifies the concept of returning to a normal condition after a disaster, and the frog symbolically expresses this hope. Also, *gama no abura* (toad oil) has been a common folk medicine. The three-monkey figure (see no evil, hear no evil, and speak no evil) is also prominent among souvenirs. If one follows these three behavioral taboos, one will live in harmony with other people – a good preventive medicine, at least to some.

As one gets closer to the shrine, the presence of the Sakamoto *kanpō* dealer becomes even more apparent. There is a *tengudō*, an edifice for worshipping *tengu* – a type of mountain deity usually depicted with a long nose, although this image is of recent origin (Yanagita, ed. 1951:388–9). According to the explanation on the wall where several pictures of *tengu* are displayed, the grandfather of the founder of the Sakamoto *kanpō* dealer worshipped *tengu*. On the wall of this edifice, facing the road, are several large framed pictures and writings describing the founder's meeting with "dignitaries," including Hitler, Mussolini, the present emperor of Japan, and former prime ministers Sato and Tanaka. Pictures of face-to-face meetings are not always included, however. Visitors to the shrine often stop briefly and glance at the writings and pictures, without displaying any particular reaction. Just before the entrance to the shrine itself is the headquarters of the Sakamoto *kanpō* store. The display at this store emphasizes more animal *kanpō* medicines than do the displays at other stores owned by the same dealer. These medicines include dried sea otter penises and charred monkey heads and cobras.

As one enters the compound of the shrine, just past a *torii* (the structure signifying a gate to a shrine), one sees a group of people, sometimes as many as thirty or so, walking rapidly between the two aforementioned stone slabs, touching the stones each time they pass them. People have a choice of making the rounds either one hundred times or as many times as their age. Elderly people often choose their age, counting one round for every ten years; a person who is sixty-five would go around six times plus five, or eleven times. Some people purchase a bundle of one hundred paper strings, removing them one by one as they complete each round. The compound, especially toward the front, is also studded with stone pillars. These pillars are covered with engravings of Sakamoto's name, and amounts and descriptions of donations to various causes, which include such civic projects as road construction in Osaka.

In a section to the right of the shrine are sold various religious paraphernalia, such as incense and small rectangular boards on which prayers are written. A few money-changing machines stand nearby to facilitate the process. There are two offices in this section. One office recruits people for the shrine's *kō*. *Kō* refers to any group organized for religious purposes; such groups have been very active throughout Japan in the past as well as the present (see Yanagita, ed. 1951:189–90). According to the newsletter of the *kō* for Ishikiri Shrine (Ishikiri Kyōhonchō, ed. 1980), the greatest number of *kō* for this shrine are found around Osaka, but some are based as far away as Wakayama, Kōchi, and Himeji, and even São Paulo, Brazil.

The second office registers people who wish to have special prayers offered for them by the priest. There are several types of such prayers, or *kitō*. Those who seek *kitō* are advised to avoid vinegar and fish with blue-green backs, such as mackerel. The office also sells a number of special items for healing, with instructions on how to use them. For example, after its purchase an amulet must be wrapped in a white piece of paper and rubbed against the ailing part a number of times. Long white pieces of cloth (*sarashi*) and cotton undergarments to be worn by the patients are also sold. Upon the patient's recovery, items used during the illness must be thrown into a river, burned, or returned to the shrine. Bundles of rice are another item sold here. Patients swallow one grain every morning with their first drink of water. In the case of infants, mothers must swallow the rice on their behalf.

To the right of the shrine is a sacred white pony in an enclosure. There are also a number of structures in the area, where prayer boards, paper cranes, and various other items are hung. Written on these boards (*ema*) are prayers for recovery from particular illnesses and statements of appreciation for recovery, sometimes written by the patients themselves, and sometimes by family members. Many people include their names, especially their first names, and their ages on the boards; a surprising number of them are fairly young. The prayers written on the boards, however, are not confined to matters of illness – some even ask for successful entrance to a particular university. The paper cranes hanging from the boards follow the Japanese tradition in which a woman folds one thousand paper cranes to help fulfill a wish. Hung among these bundles of paper cranes are various items used in curing, such as underwear in a plastic bag or canes used during an illness.

As noted earlier, the road to the shrine, the shrine compound, and even the train ride from Osaka to the Ishikiri Station turned out to be excellent for fieldwork, since most of the people were there because of some illness, either of themselves or of a close relative. The first time I visited the shrine alone, I rested on a bench in the shrine compound next to a woman of forty-five. Her daughter, twenty, had had surgery two weeks earlier, during which the doctor found a number of small growths in her uterus. The growths were benign according to the doctor, who did not remove them. Both the woman and her daughter were still apprehensive about the possibility of cancer. The woman stressed that she was concerned because she felt childbearing to be the most important role of women, and any complication of the uterus could affect this vital role. She had therefore visited a male *kamisan* (deity; in this case, a shaman) in Kyoto in the morning, and then took the long bus ride to Ishikiri in order to receive diagnoses from two additional sources besides the medical doctor. The shaman in Kyoto reassured her that her daughter did not have cancer, and would have a normal married life with children. The woman explained that she used to consult another shaman, whose spirit was Kōjin-san (the Kitchen God). She later switched to her current shaman who, as she repeatedly emphasized, is very decisive in his proclamations, although she is not sure which spirit possesses him.

Another woman of sixty-two, whom I met on a train, had been a widow since her husband was killed during World War II. Ever since her childhood, when her family had lived in the middle of the city of Osaka, she and her family had visited Ishikiri Shrine regularly. She remembered one time when she had had a growth (*dembo*) and had rubbed it with a piece of paper on which the name of Ishikiri Tsurugiya Shrine was written; the growth disappeared in a few days. She visited the shrine always on the first and the fifteenth of the month, and sometimes on a few other days. She usually prayed for the safety and general welfare of the family, but at times she went through *kitō*, or prayer sessions. Sometimes she would pay only about ¥ 1,000 for *kitō*, for which a priest would write her name, age, and wish on a sheet of paper, which she would then take home. If the matter was more serious, she occasionally paid more and was allowed to go into the *honden* (inner shrine), where a priest offered a prayer to the deities on behalf of all the people gathered there. She used to go around the two stones one hundred times, but now she goes around only eight times (six times for sixty years, plus two).

Nakayama Temple: Its role in obstetrics, gynecology, and pediatrics

As with Ishikiri Shrine, Nakayama Temple was not part of my planned fieldwork. The unquestionable importance of this temple in health care, especially for women and children, became evident during my observations at the obstetric clinic at hospital X. As will be noted in Chapter 8, many pregnant women in Japan continue to wear the traditional long white sash, called *iwata obi*, over the stomach during pregnancy. Of 106 women who answered my questionnaire, 81 had obtained a sash from Nakayama Temple.

The temple is situated on a large hill not far from a railroad station. Its compound is enormous and occupies almost one whole side of the hill, which is the central of three hills – hence the designation Nakayama (Middle-Mountain)

Temple. According to its own historical account, the temple was originally built by Prince Shōtoku (A.D. 574–622). Although the origin of its close association with childbirth and child welfare is not well documented, it may date to the end of the sixteenth century, when the wife of Toyotomi Hideyoshi, the military ruler of Japan at that time, became pregnant after prayers at the temple. She subsequently gave birth to a son, thus providing the long-awaited heir (Kanaoka 1970:263). The mother of the Meiji emperor, the grandfather of the present emperor, also paid homage to this temple before she gave birth to the emperor. Whatever its origin, the temple is known throughout Japan for its role in matters of childbirth and general child welfare.

The following description is based on two visits to the temple, one on an ordinary day, and the other on the day of a special ceremony held for the souls of the dead who have no relatives to provide memorial services for them (*muen botoke*). For lack of space I must omit much of what I observed, including a description of the ceremony itself.

The major hall (*hondō*) of the temple is situated on top of the hill, and is flanked by numerous *jizō*, the guardian buddha of children, on the hillside. The gate to the temple is situated at the bottom of the hill, and is connected to the main hall by a straight path consisting of many stone steps. On both sides of this central pathway are separate temples enshrining various buddhas, each specializing in a certain function. For example, on the left just after the gate is a temple that specializes in success in the university entrance examination. Another temple enshrines a buddha who specializes in taking care of infants who have temper tantrums, do not sleep, cry at night, or are constitutionally very weak. Another temple, which bears a sign in the front for traffic safety and the naming of newborn infants also houses *Mizuko Jizō* (*jizō* for aborted fetuses). Inside this temple, to the left, are a *jizō* for aborted fetuses, and numerous votive plaques hung on two wooden structures (Photo 17). For lack of space, these prayer boards are hung on top of each other in layers, indicating the large number of people who have visited the temple.

At the top of the hill, in front of the main hall, is a large metal incense burner (Photo 18). People buy bundles of incense, light them, and place them in the burner; many then "scoop" up the smoke with a hand and bring it onto an ailing part, such as the hip, to utilize its "healing power." Visitors, especially women with infants, also purchase white bibs, write prayers and their names and addresses on them, and hang them on a stake around the buddha (Photo 19) in front of the main hall. The main hall itself houses two offices. On the right side is a small office where the temple employees sell sashes. After purchasing a sash, a woman would ask the priest of the temple to write a sutra on it. On the left is another small office where used sashes must be returned.

The composition of visitors to Nakayama Temple also reflects the complex

17. Votive plaques for aborted fetuses, asking for forgiveness or praying for their peaceful sleep.

18. Large incense burner at Nakayama Temple. People "scoop up" the smoke from the lighted incense with their hands and place it on an ailing part of the body.

19. At Nakayama Temple, visitors write prayers and their names and addresses on bibs and hang them on stakes placed around the buddha.

human network involved in childbirth. Although pregnant women and mothers with young children comprise the core of the visitors (Photo 20), many of them are accompanied by older women, and sometimes by older men. A number of women are accompanied by their husbands, reflecting the recently increased emphasis on the conjugal bond and the nuclear family.

As the sketchy description provided here indicates, the central focus of the temple is childbirth and matters related to infancy, including easy and safe delivery, the healthy growth of children, and memorial services for aborted fetuses. According to the people I interviewed, both visitors and temple officials, the temple has long served also as a place for the *shichi-go-san* celebration – a celebration marked by a visit to a shrine, usually on November 15, when a child is three, five, and seven years old (*shichi-go-san* means seven, five, and three).

The various functions performed by the temple reveal the considerable flexibility in the roles played by temples and shrines that is characteristic of Japanese religion. As a general rule, Buddhism is closely tied to matters dealing with death; funerals and memorial services for the dead are provided at its temples. Shintoism deals with birth and growth, ceremonies for births, marriage, and other matters related to growth are provided at its shrines. The functions carried

20. Many visitors to Nakayama Temple are women with infants. In the background are numerous *omikuji* (fortune papers), which visitors buy at the temple and tie to the wooden structure for their good fortune to come true.

out by Nakayama Temple, then, are those usually assigned to a shrine (except for the memorial service to aborted fetuses, which has become important only in recent years). The visitors I interviewed found nothing unusual about the services performed by the temple. A few said, however, that although they consider this particular temple to be associated with childbirth, they usually associate the seven-five-three ceremonies with shrines. Those who do bring their children to this temple for the seven-five-three ceremonies added that, since they had come to the temple for the safe delivery of the children, they found it logical to continue to come to this temple for the welfare of the children.

Unlike Ishikiri Shrine, Nakayama Temple does not display intense commercialization or the presence of one particular entrepreneur. On the other hand, "religious services" at the temple are by no means free. One must pay for incense, bibs, prayer boards, fortunes written on pieces of paper (*omikuji*), and even a sutra written on the sash. Some of the functions, such as the prayers for success in the entrance examination or the memorial services for aborted fetuses, reflect current concerns of the people themselves and also demonstrate the financial incentive for temples such as this one to take on these functions.

Overview

Although extremely sketchy, this general discussion of the current roles of temples and shrines and the description of two religious institutions tell us something about the medical roles played by religious institutions in modern Japan, and also about Japanese religions in general. Theoretical discussions of the problems raised in this chapter are relegated to the concluding chapter of the book; here I will briefly summarize the major points made so far.

Despite their high degree of modernization and industrialization, contemporary Japanese continue to use temples and shrines for medical and other purposes. There is, however, a wide range of individual beliefs underlying visits to religious institutions. Some people do in fact believe deeply in deities and buddhas and in their efficacy in medical and other matters. Other people are half-hearted and pay visits simply because "it does not hurt anything," or because the act pleases someone who does believe.

The behaviors and experiences of visitors to shrines and temples are multi-dimensional; in addition to the medical and religious dimensions, there are social and recreational dimensions. The visits provide an opportunity for family members and friends to go out together. Even when a person pays a solitary visit on behalf of a sick family member, a pregnant woman, or some other person, the act inherently involves a significant social relationship. It is for these social relationships, explicit or implicit, that the sale of amulets and other religious items, and the presence of stores along the road to a temple or a shrine, becomes meaningful. The purchase of souvenirs and amulets is a concrete expression of social relationships that are an important factor in the act of visiting a temple or shrine. There is also a recreational aspect to the visits: Visitors take off from their daily routine, and stop to eat or purchase souvenirs along the way. Since most temples and shrines are situated on hills, often far away from railroad stations, the visits provide physical exercise as well.

The use of temples and shrines by contemporary Japanese reveals, then, the very secular orientation of the people toward their religions. People ask deities and buddhas for health, prosperity, traffic safety, and various other worldly benefits; they do not focus exclusively on their spiritual well-being or on life after death.

As a corollary, these deities and buddhas are seen by the people as performing specific functions. In anthropological literature, we traditionally regard magic as associated with specific functions, and religion with generalized purposes. Specialists in magic, be they shamans or diviners, are asked to achieve specific goals for a specific individual at given times ("cure this individual's heart illness now"), whereas specialists in religion, such as priests or monks, are asked to pray to the deities for the general welfare of the group through all time. Most contemporary anthropologists do not regard the distinction between magic and religion as clear-cut, and they tend to regard the two as opposite ends of a continuum. Nevertheless, it appears that as they are used by the people, Japanese religions are magical in nature, although they are highly institutionalized, with an elaborate body of theology. The predominantly magical character of Japanese religions demands some attention by scholars of religion and modernization, since another anthropological assumption, still held by some, is the association of magical institutions with "primitive" societies and religious institutions with "civilized" societies – a topic I will address further in the concluding chapter.

Japanese religious institutions are often intensely commercial. The commercialization at Ishikiri Shrine is somewhat unusual only in its intensity. Just as the people who pay homage to Ishikiri do not seem bothered by the commercial pressure of the *kanpō* dealer at the shrine, those who pay for purification of their cars or for paper amulets at Kōganji are not bothered by the feature of mass production evident in these practices. To the Japanese, who may literally throw ten thousand yen or hundred-yen coins to deities and buddhas when they go to shrines and temples, the commercial side of contemporary religious establishments is quite within tradition – they have always paid for religious services. It should be noted here that the use of money is highly symbolic in any society (see Simmel 1978); the "payment" for religious services by the Japanese is not the same as the payment for ordinary merchandise.

What we see in the visits to temples and shrines is a microcosm of urban Japan. "Urban magic" is wrapped in commercialism, with religious beliefs ranging from deep conviction to almost none. In one sense, the entire society gives the impression of being engaged in an intense and perpetual struggle between people and commercialism, with each trying to utilize and outdo the other, and with no clear vision of which one will ultimately have the upper hand. (For a most incisive interpretation of the use of the supernatural by the Japanese and the profusion of urban magic, see Umesao 1980:191–208; 1981:43–65; see also Befu 1979 for his insight that animism and ancestor worship are the dominant religions of Japan.)

7　Medical roles of Japanese religions: A historical-symbolic interpretation

To reveal further the medical roles Japanese religions have played, the emphasis in this chapter switches from description to a more interpretive perspective within a historical framework. In presenting both types of information in these two chapters, I hope to arrive at a comprehensive picture of the medical roles played by Japanese religions.

Background

Shintoism, Buddhism, Confucianism, and shamanism and various other folk religions have been the religions of Japan. Shintoism, the only religion of indigenous origin, and Buddhism have traditionally been regarded as the most important. It has often been pointed out that these religions have permeated the daily lives of the Japanese; they have become part of their customs without requiring any psychological commitment on the part of the individual. Most Japanese subscribe to more than one religion, often without consciously realizing it. The annual statistics on Japanese religious affiliation consistently list the total membership in various religious organizations as one and a half times the total population of Japan. In other words, over half of the people in Japan belong to more than one religious organization. The most recent figures available are for the six years between 1967 and 1978 and are presented in Table 2 and Figure 2. All these religions are polytheistic, and together they provide the Japanese with a rich and colorful pantheon composed of millions of deities, buddhas, deified ancestors, spirits, and other supernatural beings.

There is a long history of scholarly debate on the nature of the religious beliefs and attitudes of the Japanese, especially regarding the meaning of simultaneous subscription to more than one religion. The following statement by Beardsley (1965:312–13) presents the picture:

...the Japanese attitude toward religion is often described as eclectic and syncretic. Whether such a description is correct depends on one's viewpoint. Organizationally and

145

Table 2. *Number of religious organizations and membership*

Religions	1967	1974	1975	1976	1977	1978
Shintoism						
No. of organizations (%)	—	97,633	97,754	92,043	91,923	91,876
		(31.7)	(30.3)	(40.2)	(39.9)	(39.2)
Membership (%)	80,920,000	84,520,497	89,062,866	89,038,151	90,735,351	98,545,703
	(47.8)	(46.3)	(47.3)	(46.6)	(46.9)	(48.7)
Buddhism						
No. of organizations (%)	—	148,730	157,222	86,007	86,233	88,815
		(48.3)	(48.8)	(37.5)	(37.4)	(37.9)
Membership (%)	81,490,000	86,205,697	86,607,272	87,851,792	88,460,182	88,020,880
	(48.2)	(47.2)	(46.0)	(46.0)	(45.7)	(43.8)
Christianity						
No. of organizations (%)	—	7,758	7,775	7,589	7,681	7,960
		(2.5)	(2.4)	(3.3)	(3.3)	(3.4)
Membership (%)	770,000	873,286	885,862	901,797	929,502	950,491
	(0.5)	(0.4)	(0.5)	(0.5)	(0.5)	(0.6)
Other religions						
No. of organizations (%)	—	53,972	59,447	43,595	44,678	45,688
		(17.5)	(18.5)	(19.0)	(19.4)	(19.5)
Membership (%)	5,930,000	11,015,826	11,655,201	13,234,390	13,438,211	13,729,376
	(3.5)	(6.1)	(6.2)	(6.9)	(6.9)	(6.9)
Total no. of organizations	—	308,093	322,198	229,234	230,515	234,339
(%)	—	(100.0)	(100.0)	(100.0)	(100.0)	(100.0)
Total no. of membership	169,110,000	182,615,306	188,211,201	191,026,130	193,563,246	201,246,450
(%)	(100.0)	(100.0)	(100.0)	(100.0)	(100.0)	(100.0)

Sources: The figures for 1967 are from Tōkei Sūri Kenkyūjo Kokuminsei Chōsa Iinkai, ed. 1970:44. The figures for 1974 are from Bunkachō, ed. 1976:68–9. Those for 1975 are from Bunkachō, ed. 1977:70–1. Those for 1976 are from Bunkachō, ed. 1978:70–1. Those for 1977 are from Bunkachō, ed. 1979:70–1. Those for 1978 are from Bunkachō, ed. 1980:38–9. All figures are as of December 31 of the year.

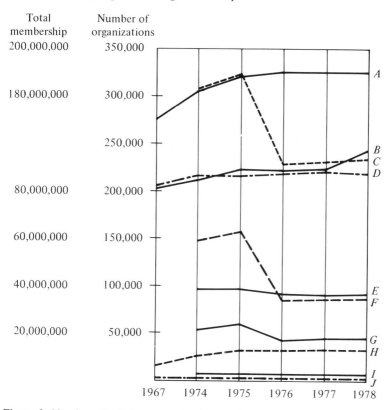

Figure 2. Number of religious organizations and membership.

ideologically, religions that have coexisted for centuries in Japan still remain separate and distinct systems.

. . .[W]hen we consider individual participation, a combination, if not a merger, of religions meets our eye.

The scholars involved in the controversy may be divided into two camps, as it were: Those who see religions in Japan as consisting of multiple "layers," and those who believe these religions to be "fused" into one system.

The following statement by Smith (1974:214–15) represents the view of some scholars who emphasize the presence of multiple layers in the Japanese religious structure (see also Itoh 1976:215; Tsurumi 1972):

Precision of definition and explicitness of formulation are not highly valued in Japan; the Japanese have perhaps more than most peoples explored to the fullest the uses and delights of ambiguity. . . . The reader may recall that throughout the foregoing chapters the words "multilayered" and "coexistent" have been used in discussing Japanese religious beliefs and practices. They are entirely apt, for there is less blending than one might expect, and more willingness simply to add new and appealing propositions and concepts to the inventory of those already current.

Although not dealing strictly with religion, Dore (1973:87–8) also points out that the Japanese in his ward in Tokyo comfortably embrace both "traditional" and "modern" ideas and practices without seeing any logical incongruity.

The other school of interpretation (Befu 1971:96; Hori 1968:10, 81; Norbeck 1976:56) holds that various magicoreligious beliefs and practices, many of foreign origin, have "merged" or "fused" to form one entity. After discussing the introduction into Japan of various foreign religions (Buddhism from India via Central Asia, China, and Korea; Confucianism, Taoism, and several other religions from China; Korean shamanism; and so on), Hori (1968:10) states:

> These borrowed ethical, magical, and religious elements were blended, reinterpreted, and resystematized into Japanese religion as one entity, through the process of cultural contact and interchange with the indigenous beliefs, rituals, and customs of primitive Shinto. They intermingled so completely that they lost their individual identities...

Hori's argument is quite complex. He sees the blending and reinterpretation of religions not as a hodgepodge, but as a process in which all the supernatural entities, regardless of their origin, are reinterpreted in terms of two basic types whose prototypes originate in primitive Shintoism (for a complete discussion of these types, *uji-gami* and *hito-gami*, see Hori 1968, 1977).

Two crucial points must be made in reference to this scholarly controversy. First, a clear distinction must be made between the two different perspectives – whether one looks at these Japanese religions in terms of their institutional-organizational frameworks and their orthodox doctrinal structures, or in terms of the way people view and practice them. In both organization and doctrinal framework, the major religions are distinct from each other, at least at the overt level. For example, most Buddhist temples are distinct from Shinto shrines, and each has a formal body of doctrine. Even in the way they have penetrated into the daily life of the Japanese, they display a division of labor: Buddhism is associated primarily with death and the dead; Shintoism is tied to birth, growth, and life in general. Of course, there are numerous exceptions to this general dichotomy. For example, there are Buddhist temples on the premises of Shinto shrines (Befu 1971:96), and a particular temple may adopt a specific function that relates to life. One can also often find symbols at local religious edifices that are both Buddhist and Shinto at the same time (Itoh 1976:215–16). Even in the realm of "official" doctrines and belief structures, much intermingling and fusion have been apparent, and there has been considerable research on the subject. On the whole, however, Shintoism and Buddhism have remained distinct in their structural organization and orthodox doctrines.

The problem of whether Japanese religions have merged or remained separate becomes even more taxing when the perspective of ordinary people is examined.

No one will deny that most Japanese are at least nominally both Buddhist and Shintoist at the same time. There is almost no alternative, since birth is celebrated only in a Shinto ceremony, and most funerals are Buddhist (see Smith 1974:73–74 for Shinto funerals). At least in terms of these customs, then, Japanese must be both Buddhists and Shintoists. The problem is whether these religions are viewed and practiced as one cultural system, or as separate systems used in combination.

The problem of lay perception of these religions brings us to the second point in the "multilayered" versus "fused" controversy. At the level of making distinctions between a buddha in Buddhism, a Shinto deity, a Taoist deity, and so on, most Japanese, no matter how indifferent they may be toward religions, would not confuse a buddha with a deity, even though the affiliation of some deities, such as Kōshin-sama of Taoism, are not well articulated. But in terms of the meaning and functions assigned to each of them by lay people, the scale tips toward the "fused" end, at least in the case of the supernaturals who perform medical functions.

I will address the multilayered versus fused controversy, a central issue in the study of Japanese religions, using data on the medical functions buddhas and deities have performed. The discussion begins with a description of the general occupational specializations of these supernatural entities and then focuses more narrowly on their medical functions.

Occupational specializations of Japanese supernaturals

To the Japanese, perhaps the most meaningful feature of this multitude of deities, buddhas, and other supernaturals is their *goriyaku* – the benevolent functions they perform. Somewhat like saints in Christianity, the supernatural entities are assigned fairly specific roles and functions, such as healing of a particular illness or protection from accidents.

Based on the information provided by Yanagita (1951, 1963), Itoh (Itoh in Katō et al. 1972:24–5; Itoh 1976:226–7) provides an excellent summary of these functions in graphic form. Table 3 is a translation of a portion of Itoh's chart that deals with illness and related matters, with minor changes. I also added to Itoh's list the third column, "Taoist deities," although only one deity is involved. Taoism has remained an important folk belief system in Japan, although its significance tends to be underestimated because it has never been developed into a distinct institutionalized religion (see Katō et al. 1972:69–70; Kubo 1961). Originally introduced from China, this system has gone through such thorough transformations in Japan that it is misleading to label it Taoism. I have translated the names of Itoh's deities and buddhas only when the translation is meaningful to the English reader; some bear proper names whose translations are meaning-

Table 3. *Medical specializations of Japanese deities and buddhas*

Specializations	Shinto deities	Buddhas	Taoist deities
Illness			
Illness in general	Kōjin (Kitchen God), Shibagami Daimyōjin	Roped Jizō (Shibari Jizō), Substitute Jizō (Migawari Jizō)	
Illness of the face	Wart-Stone Deity (Iboishi-sama)	Lifting Jizō (Mochiage Jizō)	
Illness of the eyes	Deity of the Blind (Mekura-gami), Deity of the Well (Ido-no-Kami)	Konnyaku Enma	Kōshin-sama
Illness of the ears (running cerumen; ringing in the ears)	Deity of the Boundary (Sae-no-Kami), Deity of the Ears (Mimi-no-Kami)	Jizō of the Ears (Mimi Jizō)	Kōshin-sama
Illness of the throat	Rooster Daimyōjin (Tori Daimyōjin)		
Illness of the teeth	Deity of the Toilet (Kawaya-no-Kami)	Prayer Jizō (Gankake Jizō)	Kōshin-sama
Illness of the chest and other respiratory organs	Deity of Coughing (Shiwabuki-sama)	Roped Jizō (Shibari Jizō)	Kōshin-sama
Illness of the stomach	Tsuri Tenjin	Roped Jizō (Shibari Jizō)	Kōshin-sama
Illness of the hip and the limbs	Deity of the Hip (Koshi-no-Kami), Deity of the Lower Limbs (Ashiō-sama), Kōjin of the Limbs (Ashide Kōjin), Deity of the Boundary (Sae-no-Kami)		

Illness of the skin		An Jizō	Kōshin-sama
Contagious illness	Deity of Smallpox (Hōso-shin)		Kōshin-sama
Illness of women	Awashima-sama		
Illness of children	Deity of Dirt and Poison (Odoku-sama)		Kōshin-sama
Life cycle			
Pregnancy and childbirth	Deity of the Broom (Hōki-no-Kami)	Jizō of Easy Childbirth (Koyasu Jizō)	Kōshin-sama
	Deity of Childbirth (Ubugami)		
	Deity of the Mortar (Usu-no-Kami)		
	Deity of the Pregnancy Stone (Yōsekiten)		
	Deity of the Boundary (Sae-no-Kami)		
	Deity of the Toilet (Kawaya-no-Kami)		
	Deity of the Mountain (Yama-no-Kami)		
	Deity of Easy Childbirth (Koyasu-sama)		
Growth	Deity of the Boundary (Sae-no-Kami)	Kannon of Easy Childbirth (Koyasu Kannon)	Kōshin-sama
	Deity of Easy Childbirth (Koyasu-sama)	Jizō of Easy Childbirth (Koyasu Jizō)	
Marriage	Deity of Motherhood (Komochi Gozen)		

Source: After Itoh (1976).

less. The recurrent term *sama* is an address form in Japanese used in referring to deities; when particular deities are always referred to with this address form, I left it in the romanized versions. Although the table by no means exhausts the huge pantheon of Japanese deities, it gives a good example of the functions these supernatural beings perform, which constitute perhaps the most important means of communication between humans and supernaturals.

Itoh's table does not include the frequency with which a particular specialization is assigned to deities and buddhas, or the frequency with which any particular deity or buddha is assigned various functions. However, a complementary study that includes these data has been conducted by Mizobe (1970), who examined the specializations of 103 temples and shrines randomly selected from all over Japan. Mizobe's data consist of specializations officially proclaimed by the temples and shrines themselves. As shown in Table 4 a total of 204 specializations are assigned to the 103 temples and shrines.

What is missing from both sets of data is the frequency of visits by people to particular types of deities and buddhas – in other words, their individual popularity. Ishikiri Shrine, for example, is exceedingly popular, as we have seen, and thousands of people visit it; but there may be many deities and buddhas who have their shingles up, as it were, and yet are less popular with the people.

In looking at Tables 3 and 4, it is immediately obvious that most deities and buddhas perform multiple functions. In the column for Taoist deities in Table 3, only one deity, Kōshin-sama, appears, but it appears several times. Kōshin-sama is of Taoist origin, although it appears in the contexts of both Shinto and Buddhism. Though insignificant in the hierarchies of the established religious systems, it is almost almighty; Kubo (1961:342) lists fifty-seven roles assigned to this deity. In the case of buddhas, all but two are some kind of *jizō* – a particular type of buddha discussed in detail later. Among the Shinto deities, the Deity of the Boundary appears four times and the Deity of the Toilet and the Deity of the Kitchen each appear twice. Although the Deity of Easy Childbirth appears twice, the two functions are too closely related to be counted separately.

A major difference between the findings of Itoh and those of Mizobe is that in Itoh's data Kōshin-sama and *jizō* appear most frequently, whereas in Mizobe's data Kannon is most frequent. These differences are directly related to the nature of the data each scholar used, and in fact reveal a significant fact: Itoh emphasized the way ordinary people resort to the supernaturals, so that Kōshin-sama and *jizō* came out on top. Since Taoism has never been institutionalized, its deity, Kōshin-sama, does not appear in any institutionalized edifices. It is, however, a highly significant deity, as Itoh's data suggest. *Jizō*, on the other hand, ranks second in frequency in both Itoh's and Mizobe's data. *Jizō* is a low-ranking buddha, which is often enshrined at roadsides or as an auxiliary to a major buddha of a temple. Therefore, it is expectedly the most frequently appearing figure among the buddhas in Itoh's data, but assumes the second position in Mizobe's data, in which Kannon, a major buddha, claims the top position.

Medical specializations of deities and buddhas in historical perspective

Changes and transformations of medical specializations

Miyata (1975) provides rich documentation on the histories of popular deities and their medical functions since the beginning of the seventeenth century. The lives and fates of these deities do indeed reflect the major concerns of people of the time. Outmoded specializations are often discarded or transformed into new, more meaningful, roles. The roles related to childbirth, child welfare, and general matters of illness and health comprise 54% (111 out of 204) of the total number of specializations in Table 4, indicating that these are perennial concerns of the people.[1] In contrast, functions related to calamities, including traffic accidents, comprise only 17%. Although Miyata (1975) does not provide statistical frequencies, natural disasters and fire were major concerns in the past, and were reflected in the specializations of deities and buddhas at the time. Contemporary Japanese seem to place more emphasis on luck and success in life, which comprise 28% of all the specializations.

The smallpox deity in Table 3 is an example of adaptation of specializations to changing epidemiological patterns. Of paramount importance in the past, the deity of smallpox is no longer meaningful in contemporary Japan, and its function had been expanded to incorporate contagious diseases in general. Likewise, the Deity of Coughing (Shiwabuki-sama) was originally a very popular deity when influenza was a major threat (Miyata 1975). Because influenza is better controlled in contemporary Japan, the deity is now also consulted for chronic respiratory illnesses, including asthma. Another example is the deity of Ishikiri Shrine, not included in the 103 temples and shrines in Mizobe's study. As described earlier, this deity used to be good for various kinds of boils and growths, but its major appeal at present is its efficacy in treating cancer. Cancer as a disease category is a relatively new phenomenon in Japan, as elsewhere, but no doubt some of the growths formerly treated at Ishikiri Shrine were carcinogenic. Tatsukawa (1976:197–202) provides a good historical account of cases that were indisputably carcinogenic and their treatments, including what was undoubtedly the first radical mastectomy performed in 1815.

[1] Umesao (in Katō et al. 1972:76) notes that one advertisement by a railroad company, urging people to travel by train to different temples and shrines, advocates to "be greedy in your wishes and requests (*negaigoto*)" and lists twenty-seven efficacious functions of these supernaturals, of which only three deal with illness; the majority deal with success in school, work, and life in general. Perhaps this advertisement was aimed at young people, so the emphasis on illness may have been consciously discouraged. The advertisement does at least reflect the wishes of contemporary Japanese for success in life.

Table 4. *Practical functions performed by deities and buddhas*

Names of deities and buddhas	A Safe childbirth, healthy growth of children	B Healing of illness,[a] health maintenance	C Prosperity in business, exorcism of evil, invitation of good luck	D Protection from fire, good catch at sea	E Total no. of functions carried by deity or buddha	F No. of temples or shrines enshrining deity or buddha
Kannon	24	16	22	13	75	49
Jizō	4	5	2	3	14	12
Daishi	4	2	4	1	11	8
Yakushi	4	3	2	0	9	7
Fudō	0	1	1	4	6	4
Myōō	0	1	2	1	4	2
Kishimojin	2	0	0	0	2	2
Soshi (Honzon)	0	1	1	1	3	3
Gongen	0	2	3	2	7	6
Other deities and buddhas	3	4	12	4	23	17
Others	10	25	9	6	50	36
Total	51	60	58	35	204	146

Note: Breakdown of the functions is as follows: *A.* Safe delivery, 28; abundant milk, 6; healthy growth of children, 17; total = 51. *B.* Maintenance of health and healing of illness, 45; substitutes, 2; longevity, 5; health, abundance of domestic crops, animals, and so on, 8; total = 60. *C.* Good marriage, 4; exorcism of evil and bringing of good luck, 34; safety of the nation and family, abundance of crops, and business prosperity, 13; other wishes, 7; total = 58. *D.* Traffic safety, 3; fire safety, 11; asking for rain, 4; good catch at sea and safety at sea, 8; avoidance of lightning, 3; avoidance of tidal waves, 2; avoidance of dangerous places, 1; others, 3; total = 35.

^a Breakdown of "healing of illness": Illness in general, 11; illness located above the neck, 2; illness of the eyes, 9; illness of the head, 1; illness of the mouth, nose, and teeth, 4; illness of the lung, 1; illness of the lower limbs and the hip, 2; paralysis (stroke), 1; mental illness, 1; itchiness and pain, 2; whooping cough, 1; splinters, 2; warts, corns, hemorrhoids, 2; birthmarks, 1; illness of women, 1; measles and smallpox, 2; tenseness and irritation in children, 2; boils and cuts, 2.

The term for tenseness and irritation in children is *yamai-fūji,* which is a broad term for healing various illnesses. The term *mushi-fūji* means healing *kan no mushi,* a worm believed to make children tense and irritable (for *mushi-fūji,* see Imamura 1979:208; Morisue and Hinonishi, eds. 1967:693).

Mizobe notes that the inclusion of a larger number of temples than shrines in the sample explains the small numbers in the table both for good marriages and traffic safety. However, as noted in this book, the function for traffic safety is relegated to both shrines and temples. "Substitutes" in *B* means when a mother, for example, wishes to substitute her own body for her ailing child. The same notion appears in Substitute Jizō in Table 3.

Source: After Mizobe (1970:414).

Illness as a multivocal symbol

Although general trends in people's needs and wishes are reflected in the functions that have been performed by deities and buddhas, we cannot conclude that there have been one-to-one correlations between the medical roles of these supernaturals and epidemiological patterns. The names of the illnesses a particular supernatural is said to be capable of healing must be interpreted broadly. Thus, illnesses of the stomach must be understood to incorporate both stomach ulcers and cancer, as well as any other illnesses located in the stomach in its broadest sense. Illnesses of the chest and other respiratory organs is also a very broad category.

Most important, some illness labels must be interpreted as being "metaphorical" – as being expressive of multitudes of physiological-psychological problems, rather than being biomedical disease categories or pathogens. The recent upsurge of concern about aborted fetuses illustrates this point. As I noted in Chapter 4, the rapid increase in the "worship" of aborted fetuses is not just a reflection of a narrowly conceived concern about the fetus itself; Japanese women do not perceive the fetus as a pathogen, or as a direct cause of a problem. The fetus is a polysemic symbol through which a great number of women express various kinds of concerns.

The strongest evidence for this interpretation comes from historical data. Abortions have always been performed with a very high frequency. Also, the belief in and memorial service for the water child (aborted fetus) has a long history in Japan. However, it is only recently that it has become the focus of attention. If we expect one-to-one correlations between epidemiology, be it illness or pathogen, and medical specializations performed by supernatural entities, then the frequency of the former should be directly reflected in the latter. In the past, when the number of abortions was much higher because of lack of effective birth control methods, the memorial service was never carried out on such a large scale as it is now.

Additional evidence for this interpretation comes from the increasing popularity of so-called *kakekomi dera*, or "runaway temples" (*kakekomi* = to run into; *dera* = temple) throughout Japan. These are *amadera* or temples operated by nuns where women seek help and refuge from their problems, often marital. One of these *kakekomi dera* that recently received some attention is Jikishian in Kyoto, which originally was operated by nuns. When a nun by the name of Hirose Zenjun became head of the temple in 1965, she began to provide a notebook called *Omoidegusa* (Grass of Memory) in which visitors were to write down their thoughts. She listened to the problems of visitors and gave advice. A young monk, Oda Yoshitake, born in 1948, started more systematic "counseling" of women when he took over the temple in 1978. Before he was put in charge, he had noticed that the number of women coming for consultation was increasing sharply, and that the problems they wrote down in their notebooks were of a serious nature. Intriguingly, among the 300 notebooks already filled since he became director of the temple, the most common "problem" is the confession and apology to an aborted fetus (*Asahi*, April 12, 1980).

We must therefore conclude that abortion and the aborted fetus express something beyond the narrowly defined phenomenon of abortion itself. I interpret it as a multivocal symbol in the Turnerian sense. According to Turner (1975a:155; see also Cohen 1974:ix), many important symbols in a culture, which he calls "dominant symbols," are multivocal or polysemic; they have various meanings, enabling "a wide range of groups and individuals to relate" to the symbol in a variety of ways. These symbols thus "stand ambiguously for a multiplicity of disparate meanings" and yet have the power to evoke sentiments and emotions, and mobilize people to take social action. The aborted fetus, like menstrual blood, is an apt choice to become a powerful symbol that can embody a variety of meanings and feelings, any one of which may be identified by a particular woman.

In the case of Japanese culture, it is particularly an appropriate symbol: The role of motherhood traditionally has received a high cultural value and given women a sense of self-worth and satisfaction, and yet these values are undergoing critical scrutiny and reevaluation. In some cases abortions may reflect marital conflicts, and women may even use the memorial service, at least subconsciously, to draw their husband's attention to their sufferings (see Good's analysis of the semantic network of the heart disease of Iranian women, Good 1977). Although further investigation is necessary to identify the precise nature of the problems expressed through the memorial service to the aborted fetus, it is clear that the phenomenon is a complex one and cannot be taken literally.

As the case of the aborted fetus illustrates, we must avoid a naive, positivistic equation of the illness categories or causes used to label the medical specializations of deities and buddhas with strictly biomedical or physiological disease categories and pathogens. The specializations of supernatural entities in Japanese religions reflect the concerns of people. In this sense, Japanese supernaturals are largely created by the wills and desires of the people, who determine their popularity and fate.

The role of the individual in historical processes

In addition, certain individuals play a positive role in shaping the nature of supernatural power in Japanese religions. As Miyata (1975) illustrates with a number of detailed examples, the installment of a new specialty of a deity or a buddha, or the transformation of an existing role to another one more meaningful to the people at the time, usually takes place after an unusual phenomenon occurs, such as a vision, a dream, or a miracle of some sort that is seen or performed by an individual. These individuals, often of humble social status, play an active role in shaping Japanese religions, thereby serving as agents of culture change. Other individuals who play an active role in such a flow of events are the entrepreneurs associated with temples and shrines. They are often Buddhist monks or Shinto priests who are quick to perceive people's needs, and who seize the opportunity to promote the religious establishment by adding a new specialty, or by transforming an already existing specialty of a buddha or a deity enshrined at the edifice. At Ishikiri Shrine, for example, a single *kanpō* manufacturer promoted himself, his business, and the shrine itself.

These individuals, however, do not act in a vacuum. When an individual sees a vision or performs a "miracle," he or she often projects the needs and thoughts of the people into an unusual phenomenon, such as a dream in which a particular buddha heals an illness, or the sight of a stone cracking in half in front of one's eyes. Involved in these "miracles" is the dialectic interplay between the individual's input into the culture and the cultural system itself. In order for a dream interpretation to be convincing to others, its meaning must be "public," as Geertz would put it – that is, it must derive from "socially established structures of meaning," or culture (Geertz 1973:12). The meaning cannot be completely private or idiosyncratic. If a stone cracks, for example, someone seeing meaning in the phenomenon probably would be laughed at in an American city today. In Japan in the past, however, the person's interpretation probably would have made "cultural sense," since stones and rocks had rich symbolic value, and many of the *goshintai* (the body of a deity or a buddha) were in fact rocks, stones, and pebbles (Yanagita 1963). Even today, people receive pebbles at some temples and shrines, write prayers on them, and enshrine them at home. Upon either fulfillment of the wish or recovery from the illness, they return the pebbles to the shrine, as we saw in the discussion on Ishikiri Shrine (Photo 12).

The manipulative attitude of the Japanese toward their supernaturals should not give the impression that individuals have a free hand in shaping the flow of events. A close examination of the process whereby the supernaturals are assigned their various roles reveals an intricate interplay between the cultural system and the individual. Although people's desires and needs are reflected in the roles assigned to the supernaturals, these functions cannot be created at will or randomly. Instead, individual needs must be systematically incorporated into the cultural system – that is, the symbolic system underlying the cultural characterizations of deities and buddhas.

Patterns in role allocation

As examples on a general level, only some among the multitude of deities and buddhas are assigned particular roles. In the realm of medicine, we see that a buddha called *jizō* is assigned a prominent place in both Itoh's and Mizobe's lists, and Kannon, a buddha, appears most frequently (49%) in Mizobe's list, whereas other buddhas and deities keep a low profile. Of the sects within Buddhism, 56% of the temples in Mizobe's study that provide medical and other functions belong to Shingon; the sect with the next highest frequency is Tendai, which comprises only 14% of all the temples. All other sects are insignificant. Although these data are much too general to substantiate any claim for patterning in the allocation of roles to supernatural entities, they do nevertheless reveal some regularities in the way these deities and buddhas are assigned their specializations.

There are more concrete examples of regularities in the historical process whereby roles are assigned to particular deities and buddhas. For example, the need for supernatural protection for air travel has arisen as planes have become an increasingly common mode of transportation for contemporary Japanese. One might expect that any shrine or temple operated by an entrepreneur would think of the idea and promote the power of a deity or buddha enshrined there for that purpose. However, the air safety function has been assigned only to the temple that enshrines Narita Fudōsan, a buddha already in charge of motor traffic safety (Katō in Katō et al. 1972:102). The Narita Fudōsan temple, in Narita City in Chiba Prefecture, is said to have been built in A.D. 940 (Kaneoka 1970:265–8). It belongs to the Shingon sect which, as noted earlier, is most closely associated with medical roles. The temple has been known throughout history for its power of protection from man-made calamities such as fire (Miyata 1975:126–8). In recent years its enormous expansion, with branches throughout Japan, can be credited to an ingenious monk (Araki Shōtei) who capitalized on the ability of the buddha to promote motor traffic safety and prosperity in business (Kaneoka 1970:267). Narita Fudōsan illustrates patterned change and adaptation of the functions of a temple, from fire protection to motor and air safety – protection from all man-made calamities. Given this process, we can view Tables 3 and 4 as an end product of a long process of dialectic interplay between culture and the individual.

Individual deities and buddhas with medical specializations

A brief description of each of the supernaturals in Table 3 is presented in this section as background for the interpretation of the symbolic structure underlying their medical specializations.

Kōshin-sama

At various times and regions in Japan, the original Taoist concept concerning Kōshin has gone through a series of transformations, often resulting in diverse syncretic beliefs as a result of influence from other beliefs in Shintoism and Buddhism. The most dominant and persistent characteristic is the concept expressed in the term Kōshin (Kō = monkey or Kōshin day), which is the fifty-seventh day of each sixty-day or year cycle in the Taoist calendar. On this day, the three worms (sanshi), black, green, and white in color, that are believed to dwell in a person's body are said to ascend to Heaven and report to the Emperor of Heaven their host's transgressions during the previous cycle (Blacker 1975:329; Yanagita, ed. 1951:196–7). On this evening people get together and pray to Kōshin-sama for protection. Kōshin-sama thus protects humans at the time of temporal liminality – between the two cycles of sixty days or years. As noted earlier, Kōshin-sama has remained an important folk deity and is assigned innumerable roles and functions. Here we see an inversion of hierarchy between the established theology and folk religion: Kōshin-sama, not a major deity in an institutionalized religion, is almost almighty as a folk deity with his innumerable roles, at least fifty-seven in all.

Buddhas

Jizō. The same holds true for jizō in the column for buddhas. Jizō is a low-ranking buddha in Buddhist theology and yet is of great importance to lay people. It is the most frequent entry in the column for buddhas. Although jizō is one type of the bodhisattva in Buddhism, it is not certain if it had originally existed in Buddhism in India. In Japan, jizō became a popular buddha during the late Heian period (A.D. 794–1185) among aristocrats, but the belief soon spread to commoners (Yanagita, ed. 1951:257). Of paramount importance to people throughout Japanese history has been the role of jizō as the deity of the boundary between this world and the world after death (Miyata 1975; Yanagita, ed. 1951:257–8). He is seen as the savior of people who otherwise would be tortured in hell after death. Therefore, as the deity of this boundary, jizō is often placed at other boundries, especially between villages or on any spatial boundary lines.

This general characterization of jizō as a merciful savior leads to more specific subtypes of jizō at various times in history, some of which have remained important jizō up to the present day. One of these is Shibari Jizō, or Roped Jizō, which appears three times in the table. A sick person would tie up a Shibari Jizō in order for the jizō to experience the suffering, and would pray to the jizō to save him or her. When he or she was successfully cured, the jizō would be freed (Miyata 1975:131–2). Another subtype is Migawari Jizō, or Substitute Jizō. These jizō save an individual from suffering by volunteering to be the victim of the suffering instead. There are numerous stories in which an individual suffering from an eye disease, for example, would wake up one day from a dream in which a *jizō* had appeared to find that the eye disease had disappeared and had been transferred to a *jizō* enshrined nearby (Miyata 1975:132–3; Yanagita, ed. 1951:257).

As a merciful figure, *jizō* has become a guardian of children. In fact, many *jizō* bear the face of a child and wear a red bib, as described in the section on the Ishikiri Shrine. Another subtype is Koyasu Jizō (Child Jizō). This *jizō* received its name, Koyasu (child peace/safety) because it is believed to provide safety and peace to children, especially by preventing them from falling into the world of the dead during their unstable periods of growth (Miyata 1975:130; Yanagita, ed. 1951:257). Gankake Jizō, or Invocation Jizō, is a more general category of *jizō* to which people make invocations and which therefore includes, for example, the Roped Jizō discussed above.

Merciful Buddha (Kannon). This buddha is a merciful bodhisattva whose role is to save people from suffering. As noted earlier, as a high-ranking buddha, Kannon appears most often in Mizobe's list (Table 4). Koyasu Kannon is a Kannon in charge of the welfare of children.

Konnyaku Enma. Originally *enma* was one of the buddhas in Heaven and was the guardian of Buddhism and in charge of longevity. In time, however, *enma* came to be characterized as an evil buddha or "devil" who, as the ruler of Hell, judges the past behavior of those who arrive in Hell and tortures them. During the Hōreki period (A.D. 1750–1760), the "worship" of *enma*, who by then was associated with Hell, became very popular. The precipitating factor for this popularity was the successful healing of an eye disease in an elderly woman. The woman had been asking the *enma* enshrined at Genkakuji to heal her eye. On the thirty-seventh day, as she kneeled in front of the statue of *enma*, as she had been doing all along, she fell asleep. In her dream, *enma* appeared and told her that he would heal her eye at the sacrifice of his own eye because of her earnest prayers to him. When she woke up her eye had been healed, but she noticed that the right eye of the *enma* statue had been damaged. In other words, *enma* performed the healing function exactly in the manner of Substitute Jizō. Miyata (1975:136–7), who provides this information, infers that people prayed to *enma* and other supernaturals associated with Hell with the idea that if they prayed to them, they would be spared from falling into Hell. *Enma* will be interpreted further in the next section.

Shinto deities

There are primarily three different kinds of Shinto deities: those that bear the names of spatial categories, such as the deities of the boundary and the kitchen;

those that bear the names of illnesses for which they are thought to be efficacious; and those that bear the names of afflicted body parts. Many of the deities in the last two categories are not usually bona fide deities, but are often objects where a spirit having certain healing power abides.

Deity of the Boundary. Of all the Shinto deities, the Deity of the Boundary, pronounced as either Sai-no-kami or Sae-no-kami, appears most frequently. This deity, always represented by a large rock, is believed to stop evil spirits and devils at a crossroad; hence the term *sai*, whose original meaning is "to block." This deity appears as early as the *Kojiki*, the earliest document in Japan. Recall that Izanagi-no-Mikoto visits his deceased wife, Izanami-no-Mikoto, in the underworld of the dead. As he is returning to the world of the living, he meets this deity at the boundary between the two worlds (Philippi 1969:65; Shimonaka, ed. 1941:93). Although its dominant characterization has always been as the deity of the boundary, especially the boundary between villages, over time its symbolic meaning also has become associated with male and female sexual organs – the body parts that form both the boundary line and the meeting place between the two sexes. In my interpretation, this sexual connotation for the deity is already present in the *Kojiki*. At any rate, more recently, especially since the sixteenth century, the deity has become closely associated with matters of reproduction, having the power to oversee marriage, fertility, pregnancy, and childbirth, as well as to heal illnesses of the sexual organs. In particular, it has become the guardian deity of children. (The factual information on this deity is taken from Shimonaka, ed. 1941:93.)

This description suggests obvious parallels between Sae-no-Kami and *jizō*. Although the name Sae-no-Kami includes the term *kami* (deity), and although the unquestionable official identity of *jizō* is as a buddha, both entities are associated with spatial boundaries, and both are the guardians of children. These parallels appear as early as the Muromachi period (A.D. 1338–1558), when *wasan* (praises of teachings in Buddhism in Japanese, as opposed to in Sanskrit or in Chinese) about *jizō* appeared. These literary pieces, twelve in all, bear the title *Sai no Kawara Jizō Wasan* (Praises in Japanese of *Jizō* at the River Bank at Sai) and vary somewhat in words, but not in content. The term *sai* is written using either the character for the direction west or the character for "blocking," as in Sae-no-Kami. The common theme in all twelve is the crying of abandoned small children on the western riverbank, where they build a pagoda of pebbles. At dusk, a devil appears from Hell, destroys the pagoda, and starts to torture the children, whereupon a *jizō* appears and protects them (Manabe 1959:72–4; 160–2; the original of these "praises" are in Manabe 1960:198–223).

Despite the formal distinction between Sai-no-Kami as a deity in folk Shintoism and *jizō* as a buddha, these two supernaturals are almost identical in their major characterizations, with their prototype already in the *Kojiki* (see Manabe 1959:200–1 for a discussion of whether or not in the characterization of *jizō* is unique to Japan). I might even see the prototype for both supernaturals in the *Kojiki*.

Smallpox Deity (Hōsōshin). This deity, also associated with the notion of a boundary, was thought to be an evil deity, traveling from village to village spreading smallpox. Therefore, unlike other deities who possess healing power, the smallpox deity was considered a pathogenic agent. To prevent a smallpox epidemic, or to chase off this deity when a village was already afflicted, villagers made an effigy and placed it at the village boundary, where they performed a ritual to chase the deity out of the village (Miyata 1975:92–100).

Kitchen God (Kōjin-sama). This deity, listed twice in the table, is characterized in various ways depending on times and regions. Two major characteristics, however, are fairly consistent. First, this is the deity of the kitchen, or more specifically, of the cooking stove and/or the fire that represents the kitchen. The kitchen or stove is assigned an important symbolic meaning and represents the household itself. Second, Kōjin-sama is a fierce deity, as the term Kōjin (*kō* = fierce, rough; *jin* = deity) indicates (Shimonaka, ed. 1941:135; Yanagita, ed. 1951:197).

Deity of the Toilet (Kawaya-no-Kami). This deity is comprised of both a male and a female, who are the deities of the ground and water, respectively. They were born of the excretion and urine of Izanami-no-Mikoto, the Goddess of the Underworld. The Deity of the Toilet is endowed with powers for healing illnesses of the eyes and the teeth, as well as gynecological illnesses (*Jingū Shichō* 1967:916; Shimonaka, ed. 1941:384).

Awashima-sama. With a more proper name of Awaji-myōjin, this deity became a popular deity for gynecological illnesses during the Genroku period in the seventeenth century, when a group of itinerant priests called *ahashima* traveled all over Japan, carrying a small altar enshrining Awaji-myōjin from which pieces of cloth of various colors were hung. As these priests walked around a village, they proclaimed in loud singing voices the healing power of this deity for "the illnesses of women located below the belt" (Shimonaka, ed. 1941:71; Yanagita, ed. 1951:15–16).

Others. As noted earlier, the deities of body parts and those of particular illnesses are not established types of deities. Someone might engage in *gankake* – praying to some supernatural power requesting the cure of an illness, but promising in return abstinence from a particular food or some other act of personal sacrifice. Since in the past a bridge, a river, or a slope was often considered to possess supernatural power, during *gankake* people often prayed to them. Therefore, one particular part of a bridge might become a deity of toothaches or coughing. (For information on the supernatural power of a bridge, river, and so on, see Miyata 1975:40–7; Yamaguchi 1977. For examples of these entities as deities of particular illnesses, see Miyata 1975: 40–7, 141, 143.)

Symbolic interpretation of medical specializations

The preceding description of deities and buddhas with medical specializations reveals two major patterns in the symbolic structure that underlies the overt meanings attributed to each of these entities. First, some of these entities are associated with the notion of a boundary. Second, some embody the concept of a stranger-deity with dual power.

Jizō and the Deity of the Boundary (Sae-no-Kami), both appearing frequently in Table 3, are associated with spatial boundaries such as a village border. We noted also that effigies of the Smallpox Deity are placed at the village boundary. Many of the deities whose names refer to a particular illness or body part are also associated with a spatial boundary, often represented by a river or a bridge over a river. A river often marked a boundary line between villages in the past, and it continues to constitute a demarcation line between towns and cities in contemporary Japan. Kōshin-sama, a Taoist deity, which appears most frequently of all the supernaturals in Table 3, is associated with temporary liminality – the "boundary" between two cycles of sixty days or years in the Taoist calendar.

The concept of the boundary, which embodies the notion of "betwixt and between" (Turner 1967), brings us back to the spatial marginality discussed in Chapter 2. I suggested there that impurity in the Japanese symbolic structure is expressed as the spatial marginality – that is, the boundary. This location is where cultural germs are located, and where some of the *burakumin* (outcastes) associated with impurity used to reside. My symbolic interpretation in this chapter of the medical roles of supernatural entities reinforces the symbolic equation of the marginality or fringe with impurity: These supernaturals are situated at the boundary, where cultural germs are located, in order to prevent germs and impurity from entering the village, or to chase them out of the village or any other spatial unit if they have already invaded it.

The second major pattern in the symbolic meanings assigned to the supernaturals is that several of them, whether they are deities or buddhas, belong to the *marebito* (stranger-deity) deities in early Japanese religion. As noted in Chapter 2, the stranger-deities were outsiders to agrarian communities, and went from village to village. They were endowed with dual powers, and could be in a state of either *nigitama* (benevolent or peaceful state) or *aratama* (fierce state). It was up to the villagers to control their power by turning the positive power to their own advantage through proper ritual acts, or by turning the negative power against themselves.

Included in this category of supernaturals are Konnyaku Enma, Kōjin-sama, Awashima-sama, the Deity of the Toilet (Kawaya-no-Kami), and the Smallpox Deity. Konnyaku Enma, as mentioned previously, was originally a deity of Heaven who later became an evil deity of Hell. He nonetheless continued to perform the positive function of healing. Clearly, then, he became a deity outside this world, endowed with dual power. Perceived as a fierce deity, Kōjin-sama is a linear descendant of *aratama*, a deity in a violent state, who nevertheless possessed the opposite quality, *nigitama*, as revealed in his power to heal and to protect the fire and kitchen. A direct symbolic link to the stranger-deity is also immediately apparent in the case of Awashima-sama, whose healing power was delivered by itinerant priests from outside a settlement. The Smallpox Deity presents a somewhat different situation; it is represented as a stranger-deity with malevolent power, although as noted above, the villagers treated this deity as a visitor. The notion of dual powers is most apparent in the Deity of the Toilet (Kawaya-no-Kami), a composite deity consisting of both a male and a female deity. Being born of the excretion and urine of a goddess of the underworld, this deity is an outsider.

In other words, the first group of supernaturals are those placed at the boundary to protect the inside from the invasion of impurity. The second group are stranger-deities who clearly belong to the outside and who have dual power; they can provide medical care or bring an illness, as in the case of the Smallpox Deity.

The symbolic association of the outside with dual power finds further support when we survey the supernaturals considered to bring good luck. The list by Itoh (1976), of which only the first half is translated in this book, includes another section that provides the names of supernaturals considered to bring good fortune in agriculture, lumbering, fishing, and so on. A conspicuous pattern in the list is the recurrent appearance of two deities – Ebisu and Daikoku. These two closely related deities have remained popular and meaningful to the people throughout history (Miyata 1975), and their appeal remains strong even today. They are believed to visit people from a land beyond the sea, bringing good luck (Miyata 1975:101–20; T. Yoshida 1981). In short, they are contemporary versions of ''stranger-deities.''

After a long discussion, then, we are finally returning to the question raised at the very beginning of this chapter – the controversy over whether or not Japanese religions are fused or consist of multiple layers. As suggested here, I believe all the supernaturals, regardless of their religious affiliation, are patterned in terms of one basic symbolic structure. That is, whether they are deities in

Shintoism or Taoism, or buddhas, their symbolic meaning at a structural level derives from the symbolic opposition of purity : impurity :: inside : margin. Unlike margin, the outside is marked with dual power and meaning, positive and negative.[2] This is exactly the same symbolic structure as that underlying the daily hygienic practices of the contemporary Japanese.

A brief examination of the medical functions carried out by deities and buddhas in the Japanese pantheon suggests that a number of religions of foreign origin have been interpreted within the framework of basic Japanese symbolic structure, which may already have been present at the time of early folk Shintoism. It also suggests a concordance between the symbolic structure underlying the meanings given to these supernaturals and the one governing the rules and regulations of daily hygiene. However, my interpretation is only one of several possible ways of looking at Japanese religions, which may be fused in some areas and multilayered in others.

[2] Since this book is not on Japanese religion per se, I will refrain from further discussion of the subject. However, it should be pointed out that Hori (1968, 1977) sees two major types of deities in early Japanese Shinto religion: *ujigami* (tutelary god) and *hitogami* (man-god). The former is a deity in group religious activities, worshipped by the members of a social group; the latter's relationship to humans is on the individual basis with a powerful medium, such as a shaman, between the two. (For further discussions of these types of deities, see Hori 1968:esp. 31, 33; 1977.) As in other societies, shamans in Japan have always been medical specialists, and therefore *hitogami* (man-god) should be more closely affiliated with medical specializations. However, Kōshin-sama, Koyasu Kannon, and Daikoku, for example, all discussed in this chapter, are all *ujigami* deities (Hori 1968:39). Therefore, we cannot link the supernatural entities assigned medical functions exclusively with either *ujigami* or *hitogami* deities.

8   Doctors and outpatients: Biomedicine (I)

This chapter focuses on the sociocultural aspects of biomedical practice in Japan. The delivery of biomedicine in Japan is embedded in Japanese culture and society, which render it radically different from biomedicine as it is practiced in other societies. This chapter, then, is not about biomedical science itself.

Although the word "biomedicine" is used for the subtitle of this chapter and the next because the majority of licensed doctors and hospitals deliver biomedicine, the description applies equally well to those *kanpō* doctors who must be licensed to practice biomedicine and who often work in predominantly biomedical clinics and hospitals. There is much less contrast between *kanpō* and biomedicine in Japan than there is between alternative health care systems and biomedicine in the United States, where the former has been associated since the late 1960s with antistructural movements, and therefore operate in opposition to established biomedicine. *Kanpō* antedates biomedicine in Japan; although the basic views of illness and health in the professional culture of respective practitioners are quite different, as noted in Chapter 5, the ways they deliver their medicine are often indistinguishable.

Medical systems in Japan, as well as public attitudes toward the systems and their medical specialists, are both varied and rapidly changing. Intracultural variation, individual variation, and some current changes are, however, largely excluded from the following description, in order to present an overview of all the systems. Because the primary focus is on the individual experiences of patients visiting doctors, the institutional aspects of Japanese health care will also be excluded from the description. These institutional aspects include the medical insurance system, medical education, the welfare system, the Japanese medical association, and various other institutions that affect health care, both beneficially and adversely.

Health care delivery systems in contemporary Japan

Japan does not fall far behind other "modern" countries in terms of the availability of health care specialists and medical facilities. It shares with most other

Table 5. *Number of hospitals and hospital beds for mental patients*

	Hospitals	Hospital beds	Hospital beds for mental patients	Total population
Japan (1977)	8,470 (0.7)	1,207,003 (105.7)	290,121 (25.4)	114,154
United States (1975)	7,336 (0.3)	1,401,624 (65.6)	272,381 (12.8)	213,611

societies the problem of the uneven distribution of medical specialists and facilities, which are concentrated in urban areas. There are some statistics available,
in which doctors (*ishi*) means licensed doctors regardless of whether they practice
kanpō or biomedicine (see Chapter 5 for figures on *kanpō* doctors). In 1976,
for each 100,000 people in Japan there were 129.8 doctors, 41.9 dentists, 86.2
pharmacists, and 369.7 nurses. These figures may be compared with those for
Great Britain (England and Wales), where in 1974, 131.3 doctors, 28.9 dentists,
27.7 pharmacists, and 375.4 nurses per 100,000 people were recorded, and to
those for the United States, where in 1974 there were 165.2 doctors, 50.6 dentists,
and 636.6 nurses for every 100,000 people (Kōseishō, ed. 1978:139; no figure
is given for pharmacists in the United States). The region where my fieldwork
was conducted is close to the Japanese national average in the number of doctors
available. In 1976, per 100,000 people, the number of doctors was 127.6 for
Hyōgo Prefecture, where the city of Kobe is located, 140.2 for Osaka, and 172.2
for Kyoto (Kōseishō, ed. 1978:142). In 1977, Hyōgo Prefecture had a total of
7,391 doctors, 2,616 specialists in moxibustion, 2,670 acupuncturists, and 4,706
masseurs of various types (Hyōgoken Eiseibu 1979:359–60), with a total of
47,180 beds in 5,600 hospitals and clinics (*Asahi* January 10, 1979). The city
of Kobe and surrounding areas in 1977 had 3,149 doctors, 652 dentists, 3,163
registered nurses, 2,483 practical nurses, 93 hospitals, 1,255 clinics, and 576
dentists' offices, as well as 8 mental hospitals and 3,136 hospital beds for mental
patients (Kōbe-shi Eiseikyoku 1978:124–5; 217).

The number of mental hospitals and hospital beds for mental patients requires
further explanation. The figures in Table 5 for Japan and the United States are
informative; the figures in parentheses represent figures per 10,000 persons
(World Health Organization statistics quoted in Kōseishō, ed. 1978:155). According to these figures, Japan, which does not emphasize psychological illnesses,
has more than twice the number of hospital beds for mental patients than the United
States, where the situation is the opposite. On the other hand, in Japan there are
only a very small number of doctors trained in psychoanalysis and psychiatry,
and as we will see shortly, the number of private practitioners in these fields is

extremely small. Although a comprehensive interpretation of these figures must include a study of the types of patients in each country, we may infer that in Japan deemphasis on psychological illnesses and the resultant lack of availability of specialists for these afflictions may indeed result in a large number of in-patient facilities where doctors, who are not necessarily trained in Western psychotherapy, must care for patients.

The medical profession: Past and present

A brief historical overview of the medical profession in Japan provides a useful background for understanding contemporary Japanese biomedical practices within their sociocultural setting. It should be noted, however, that the following description pertains to the Japanese medical profession in general; historically, this consisted of *kanpō* doctors before it came to consist predominantly of biomedical doctors. *Kanpō* was introduced to Japan from China by the sixth century and was the official institutionalized medical system before the introduction of biomedicine. The Dutch school of biomedicine was established only during the late eighteenth century. With the start of the Meiji era, the Japanese government adopted the German school of medicine (Bowers 1965; Leslie 1974; Ōtsuka 1976), whose influence is still visible in biomedical practices today. Regardless of which school of medicine they followed, practitioners were and are *ishi* (doctors).

During the Ritsuryōsei period (between the mid-seventh and mid-ninth centuries), the national government provided public medical care as well as various other services, including relief for victims of floods, epidemics, and famines (Fuse 1979:19–21). The government trained prospective doctors and, upon completion of their training, sent them to various regions in Japan. These doctors were employed by the government and provided free medical service to the public. This system ceased to exist when the central government itself lost its power during the mid-ninth century. Medical specialists were forced to practice on their own, and people in turn had to seek out and pay for a doctor's services themselves. Medical practitioners had always been assigned the same social status as manufacturers and craftsmen; this social ranking drastically dropped when doctors began private practice (Fuse 1979:14–24). The low social status accorded doctors throughout Japanese history until the Meiji period derives in part from the characterization of their professional skills as "craftsmanship," rather than "scholarship." It also derives from their unavoidable proximity to two sources of pollution, sickness and death – the two agents that generate the "Japanese germs" discussed in Chapter 2.

It was during the Edo period (1603–1867) that the prototypes of contemporary private practitioners became fully established (Fuse 1979:106–7). Because medical knowledge and skills were still classified as "crafts" (kō or hōjutsu in the Japanese of that time), doctors remained equivalent to manufacturers and crafts-men, who comprised a caste that ranked third from the top in a four-caste system (warriors, farmers, manufacturers, merchants, in order from the top) (Fuse 1979:30–5). The caste system was rigidly maintained during this period, so that the assignment of doctors to the third caste was not merely a formality, but had day-to-day consequences in their lives. Many private medical practitioners during the Edo period were actually Confucian scholars and were highly respected, but could not make a living in that profession and hence practiced medicine, some-what sheepishly and apologetically (Fuse 1979 provides numerous documented cases). Some doctors published their medical work under pseudonyms.

In Chapter 2, I discussed the concept of "Japanese germs," which ultimately derive from "people dirt," and noted that in the Kojiki, the oldest known Japanese document, the same idea is expressed by the statement that death and the dead body are sources of pollution. In this connection, then, it is important to note that the early Japanese medical doctors, many of whom were eager to learn more about the inside of the human body than they could learn from Chinese medical texts, were not permitted to engage in the dissection of human bodies because corpses were potent sources of pollution. Tōyō Yamazaki, a famous doctor in Kyoto, was the first to receive permission from the Kyoto government to have human bodies dissected, in 1754. He did so at a time when five criminals were to be executed in Kyoto; he and his colleagues were allowed to examine the internal organs of one of them after he had been beheaded. Significantly, these doctors did not touch the corpse themselves. Instead, an executioner of "lowly status" (of burakumin status) followed their directions and dissected the body, while the doctors observed and took notes. It is said they were so excited at this opportunity to observe the inside of the body that they made mistakes in their observations. Nonetheless, they were able to point out erroneous infor-mation derived from a Chinese medical text and widely believed to be factual at the time (Moriya 1978:96–9; Ogawa 1982:esp. 105–32).

Although the early doctors were regarded as craftsmen, a strong medical ethic prohibited them from engaging in free enterprise. This ethic, expressed as i wa jinjutsu (medicine practices mercy), demanded that whatever doctors receive from their patients be not a payment for their work, but a gratuity offered voluntarily. Payment to doctors was therefore euphemistically called "payment for medicine" (kusuridai) (Fuse 1979:96–7). As this term for the gratuity indicates, doctors not only engaged in diagnosis and the prescription of medicine, but also dispensed medicine – an important feature of the Japanese medical system that has persisted to the present.

Some doctors who followed this medical ethic became quite successful when their fame became established; people were more than willing to offer a gratuity for the "free" service. Despite the constraint of this ethic, many of the commercial characteristics of the modern Japanese medical system originated during the Edo period. The custom of advertising, such as that adorning walls, telephone poles, and roadsides all over Japan today, was established during this period. In the early nineteenth century, for example, one obstetrician-gynecologist in Osaka dressed in a woman's kimono and walked around the street to advertise his practice (Fuse 1979:111).

Many changes have occurred since that time, including, overtly at least, the domination of *kanpō* by biomedicine. In addition, the status of doctors rose considerably during the subsequent Meiji period, which began in 1868. Nevertheless, as Fuse repeatedly stresses, the basic nature of contemporary private practitioners was established during the Edo period. Just as they were during the Edo period, doctors today are called *machi-i* or *machi-isha* (both meaning "town doctors"), or *kaigyō-i* (doctors in practice); they are neighborhood family doctors who treat patients and dispense medicine and who advertise in the yellow pages, in newspapers, and on billboards. These doctors are viewed by the public with mixed opinions. Compared to the professor-doctors at large university and other hospitals, the neighborhood doctors receive far less respect. Yet in many cases they are more thoroughly trusted for their willingness to treat people even with small problems.

Many of these private practitioners have their offices in their homes, often with their wives assisting them as pharmacists or receptionists. They often keep extremely long hours, which usually include three hours in the morning, another three hours in the afternoon, and then a few more hours in the evening to accommodate those who work during the day. Their offices are called *iin*, and some have facilities for in-patient care. If there are more than twenty beds for hospitalization, the facilities are called *byōin* and are subject to government regulations different from those governing private practices.

In addition to these private practitioners, who are the most numerous doctors in Japan, there are also doctors who work in clinics and hospitals of all sizes. Perhaps the most "modern" of all are those at the National Center for Cancer Research and the National Center for Circulatory Diseases. These two institutions, built and supported by the government, are at the forefront of medical research on these two diseases, which have the highest mortality rates in Japan. Their patients are accommodated in the best of facilities. The physical appearance of these hospitals is very similar to that of first-rate hospitals in the United States.

At most private offices, clinics, and hospitals, doctors see large numbers of patients. For example, at hospital X, during three morning hours on May 19, 1979, two doctors at the internal medicine clinic saw 100 outpatients who were there for the first time, in addition to 102 patients who had been seen there at least once before. During the same period, the one doctor on duty at the eye clinic saw 48 patients, and the doctor at the ear, nose, and throat clinic saw 45 patients. The obstetric/gynecology clinic, where I conducted most of my field-work, usually had one doctor on duty who was occasionally joined by a resident, and the average number of patients each morning was between 40 and 50. As noted earlier, at the *kanpō* clinic, the number of patients per morning also averaged about 45. These figures were checked with several doctors working elsewhere in Japan, and are not at all unusual. Obviously, the average time a doctor spends with each patient is very short indeed.

Many Japanese blame the insurance system for people making frequent but virtually free visits to doctors and for doctors accommodating and often en-couraging these visits. At the obstetric/gynecology clinic at hospital X, for example, many patients were seen weekly. The phenomenon is seen to reduce the quality of the medical care. There is, however, another factor that is re-sponsible for the phenomenon – the relative readiness with which the Japanese both recognize departures from health and consult doctors about them. Again, records from the past provide an interesting comparison. For example, Sōhaku Asada (1813–1894) was a well-known doctor who practiced the medical ethic of "medicine for mercy." During his last year he saw 14,000 patients, of whom 7,000 were seen without payment. He is said to have seen between 300 and 500 patients a day (Fuse 1979:104–5). It appears, therefore, that the relatively large number of patients seen by doctors is not a pattern suddenly created by the insurance system.

There is one development that has appeared only recently: At doctors' offices, clinics, and hospitals there has been a rapid increase in the number of older patients, whose expenses are covered by the national health insurance system. Because of rapid changes in attitude toward the aged and changes in family structure, which now emphasizes the nuclear family, these older people often feel lonely and uncomfortable, even when they are living with their offspring. Some of the waiting rooms at neighborhood doctors' offices have become local gathering places for the elderly. Some older people prefer to be hospitalized, even when their illnesses are not grave, and are unwilling to be discharged after recovery. Some doctors accommodate this behavior, either in their waiting rooms or in the hospitals, since their services to the elderly are reimbursed by the government. Others discourage the practice, pointing out that clinics and hos-pitals are not homes for the elderly (*Asahi* March 16, 1979).

All doctors in Japan must complete six years of medical school and must pass an examination administered by the government in order to receive an *ishi menkyo*, a certificate to practice medicine, be it *kanpō* or biomedicine. Recent changes have eliminated from the requirements both a medical degree and a period of internship or residency. Many doctors do opt to go through *kenshū*, an equivalent to internship or residency, in order to acquire additional experience, especially when they wish to specialize. Specialization in Japan, however, is not well developed. In fact, the government does not particularly encourage specialization, but instead emphasizes overall knowledge. Only in neurosurgery and anesthesia can one receive a formal certificate for specialization by passing a government examination. On the other hand, even without such certification, one can claim specialization in any area, including both neurosurgery and anesthesia. Twenty-six medical specialties are designated as such by the government (Kōseishō Tōkei Jōhōbu, ed. 1979:37).

Most doctors in private practice, who in fact are general practitioners, often claim more than one specialty. These specialties are listed in the front of the clinic, on advertising billboards, and in the yellow pages of the telephone book. A common assumption made by both the doctors and the public is that the first specialty listed is the primary one. Regardless of the number of specialties doctors may claim, they must establish their reputations either as family doctors or in a particular specialty in order to attract patients.

In order to show how private practitioners and hospitals present themselves to the public, and how the public receives this information, I have tabulated in Table 6 the primary specialties advertised in the 1977 telephone directory for Kobe and the surrounding cities. The "primary specialization" in the table is the specialty listed first in each advertisement. Not all doctors advertise their practice in the telephone directory. Table 6 therefore lists only 245 offices operated by one doctor, and 344 clinics operated by more than one doctor, for a total of 589 medical facilities. If we include those who are listed in the telephone directory but who do not advertise, there are 321 offices operated by one doctor, 418 clinics with more than one doctor, and 44 hospitals, for a total of 783 medical facilities.

Virtually all the doctors and hospitals in Table 6 claim more than one specialty, often up to five for a single doctor. Dentists, ophthalmologists, and ear, nose, and throat specialists never list any other specialty; their fields are regarded by people as not closely related to the other fields, although in practice this is not the case. As noted earlier, the stomach and abdominal illnesses receive a great deal of attention among the Japanese. This concern is reflected as a specialty in *ika* or *ichōka*, which literally means the stomach clinic, although I have translated it as gastroenterology. *Ichōka* is an officially recognized specialty listed by the Ministry of Health and Welfare (Kōseishō Tōkei Jōhōbu, ed. 1979:37). Although thirteen private practitioners in Table 6 emphasize their treatment of stomach disorders by listing *ika* or *ichōka* as their primary specialty, others list internal medicine, subsuming gastroenterology under this more general term. If we combine internal medicine and gastroenterology, the total of 14.9% is the most

Table 6. *Primary specializations advertised by doctors and hospitals in the 1977 telephone directory of Kobe and surrounding area*

Primary specialization	Number			Percentage (%)		
	Multiple doctors	Single doctor	Total	Multiple doctors	Single doctor	Total
Neuro-internal medicine	1	0	1	0.3	0	0.2
Neurology	6	5	11	1.7	2.0	1.9
Mental illness ("psychiatry")	1	0	1	0.3	0	0.2
Internal medicine	42	33	75	12.2	13.5	12.7
Stomach clinic (Gastroenterology)	13	0	13	3.8	0	2.2
Radiology	4	4	8	1.2	1.6	1.4
Circulatory diseases	0	1	1	0	0.4	0.2
Pediatrics	10	29	39	2.9	11.8	6.6
Surgery	45	6	51	13.1	2.4	8.7
Plastic surgery	1	0	1	0.3	0	0.2
Orthopedics	9	1	10	2.6	0.4	1.7
Obstetrics and gynecology	53	34	87	15.4	13.9	14.8
Ear, nose, and throat	19	23	42	5.5	9.4	7.1
Ophthalmology	28	16	44	8.1	6.5	7.5
Dermatology	24	7	31	7.0	2.9	5.3
Dermatology and urology	0	1	1	0	0.4	0.2
Urology	5	2	7	1.5	0.8	1.2
Venereal disease	5	0	5	1.5	0	0.8
Anus clinic (proctology)	5	0	5	1.5	0	0.8
Dentistry	73	83	156	21.2	33.9	26.5

Note: When more than one specialty is listed in an advertisement, the primary specialization is considered to be that which is listed first.

frequent specialty other than dentistry. According to an admission official at hospital X, more than half of the hospital's patients come to the internal medicine clinic, and of these patients, more than 60% are above sixty-five years of age.

Surgery as a primary specialty is misleading, in that it is not equivalent to surgery as defined and practiced in the United States. Surgery as practiced by Japanese private practitioners does not include operations of any great magnitude, which are done only at major hospitals. Therefore, some doctors specialize in both internal medicine and surgery – two fields that are considered very different in the United States. In fact, out of the 245 private practitioners listed in Table 6, 7 doctors include surgery with other specialties. The listings of their combined specialties range as follows: internal medicine and surgery; gastroenterology and surgery; gastroenterology, radiology, and surgery; surgery, internal medicine, gastroenterology, dermatology, and radiology; obstetrics, gynecology, internal medicine, and surgery. These combinations illustrate that these doctors are indeed general practitioners, rather than true specialists.

The anus clinic, which specializes in the treatment of hemorrhoids, often through surgical removal, may be equated to proctology in the United States. There is little reliance on euphemisms in acknowledging either this specialty or that for treating venereal disease, and one often sees large advertisements for these services on the street. These particular specialties are not usually combined with any other specialty. It is only very recently that some of these clinics have added other specialties so that patients seen to enter the clinics are not embarrassed. The poor representation of psychiatry, neurology, and neuro-internal medicine (somatic illnesses affected by psychological conditions, see Chapter 4) in Table 6 reflects both the lack of emphasis on psychological causes of illness among the Japanese and the fact that few private practitioners specialize in this area. In contrast, in the United States, psychiatry as a specialty has been consistently the third most popular specialty chosen by medical doctors, ranking behind internal medicine and surgery. In the United States, the number of doctors choosing psychiatry as their specialty has ranged between 6.51 and 7.04% during the period 1970 to 1979 (Wunderman 1980:25); these percentages are deceptively low because of the large number of general practitioners, however.

Visiting a doctor

Absence of appointment system and concepts of time

Unlike in the United States, the process of visiting a doctor in Japan does *not* begin with making an appointment. Virtually no clinic or hospital has an appointment system. The only exceptions are dentists and specialists in acupuncture and moxibustion, since their treatment takes longer. Most patients are seen on a first-come, first-served basis. They receive a number for their turn or are placed on a waiting list. As long as they get to the receptionist within office hours, they are usually seen, even if their turn actually comes after the clinic hours are over.

An example from the Fujimori clinic in Himeji City, reported in a newspaper (*Asahi* October 1, 1979), illustrates an extreme case of not only how the system works without appointments, but also how people select a doctor. The hospital was founded in 1915 by the father of the present hospital director in Himeji, which is a relatively small, quiet city to the west of Kobe. Today, the receptionist's window opens at 5:00 A.M., by which time about 100 people are already waiting in line. Within thirty minutes about 180 patients are scheduled, the last one of whom may not be seen until 9:00 P.M. Equipped with bedding, the first forty to fifty patients are usually those who have waited overnight, or had family members wait for them, in the clinic parking lot, which is protected above and on three sides by thin pieces of slate. Mr. Omuro, a thirty-five-year-old employee of a local company, who was interviewed by the newspaper reporter, had been sleeping in this parking lot every other night for the previous three months in order to secure visits for his oldest daughter, two years of age. His reason for going to such an extreme was that, after unsuccessful visits to many ear, nose, and throat doctors, his daughter's hearing had improved noticeably since she had started going to Dr. Fujimori.

When I asked doctors about the lack of an appointment system, many told me that if they started an appointment system they might lose patients, because the Japanese are not accustomed to such a system. Others pointed out that there is no way to institute an appointment system when each doctor sees so many patients a day.

The basic factor responsible for this lack of an appointment system, in my view, is the Japanese concept of time. Industrialization, with the invention of the clock, is said to have transformed the qualitative notion of time, defined by each cultural system, to a universally standardized quantitative concept. In some societies, such as the United States, the transformation has penetrated deep into daily life, and people are indeed governed primarily by quantitative time concepts, by punching the time clock at work. On the other hand, some qualitative ideas of time have been retained. Americans still divide the week qualitatively into weekdays for work and weekends for religion and/or play; the week does not consist of seven equivalent units. Numerous examples of similar patterns are given in Hall (1969).

Among the Japanese, time is considered even less in quantitative terms. Even at work, white-collar workers in Japanese companies, as is well known, do not confine their work from 8 to 5; instead, they work much longer hours, since they feel they are putting in a work day, rather than a strict eight-hour day. Japanese are often surprised by the almost immediate disappearance of American office workers at 5 o'clock sharp. In Japan, even social engagements are undertaken more spontaneously than in the United States. Visits among friends, relatives, and acquaintances often occur without prior notice. Colleagues at a university, for example, visit each other, often for prolonged visits, without making prior arrangements. These visits are rarely refused even when they come at a very inconvenient time. During my initial stay in Japan in 1979, I found myself somewhat bewildered when my colleagues asked me to join them for dinner, sometimes that same evening – I had been too accustomed in the United States to scheduling even a lunch engagement with a colleague several days in advance. I believe, therefore, that the lack of an appointment system at clinics and hospitals reflects the perception and management of time among contemporary Japanese, rather than just eagerness on the part of doctors to maintain their current number of patients.

This situation contrasts at least superficially with that in the United States, where one usually makes an appointment for visits to doctors and for many other services. Ironically, however, American patients, who may feel very uneasy not having an appointment, nevertheless may wait hours beyond their scheduled appointment time; in fact, there are reports that some doctors schedule several appointments simultaneously. The basic difference, therefore, between the Japanese and American systems is actually related to basic concepts of time. Americans feel uncomfortable without an appointment, whereas the Japanese feel more comfortable without one; but the wait may be very long in either case.

Introduction to a doctor

Although most patients come to a doctor without a formal introduction, even visits to doctors do not totally escape the elaborate system of "introduction" that remains so important in Japanese interpersonal relationships. I have already discussed the use of name cards and their significance in Chapter 2. In one hospital where I worked, the records of some of the patients had a name card attached to the first page. These name cards were sometimes those of a previous doctor who had referred the patient to the doctor. The use of the name card implies a more complex referral system than that in the United States, since the name card indicates personal involvement with the patient. I observed that in some cases, a referral is followed by a telephone call. Furthermore, the second doctor may call the doctor who made the referral to report the nature and progress of the treatment. I once overheard a telephone conversation made by one doctor who invited the previous doctor to come and visit the patient when she was hospitalized. The name card also may be the patient's own, if he or she is of high social standing, or that of the patient's spouse, relative, or friend – whoever is of high social standing.

Such personal introductions often ensure much greater attention by the doctor. In Japanese doctor-patient relationships, patients place the entire responsibility for their well-being in the doctor's hands, giving in turn a deep sense of trust, especially in the case of serious illness. This system of personal introduction becomes even more significant in cases involving hospitalization.

The examination room: The concept of time, body, and privacy

The process of seeing a doctor reveals a great deal about attitudes toward the body, and concepts of space, privacy, and the individual in Japanese culture. The examination room is usually separated casually, often with only a curtain, from other areas of the office, such as the waiting room. I often observed that even when a door existed between the waiting room and the examination room, it was rarely used. Even at large hospitals, the arrangement is similar. For example, at university hospital Y, a series of examination rooms is separated only by curtains, although the buildings were built only recently and are of the highest quality.

Although the curtain itself was introduced from the West, it is in fact equivalent to more traditional sliding doors, screens, and other dividers, which are neither permanent nor physically capable of shutting off sound and vision between the divided spaces. These traditional dividers are extensions of the basic means used in Japanese culture to create a separate space – *shimenawa*, a rope that creates a sacred place and demarcates it from the profane world. A sacred space can be created anywhere by putting a *shimenawa* around it. The use of *shimenawa* epitomizes the flexible Japanese concept of spatial boundaries, which often exist only in the mind and yet are strictly observed. Even today, the Japanese are extremely adept at observing invisible lines of spatial demarcation in public places. Thus, in restaurants a table may be occupied by more than one group of people, each person observing, without the slightest sense of discomfort, the invisible boundary that divides one group from the next.

Japanese devices for the division of space contrast sharply with the wall in Western architecture. The wall is permanent and physically shuts off communication between the divided areas, ideally eliminating not only visual but also auditory contact. As noted in Chapter 2, the wall is certainly used in Japanese architecture, but it is used to demarcate the inside from the polluting outside, for which the separation must be solid and permanent. Within the inside, then, divisions are temporary and "symbolic."

In a private practitioner's office, the examination room is barely separated from the waiting room. Furthermore, while the examination goes on, nurses and other personnel may pass by, and the patient's family members often stay throughout the examination. In contrast to this open atmosphere, the examination process in the United States clearly expresses the cherished cultural values of privacy and the sacredness of the body. During an American examination, the doctor and the patient are alone in a room behind a closed door, with a thick wall guaranteeing absolute privacy.

Just as the Japanese are quite open about their bodies in public baths, they consider taking their clothes off in a doctor's office purely a matter of business. They do not regard the naked body as strictly private or as necessarily suggestive of sexuality. The body has multiple functions. Therefore, when a woman nurses an infant, when a man urinates, or when a person takes a bath or is seen by a doctor, it has nothing to do with sex. The exposure of the body is carried out quite naturally in order to fulfill these functions. Several times I have seen men start taking their clothes off in a doctor's waiting room as they began heading toward the examination room. Such behavior, however, is not characteristic of women; as in almost all cultures, women are required to show more modesty than men in regard to their body. Japanese women, on the other hand, seem quite comfortable being next to male patients while they are treated by acupuncture or moxibustion, and the body is partially exposed for the treatment.

Surrogate patient

At least to an outsider to Japanese society, one phenomenon in the doctor's office that stands out as unusual is what I call a "surrogate patient." I was first reminded of this custom, which I was aware of but which was not articulated in my mind, at the *kanpō* doctor's clinic described in Chapter 5. A middle-aged woman came into the examination room and sat on the chair like a patient. She then described the symptoms, which did not sound at all like those of a middle-aged woman. This was because in Japanese a speaker does not use personal pronouns, especially in polite speech, as when a patient is addressing a doctor. Thus it is sometimes not clear about whom the speaker is talking. The mother was using humble forms of speech that could be applicable to herself or to a member of her family. After she left with the prescribed herbs, I asked the doctor about her. He explained that she had come on behalf of her son, who was at school. He said that it is not uncommon for a person to come and get medicine for someone else, and that doctors will prescribe the medicine, provided that they had seen the actual patient and were familiar with the patient's problem. This attitude was shared by several other doctors whose opinions I asked on this matter. After the incident at the *kanpō* clinic, I observed numerous "patient substitutes" elsewhere. The following section describes only a few.

At the obstetric-gynecology clinic at hospital X, it was not uncommon for a mother to represent her daughter, married or unmarried. In several cases involving unmarried daughters, the mother came because the daughter was too shy to describe her condition herself or to be seen there. Even in the case of married daughters mothers are often involved, either as the surrogate patient or to accompany the patient. For example, one married woman came to the doctor herself, but as she was leaving she told the doctor that her mother would come to hear the results of her tests, since she was going to her own home, far from the hospital. Several other cases at the same clinic involved friends of patients. For example, one woman schoolteacher came on behalf of a colleague who could not take off from teaching that day. She sat in the patient's chair and listened to the results of her friend's tests, and asked the doctor for instructions on what her friend should be doing. As the woman was leaving, the nurse, apologizing for the bluntness with which she must "talk about money," asked her if she could take care of her friend's payment for that month. The woman readily agreed to do so.

One memorable encounter of this type involved a fifty-seven-year-old male patient at university hospital Y, who held a socially respectable position. Greater details are included for this case, since it illustrates many aspects of health care for the individual in Japanese society. The man came in on my first day of observation at the internal medicine clinic of the hospital. The man looked healthy and in his prime, and came into the examination room with his wife and his daughter, who looked to be in her mid-thirties. According to his record and the doctor's account, he had some problems with the heart, kidney, and prostate. The man described his bad circulation, frequent urination, and occasional head-aches and dizziness, all of which, he said, disappeared after he took a bath. After his initial description of the symptoms, however, he remained silent, and his wife and especially his daughter took over the descriptions and questions.

As the doctor examined the back of the man's eyelids and took his blood pressure, his wife supplemented her husband's description by stating the number of times he urinated per day. The daughter had checked how hot his bath should be and complained that, although she had run the bath at the right temperature, he had insisted on raising it higher. She asked the doctor if the swelling of the man's leg had subsided and how his kidney was doing. Implying that the doctor should join in her accusations, she complained that her father would not include enough vegetables in his diet. She also had checked every medicine that was prescribed for him, in order to make sure that the dosage and frequency were correct. The daughter, in fact, was very informal in dealing with this young doctor, who was in his early forties, and did not use honorifics, whereas her parents were much more respectful toward him.

Although the patient was present in this case, his wife and daughter in fact became surrogates by taking over the interactions with the doctor. The case vividly illustrates that the illness of one member of a family is of concern to all; health care in Japan is an affair for the entire family. Furthermore, the case also illustrates the important role of women in health care; they are in charge, with the entire responsibility for a patient, whether he is an infant or an adult male, and they make sure all the doctor's orders are followed. These women's knowl-edge of the man's daily behavior, including the frequency of his urination, illustrates the Japanese interest in minute details of bodily functions, their own or those of family members, as I pointed out in Chapter 3.

Finally, this case also portrays the man-woman relationship in the Japanese domestic sphere. A wife often assumes a "maternal," at least in an American sense, role in taking care of the daily details of her husband's life, including the management of the body. Thus, even today some women continue to dress their husbands in the morning or undress them upon their return. This custom is becoming somewhat attenuated not because of the negation of this particular role or the concept behind it, but because some wives no longer feel it is their responsibility to get up early enough to "prepare" their husbands for their "daily combat" outside the home. Male independence in the public domain is in no way contradicted by what we might call a "passive" role in the domestic sphere. In fact, many Japanese men virtually have no power at home; their wives make all the decisions, including those about the children.

This same logic underlies the practice in which the husband hands over his entire paycheck to his wife, who then decides the sum for his allowance. Once I was asked by a male relative to support him in his plea to his wife to increase his allowance; he thought that I, as a professional woman, would understand how expensive but essential it is to socialize with one's colleagues. This man was a well-paid executive of a large trading company. Some men used to "steal" money before they turned over the *gekkyū bukuro* – a bag containing their salary in cash – to their wives. The recent change to the direct deposits of paychecks into employees' bank accounts was a blow to these men. One anthropologist complained that he now felt like a cormorant: In the famous ritual fishing method in Japan, cormorants dive to catch fish, but they cannot swallow the fish they catch because ropes are tied to their necks. The cormorant feels it has fished, just as the "rice-winner" feels he has earned money; however, neither is in control of the results.

Pregnancy and childbirth

Although previous sections have amply illustrated the sociocultural nature of biomedical health care, a brief description of selected features of contemporary beliefs and practices involved in pregnancy and childbirth, and my observations at the obstetric clinic at hospital X, should illuminate not only its Japanese nature, but also an important aspect of medical pluralism – the syncretic nature of each medical system, which is a product of mutual influence among the various coexisting systems. We will see in the following description a combination of biomedicine and traditional magicoreligious practices and beliefs, the stark realization of which came to me on the first day of the dog as I began my observations at the obstetric clinic of hospital X (each day of the lunar month is assigned one of the twelve animals). On that day, as Dr. S, the obstetrician and also the head of the hospital, sat at his desk, the head nurse placed a brush and red ink on his desk. As women came in, they presented a long white cotton sash, on which he wrote the elegant character *kotobuki* (happiness) in one brush stroke (Photo 21).

Pregnancy sash (iwata-obi)

A white cotton sash, called *iwata-obi* or *hara-obi*, 4 meters in length, has been used by pregnant women in Japan for a long time; it was definitely in use during

21. An obstetrician at a biomedical hospital writing a red character for celebration on the pregnancy sashes of his patients.

the Edo period (1603–1867), and some say it dates back to the Heian period (794–1185). Although a few women today use a loose corset, most Japanese women continue to use the sash, which they wrap around their abdomens fairly firmly. At hospital X, of 149 women who returned my questionnaires on the sash, 139 women used the sash, 6 used a corset, and 3 used a girdle; 3 women did not answer. The predominance of women who use the sash was also confirmed at the maternity ward of university hospital Y and at one other medium-sized hospital. The sash is acquired usually from a temple or a shrine noted for its efficacy in childbirth. Of the 139 women who used the sash, 106 had acquired them from a temple or a shrine. Some of the rest were using the sash from a previous pregnancy. As noted in Chapter 6, of the 106 women who acquired a sash from a temple or a shrine, 81 had obtained them from Nakayama Temple, indicating the highly selective process of determining which religious institution is considered "effective." Some temples and shrines instruct that the sash be burned after use, but most require that it be returned to them.

The sash is first worn on the day of the dog during the fifth month of pregnancy, which corresponds to the fourth month in the American way of counting, although in some regions they choose the third or the seventh month (Ōshima et al., 1980:151). The Japanese system of measuring the duration of pregnancy starts with the last menstruation, so that there are ten months of pregnancy. This system of counting is now being "officially" changed to the nine-month pregnancy system, following a directive issued by the World Health Organization in 1978 (*Asahi* January 25, 1979). This change has been slow at the popular level. The day of the dog is chosen because the dog is associated with easy delivery. Each day of the month is assigned one of the twelve animals of the lunar calendar. Most Japanese are quite oblivious to this "old custom," and women may not acknowledge any personal belief in the effect of choosing the day of the dog in their manner of delivery. But the custom of tying the sash for the first time on this day is still very commonly practiced.

A woman used to receive instructions about how to tie the sash around the abdomen from her mother, mother-in-law, or another woman. With the increased prevalence of the nuclear family, who often live away from their parents, the maternity wards of many hospitals have taken up this role. In fact, during my fieldwork, I was eager to be at the obstetric clinic at hospital X on the days of the dog, since I was sure to see many women. Some women brought sashes that were not only obtained from a temple or a shrine, but had sutras written in brush strokes by a monk. After Dr. S wrote the character for happiness on her sash (see Photo 21), each woman was led to an area behind a curtain, where the head nurse showed her how to tie it around her abdomen. Dr. S took great pride and delight in writing the character on the sash, and the women were indeed appreciative of his effort. A young doctor, who occasionally came to help Dr. S when there were too many patients, felt very awkward in this role, since he was not good in using the brush. He told me that he usually asked Dr. S to write the character, even for his own patients. Dr. S recalled that on the days of the dog he used to receive sea bream and *sekihan* (rice cooked with red beans, which give a reddish color to the rice) – two traditional dishes for happy occasions – from women beginning to use the sash. Today they no longer bring these dishes to the doctor, but many present him with a gift.

Traditionally, the sash was a symbol of the confirmation of pregnancy. By the fifth month the pregnancy was certain, and the sash expressed its recognition and the happiness felt not only by the woman, but by those close to her. The association between the sash and the confirmation of pregnancy seems to continue even today, as the conversation between Dr. S and one woman indicated. The woman was in her fourth month of pregnancy, and asked Dr. S if she could make a trip to Tokyo or if she should wait until she started to wear the sash. Dr. S told her that most miscarriages do occur during the first three months, but that just to be sure she should perhaps postpone the trip until she was using the sash. In other words, the sash signifies not simply that the woman is pregnant, but also that the pregnancy is stabilized and that childbirth is more or less assured.

Beyond the symbolic meaning of the sash, contemporary women also see several functions in its use. On questionnaires returned to me by 104 women, there were 207 answers, since some women circled more than one reason for wearing the sash. Of the 207 answers, "to protect the stomach from chilling" received the highest score of 100 (50%). Other answers were: because it is customary (38 answers, 18.3%); because it feels good (27 answers, 13.1%); so that the fetus will not grow too large (25 answers, 12%); miscellaneous reasons (9 answers). Some women think a hard labor results if the fetus becomes too large, and some even pointed out how Western women have more difficulty in labor because they do not use a sash and consequently let the fetus grow too large. As I talked with the women, many also mentioned that the sash stabilized the fetus, which starts to move around during the fifth month. Dr. S emphasized comfort and the prevention of chilling of the stomach as his reasons for recommending the sash. He regards corsets and girdles as very poor substitutes for the sash, since they cannot be adjusted in size on a daily basis, as can the sash.

As noted above, these sashes are obtained from a temple or a shrine. The decision of who goes there to obtain it reveals the intricate balance between culturally prescribed kinship patterns and the actual interpersonal relationships among those involved with the childbirth. Of 108 women interviewed at the biomedical hospital, only 19 said that they had chosen the temple or shrine themselves. In 22 cases, the mother of the woman's husband made the decision, and in 47 cases the woman's own mother made the selection – although the mothers did not make decisions on their own, but in consultation with the pregnant woman. When it came time to actually visit the temple or shrine to obtain the sash, only 3 women had gone on their own. The other women went with someone else – in 12 cases, with their own mothers, in 7 cases with the husbands' mothers, and in 42 cases with their husbands. Sometimes the pregnant women did not even go to the temple or shrine: In 24 cases their mothers went on their behalf; in 12 cases, the mothers of their husbands; and in 3 cases, their husbands. Traditionally, it was the mother of the pregnant woman who was most frequently involved, and next the mother of the woman's husband, especially when it was the first birth. The husbands were seldom involved. Therefore, the recent statistics show one marked change – the increased emphasis on the conjugal bond and consequently more involvement of husbands, which was clearly evident in observing the visitors at Nakayama Temple.

These statistics are relevant to any discussion of pregnancy and childbirth in a modern Japanese biomedical hospital, since they clearly illustrate that the event is not important just to the woman or to the expectant parents. The recent emphasis on the husband's involvement has simply expanded the list of the people involved in the event, which includes, not simply psychologically but in a very real sense, at least three nuclear families – the expectant parents and both of their sets of parents.

Satogaeri (return to one's natal home for child delivery)

As we briefly discuss the custom of *satogaeri*, family involvement in childbirth should become clearer. *Satogaeri* (returning to the natal home) is a long-practiced custom in Japan that has been modified over the years as the kinship structure has changed, and there are some regional variations in its form (Yanagita, ed. 1951:238–9). Basically, it is a custom whereby a woman returns to her natal home at certain key times, including childbirth, often "for a vacation." In the traditional kinship structure, a woman relinquished her membership in her natal home and married into her husband's household. Her return at the time of her first childbirth in some cases signified, in this traditional setting, her permanent switch of membership, since she was often returned to her natal home if she failed to produce offspring, especially male offspring.

In recent years, even though cultural emphasis on the reproductive role of women has decreased, *satogaeri* continues as a common practice. The practice of *satogaeri* has been especially important in providing psychological as well as physical help from kin during childbirth, although *satogaeri* is practiced on other occasions as well. In the case of child delivery, the most common pattern has been for the woman to return home, sometimes a long distance, for the birth of her first child, but for her mother to come to help her for her second and subsequent childbirths.

Of the 148 women who responded to my questionnaire, 77 (52%) planned to return to their natal homes, 64 (43%) to their own homes, and 7 to the home of their husband's parents. Of the 64 women who were planning to return to their own homes, 3 had made this choice because their natal home was very close and 6 did so because their mothers were coming to stay with them to help. In other words, of the 148 women, 81 (54%) would have their mother's help in one way or another. Of the 77 women returning to their natal homes, 21 had older offspring whom they were taking with them; however, of the 64 who chose to stay at their own homes, 13 gave as the reason for staying the care of their older offspring. In summary, over half of the women were planning to go back to their natal homes, and even more would have done so were it not for their older children.

The length of stay at the natal home ranged as follows (the number of women in parentheses): two to three weeks (5); one month (36); a month and a half (4); one to two months (2); two months (5); two to three months (1); three months (2); four months (1).

Of 137 of the women who answered the questionnaire, for 111, both their own homes and their natal homes were in the Hanshinkan area, which includes the area between Kobe and Osaka. The natal homes for 9 women lay immediately west or east of this area. Homes of the remaining 17 women were located all over Japan, except Hokkaido. Of these 17, 7 in fact were already staying at their natal homes, which were located close to hospital X. Of the women who chose to stay in their natal homes two months or more, for 4 women both homes were within the Hanshinkan area; for 3 their natal home was fairly distant (Tokyo, Gifu, and Saga); and 2 did not indicate the locations of their natal home.

Although both their natal and their own homes for the great majority of the women were located in the Hanshinkan area, it is important to note that in the *satogaeri* custom women often leave their husbands behind, despite the recent emphasis on the conjugal bond. Whenever I had a chance, I explored the feelings of the fathers on this matter. Contrary to my "American" suspicion that they would feel deserted, most young fathers, including a number of my young anthropology colleagues, replied that they felt quite good about their wives returning to their mother's homes; they felt that both their wives and the newborns would be in good hands. In other words, their wish to place their wives and the newborns in the experienced hands of the wife's mother caused them to not only approve but even to encourage the *satogaeri* practice. Of course, many of them would visit their wives and babies, if the natal home was within a close distance.

The reason for returning to the natal home given by the women themselves was based largely on the fact that they would feel comfortable and could recover better because of the psychological and physical help available. Of the 70 women who specified the reason for their return, 28 cited the psychological assurance they would receive at their natal home, and 18 pointed to the help they would get (no need to do household chores and someone looking after their older children). There seems to be no feeling of discomfort or embarrassment at returning to their natal homes after establishing their own homes. One woman told me, in fact, that one advantage of marrying and having children at a young age is that her parents would be young enough to help take care of her and her children. The feeling was that it was quite natural to be taken care of by one's mother at childbirth.

The mother's attitude is also generally very positive. Many of them consider it part of their role as mothers and in fact look forward to taking care of their daughters at childbirth. One woman who lived in a very small house and was not at all well-off economically took care not only of her daughter, but also of her son and his wife during and after childbirth. Her daughter-in-law asked if she would wash diapers if they moved in with her. When she agreed, the daughter-in-law told her that she and her family would stay with her for forty days – the entire period of her maternity leave from work. This woman had not expected them to stay that long but was glad to accommodate them, since she felt she had not done enough for her son when he was growing up just after World War II. Although this case is somewhat unusual, I have known many cases in which the mother was more than willing to help her daughter(s).

The *satogaeri* practice reflects several features of Japanese kinship and patterns of thought. Women do not seem to think they become completely "independent," in the American sense, after their marriage, and thus are quite comfortable in continuing to rely upon their parents. The mother-daughter relationship, which continues even after the daughter's marriage, and is most succinctly expressed in the *satogaeri* practice, provides evidence of a strong and lasting nonformalized kinship relationship that hitherto has been obscured by the formalized kinship system, in which the father-son succession receives the primary attention. On the ideological side, both *satogaeri* and the Japanese attitude toward the practice reinforce the "pampering" attitude toward the sick – a theme stressed in this book. Pregnancy and childbirth are treated as "sickness," and women consequently receive care and attention during this time. As we will see in Chapter 9, Japanese women are usually "stronger" than men in times of illness, because they seldom can afford to interrupt their household work to be hospitalized or to lie in bed for a long time. In contrast to other types of illness, then, taking time off for childbirth is culturally institutionalized so that women have the "right" to take a vacation. The enormous emphasis Japanese culture places on children may have been a factor in institutionalizing the *satogaeri* "vacation" for women.

Although Matsuda (1979:23), the Japanese Dr. Spock, contends that *satogaeri* at childbirth is a practice primarily in Kansai (western Japan), a survey in Tokyo, where people come from all over Japan, reveals a wider prevalence. This survey (reported in *Asahi*, November 25, 1978) was administered to 300 women between the ages of twenty and thirty, of whom 85% either were pregnant or had children. Of these women, 43% intended to and did practice *satogaeri*. In 35% of the cases of the women who did not, their mothers helped either by moving into the house or by living nearby. In other words, 78% of the women were or intended to be taken care of by their mothers. This figure is even higher than my sample. The survey also revealed that 70% of these women had gone to a temple or a shrine to pray for safe delivery and owned an amulet.

Japanese obstetricians and hospitals seem to cooperate in accommodating the custom of *satogaeri*. In fact, they do so in such a natural manner that they seem unaware that they are accommodating a traditional custom. Thus, at hospital X, and as I later confirmed elsewhere, the head nurse asked every woman at the time of the tying of her sash during the fifth month where she planned to deliver. The fact that some did not plan to deliver at hospital X did not bother Dr. S at all. I asked him if he would not feel more comfortable if a doctor would deliver the baby of a woman patient. He said that he could take care of the woman as long as he had information about her recorded in a *boshi techō* (Notes on mother and child), a small notebook issued by the government in which a pregnant woman must keep her record.

The clinic scene vividly reflects the involvement of others in a woman's pregnancy. In addition to the cases introduced in the section on surrogates, I several times saw the parents of a new mother coming to the clinic to thank Dr. S with a gift. They usually seemed very grateful to Dr. S, and often stated explicitly that it was he who was responsible for the safe delivery and healthy baby.

This description of pregnancy and child delivery in Japan has omitted many other cultural practices and beliefs, including the taboos surrounding pregnancy. The description, however, should support the argument that biomedicine in Japan is thoroughly embedded in Japanese culture and society. It should also show that a pluralistic medical system consists of systems that are more or less discrete as medical institutions but, far from being independent, have received influences from each other.

9 Hospitalization: Biomedicine (II)

In this chapter I continue to examine the sociocultural aspects of biomedical health care in contemporary Japan by focusing on the process and experience of hospitalization. Many of the following generalizations, and the specific cases that illustrate them, pertain primarily to hospitalization either for the treatment of a physical illness or for an operation. They may therefore not apply to hospitalization for mental illness, to repeated hospitalization for a chronic illness, or to hospitalization at specialized *kanpō* clinics, only a few of which exist in Japan today. The description is not meant to be exhaustive, and its primary emphasis is perspectives from patients. Therefore, the role of a nurse, for example, is not included in the treatment and the role of a doctor is examined only insofar as it directly affects the patients.

The choice of a particular hospital is based on a number of factors. In the case of a company employee, for example, the firm may have insurance arrangements with certain hospitals. The most important factor in most cases, however, is the choice of a certain doctor who has shown expertise in a type of operation or the treatment of a particular disease. To receive care from such a doctor, some people are willing to choose hospitals a long distance from their homes. To supplement the family doctor's advice, people gather extensive information by word of mouth, although they rely most heavily on the advice of family members. Other things being equal, however, proximity is an important factor because family members continue to take care of patients after they are hospitalized, rather than relegating all this responsibility to the hospital staff.

Another factor, which I thought had totally disappeared, is the choice of a hospital that is in a favorable direction from one's house. I was reminded of this when I met a *futon* (bedding) dealer in hospital X, who had come to deliver a covering *futon* (*kakebuton*) to a patient. He and his customer were both from an area southeast of the hospital that was inhabited primarily by blue-collar workers. Although the hospital had once been fairly exclusive, catering only to the well-to-do, the insurance system had made it accessible to people with lower incomes. When this occurred, I was told, people in the southeastern area started to choose the hospital because of its location, which was auspicious for them. This factor is no longer very important to most contemporary Japanese, who either do not think of it or ignore it in favor of the other factors discussed above. In nonemergency cases, many people used to choose a good day in the lunar calendar (see Chapter 3) to enter or leave a hospital. At present only a small number of people, usually the elderly, follow this practice, as Chiba (1981) observed during her hospitalization in Tokyo. As noted in Chapter 4, Taoistic beliefs in auspicious and inauspicious temporal units (certain days of the month or years in the cycle) and spatial directions still govern the conduct of at least some Japanese.

Introduction to a doctor

To many Japanese patients, a personal introduction to a doctor is very important in cases of hospitalization. One example, the case of Mr. A described in Chapter 6, will suffice as an illustration of the feeling about this practice. When he and his immediate superior at work decided that he should have his recurring ulcer treated surgically, the company doctor selected a municipal hospital in Osaka because of a particular surgeon there who was known for operations on the stomach. The company doctor himself made a special referral so that the man would be operated on by that surgeon, and not by another. When the selections of the hospital and surgeon had been made for the man, the husband of his wife's sister undertook to find someone who knew the doctor personally. He found that an old classmate at his high school, from which he had graduated some forty years earlier, had later become a classmate of the surgeon in medical school. His high school classmate telephoned the surgeon, and the personal ''introduction'' was successfully completed. Mr. A and his wife were profoundly grateful, and repeatedly talked about their brother-in-law's kind gesture. They expressed their gratitude when Mr. A was celebrating his recovery, and sent gifts to those who had visited him during his stay in the hospital. While the brother-in-law of Mr. A used his connections to secure an introduction to the doctor, Mr. A's brother took off from work in order to obtain an amulet from the Ishikiri Shrine.

Lest this description suggest merely the quaint habits of a strange people, or reinforce the stereotype of the Japanese emphasis on kinship and indebtedness, I must point out that the practice of securing a personal introduction to a doctor actually demonstrates the Japanese refusal to be passive recipients of institutionalized health care. These cultural institutions permit the Japanese to create, at least in their own minds, the optimal conditions for successful operations or treatment. They feel confident that they are the ones who have chosen their doctors, and not vice versa. They have the assurance that their doctors will pay personal attention to them and do their best, since they have established special relationships with them through proper introductions. Furthermore, the patients are reassured by the concern of others who have gone to shrines and temples to pray for them; and after all, a talisman does not hurt, and may even help, in ensuring the success of the operation or treatment. In short, the patients have done their best to personalize the situation, without becoming engulfed in a huge, impersonal institution.

On the other hand, this system can adversely affect people who cannot obtain an introduction. In fact, there has been a great deal of controversy about a related matter – that is, that "introductions" often are accompanied by a substantial gift, either in cash or in goods. Whether or not the system works against the less privileged, then, depends largely on the integrity of individual doctors. The National Center for Circulatory Diseases, for example, adopted a policy that forbade doctors to receive gifts. Some patients felt relieved about this policy, but others felt somewhat helpless at having their means for expressing gratitude eliminated.

Length of hospitalization

The average length of hospitalization in Japan is by far the longest in the world. A survey by the World Health Organization in 1977 (quoted in Kōseishō, ed. 1978:158) found that the average length of hospital stay for a patient was as follows: 42.9 days in Japan, 8.1 days in the United States, 16.7 days in West Germany, 13.5 days in Italy, 12.9 days in Sweden, 12.8 days in Denmark, and 13.1 days in England and Wales. In the case of Mr. A, he was hospitalized for a month and a half for an ulcer operation, and was on sick leave from his work for a total of two and a half months. Chiba (1981) was given an estimate of four weeks of hospitalization for her mastectomy, although this young woman journalist was determined to be discharged as soon as possible. She managed to be discharged after fifteen days, including one week of preoperative stay, setting a record for the shortest stay in the hospital. Another woman journalist, Nakazato (1981), was hospitalized for two months for a mastectomy.

My observations of doctor's recommendations at the obstetric-gynecology clinic also revealed many cases of long hospitalization periods, and showed the readiness with which women were willing to be hospitalized on doctor's recommendations. One case involved a pregnant woman who had no major symptoms. She was recommended for hospitalization so that she could rest, because she had a history of miscarriages and had experienced some difficulty in becoming pregnant. Furthermore, as the case of Chiba (1981) illustrates, the preoperative period of hospitalization is long, especially in contrast to the procedure in the United States, where a patient is usually admitted the day before the operation. Doctors at the obstetric-gynecology clinic at hospital X often recommended hospitalization for childbirth well before the due date and before any sign of labor, especially for women with a history of difficulty, or who were pregnant for the first time.

The length of hospital stays has been discussed in Japanese newspapers and other mass media. Some sources argue that in order to receive as much reimbursement as possible from the government and insurance companies, the hospitals take as many patients as they can and encourage long stays. This practice has been observed especially in treating the elderly, who are totally covered by the national health insurance plan. Some elderly patients, feeling as though they are suddenly left to care for themselves, prefer to stay in the hospital even after recovery. Opinions of doctors on treatment of the elderly remain divided. The director of hospital X said that he really did not have the heart to "kick out" old people if they wished to stay, provided the hospital had enough beds to accommodate them. Others argued that hospitals should not be old people's homes.

On the other hand, Okuyama (1976:50–2), a frequent and vocal critic of the Japanese medical system, argues that two factors are responsible for long hospitalization. First, in his view, patients in Japan are not hospitalized soon enough; they wait until they are very sick, and longer hospitalization is therefore required to treat them. Second, he says that the care provided by Japanese hospitals is so poor that recovery is slow, necessitating a long stay. He therefore suggests: "Perhaps patients should stay longer in a hospital, since too frequently they are discharged before complete recovery from their disease" (Okuyama 1976:52).

Okuyama's remarks are especially interesting in that, despite his consumer-advocacy approach, he argues for even longer hospitalization. His opinion provides additional evidence that one of the major factors behind the unusually long hospitalization period in Japan is a basic "pampering" attitude toward the sick, as we saw in previous sections of this book. The Japanese think of many more conditions as "illnesses" than biomedicine recognizes as "diseases." Even biomedically trained doctors recognize the presence of "illnesses" rather than just "diseases." In fact, contrary to Okuyama's interpretation, Japanese patients seem to be hospitalized longer and with much more minor symptoms than they would be in the United States.

Part and parcel of the Japanese attitude toward illness is the emphasis on *ansei* (peace and quiet, or bed rest) as the major treatment for virtually any illness, from a minor cold to a major disease. Exercise during pregnancy or after an operation has been effective in promoting speedy recovery in the United States. It has had a very limited success in Japan. One head nurse at university hospital Y told me that when they recommended exercise, many patients took offense and thought it inconsiderate; they insisted on *ansei*, "at least when I am sick." Biomedically, according to one doctor at university hospital Y, the practice of *ansei* has had little adverse effect on Japanese patients who, unlike Western peoples, have little problem with thrombosis. Lengthy hospitalization, then, may be seen as the official sanctioning of *ansei*, the most cherished treatment method in popular Japanese medicine. Long hospitalization periods thus affirm the legitimacy of, and provide institutional support for, sickness.

The definition of a wide range of ailments as illnesses, the "pampering" attitude toward the sick, and the belief in bed rest as a cure-all cannot completely explain the long hospital stays; some institutions, such as the insurance system, also are responsible. Another crucial factor in understanding the practice of lengthy hospitalization is the care of patients by the family and others – that is, hospital personnel are not the only ones who tend to the sick. Because of the substantial support by family and others, hospitalization is not nearly as costly as it is in the United States, where the sick are cared for exclusively by hospital personnel.

Another important characteristic of Japanese culture that facilitates long hospitalization is the way an individual worker's role is defined in Japanese organizations. A worker's job does not consist of tasks assigned exclusively to that particular individual. Instead, "diffuse job definitions" or "a lack of sharp jurisdictional definitions of job duties" (Cole 1979:200, 220) results in extensive job rotation. This practice enables co-workers to cover the tasks of the sick person with relative ease. There are few empty spots in the work allocation that no one else can fill. A long absence from work in Japan does not mean the inefficiency in production or execution of tasks that results in a society where individual work roles are more clearly delineated. In the case of a woman with a family, the period of hospitalization is often shorter, precisely because she is often the only one who can carry out all the tasks at home; she seldom has "co-workers" who can cover her job. Therefore, unless a woman has an adult offspring, usually a daughter, or other women who can help, she must go home as soon as possible. Even for women, however, hospitalization is much longer than in other societies.

For both men and women, there is an implicit and sometimes explicit expectation on the part of the patient, approved by family members and doctors, that hospitalization is a form of "vacation," a reward for hard work. This attitude may be linked to the limited use of paid vacation time by Japanese employees. Illness legitimizes the "vacation" Japanese workers otherwise feel pressured not to utilize (Cole 1979:231). Needless to say, the connection between these two phenomena is not always consciously recognized. This situation also applies to nonworking women, as we saw in Chapter 8. At hospital X I heard some women explicitly state that their hospital stay was a *kyūka* (vacation) from their families. On their vacation, patients expect to relax and be spoiled. It is predictable, then, that many Japanese patients resist postoperative exercise.

In the following sections, I will examine the role of the sick and patients against the broader background of social relationships in Japanese society. Technically, the patient role begins only when a person is placed under the care of a hospital or doctor. The sick role, on the other hand, starts whenever a person becomes ill; that is, if his or her conditions are recognized as symptoms of an illness as defined in that particular culture. She or he is then relieved of some or all their normal roles, depending on the gravity of the illness. Numerous factors create intracultural variation in this pattern. People who are not well off are excused from their normal roles much less readily than those who are wealthy. In addition, certain roles for an individual may be relinquished more easily than others. For example, a woman may be able to give up her role as a professional, a homemaker, or even a wife, but may have to continue to fulfill her duties as a mother, depending on both the emphasis on the maternal role in her culture and the age of her children. Again, I will be stressing generalized Japanese patient roles, with some discussion of male-female variation at the expense of other types of intracultural and individual differences. In a Japanese hospital, people continue to carry out the sick role in their relationship with family members and visitors, but assume the patient role in dealing with the doctor and other hospital personnel. In the following description, I do not always make a distinction between the two.

The patient role

Retention of personal identity

In the United States, where the sovereignty of the individual is sacred, the patient role ironically denies individualism, at least symbolically. It begins with admission to a hospital, when an individual must discard such traces of personal identity as personal belongings, including clothes. People must change to nondescript sterile gowns and wear wristbands as identification, and assume a new identity as a ''patient.''

In sharp contrast, the patient role in Japan reinforces individual identity, as well as each patient's identity as a social persona. This is indeed ironic, since Japanese culture is not known for its emphasis on the individual. In Japan, where one must usually wear a uniform from kindergarten all the way through high school, and formerly through the university, hospital patients use their own nightwear. The use of personal nightwear may seem trivial. However, its symbolic significance in the retention of the patient's individual identity becomes clear with increased understanding of the patient role in the Japanese medical system. Nightwear is one of the most welcome gifts to a patient, chosen especially by those who know the patient well. Attractive nightwear is thought to cheer the patient. The patient must change this clothing often, since it gets soiled, or symbolically polluted, by the sick body more quickly than usual. Extra nightclothes ease the work for the family, which usually is in charge of laundering them, and also make the patient presentable to visitors.

I casually mentioned the American custom of wearing a sterile gown to a group of young women part-time workers at the National Museum of Ethnology, and was taken aback by their emphatic expressions of distaste, which I attributed to their young age – the age when appearance is very important, especially when one has only recently been released from school uniforms. This incident happened at the beginning of my fieldwork, and I had not thoroughly analyzed the differences in the patient role between the two cultures. Also, because I had been hospitalized only twice in Japan, when I was very young, but several times more recently in the United States, I had become accustomed to the American practice. Later, I discussed the American admission process with a colleague who had spent several years in the United States when she was a graduate student. She recalled the discomfort she felt when she was forced to change to a sterile paper gown at the university infirmary. She explained that it was an important incident, in that she became sharply aware of the alien nature of American society, in which she would never really feel at home. In other words, the gown was an epitome of what she perceived as the essence of American culture, with which she felt incompatible.

To ascertain the feelings of health professionals on this matter, I described the American admission process and the use of hospital gowns to a group of eight doctors. Their negative reaction was just as strong as that of nonprofessionals. One doctor in his mid-fifties, who was once the head of a medium-sized hospital but was now in private practice, said that if a Japanese hospital decided to enforce such a rule, people would bring suit against this abrogation of human rights, and it would be all over the front pages of the newspapers. All of them stated that they would let even very ill patients wear not only their own nightwear, but also their own underwear, precisely because they are so ill, and should be made as comfortable as possible. They then pointed out that the practice was indeed inconvenient in cases of bedridden patients, especially since most Japanese use Western style underwear, rather than the traditional underwear, similar to a wraparound skirt, which would be much easier to handle.

I introduced the subject again when I visited doctors and nurses at university hospital Y. There, according to a head nurse, some hospital personnel had recently brought up the idea of instituting the use of hospital gowns. The idea met with immediate and strong objections at a meeting. Some then suggested using gowns of several different colors, with lace for women; even then the proposal was quickly dismissed. The head nurse added that people feel that ''at least when they are ill,'' they should be able to choose their personal attire.

Retention of kinship identity

Continued care by the family and others. Not only do patients remain individuals after hospitalization, but they also remain part of the basic social unit, which in most cases is the family. Care of the sick is not transferred completely to the hospital. Instead, the people closest to the patients continue to care for them, often day and night, in important ways. This care begins at the time of admission. For example, the internal medicine ward of the National Center for Circulatory Diseases allows families and other people close to patients, including children, to wait in the hospital rooms when the patients are brought in for an operation or treatment at the intensive care unit. The doctor at this facility pointed out the importance of the *seishin ian* (psychological comfort) provided by the family. A nurse added that patients feel they must share a nurse, but they can expect exclusive attention and care from their *miuchi* (inside people), families and other closely related people (see Chapter 2). She also pointed out that this practice is beneficial for the family, since they would become restless at home, not knowing what is happening to the patient.

At this hospital, where regulations are much more strict than at most other hospitals, the family must receive permission to care for the patient first from the head nurse and then from the hospital. These rules are made by the head nurse of each ward, so some wards have more stringent rules about family care than others. In fact, at the ward for infant heart surgery, families are not allowed to attend to the patients because of their critical condition. According to a nurse in this ward, some families arrange for their infants to stay in another pediatrics ward so that they can be with them.

Most other hospitals, however, almost expect the continued participation of the family in patient care. The director of hospital X, in fact, told me that he often relied heavily on the observations of family members about the patient's changing condition; he assumed that they would have better knowledge of the patient's condition, and therefore would make sharper observations, than could a nurse who would see the patient only occasionally and might not feel the same concern. A doctor in his late thirties at a municipal hospital near Osaka told me of his dismay when he visited hospitals in France. He observed that family members there would not bother taking care of "the functions of the lower part of the body"; instead, they watched as the nurses did so and went home in the afternoon rather than staying through the night. He felt quite disappointed, as he put it, especially since the French were so demonstrative toward the patients in kissing and other bodily contact. To him, it was incongruous that their expressed feelings were not supported by what he considered to be devoted care for their loved ones. In contrast, he noted that Italians were similar to the Japanese in terms of family care for the patient.

If circumstances permit, one family member will stay with a Japanese patient in the hospital room. Unless the family hires a *tsukisoi* (a round-the-clock attendant), someone stays even at night. There are three major functions for the people attending the patient. First, they attend to all personal needs, unless that job is relegated to a *tsukisoi*. Often patients feel uncomfortable about asking hospital personnel to take care of their bodily functions. Second, family members receive all visitors.

The third major duty of the family is to provide meals for the patient. Families used to bring bedding as well as cooking equipment to the hospital, and cooked for the patients right there. Although this is rarely done now, some hospitals still allow patients to bring their own bedding. Some Japanese feel that the Western-style blankets provided by the hospital are uncomfortably thin, and bring their own quiltlike traditional bedding. Although the custom of bringing cooking and eating equipment is no longer practiced, contemporary Japanese use the system of *sashiire* extensively. The original meaning of the term *sashiire* refers to goods, including food, brought to imprisoned defendants awaiting verdicts. Japanese use this term figuratively in referring to the custom of bringing cooked food for the patient, implying that the patient is "imprisoned." Between *sashiire* and the food brought by visitors, some patients never taste the food served by the hospital kitchen, although hospitals now provide three meals a day, with government funds. Patients, family members, and even doctors all have a ready explanation for the practice – the food at hospitals is very poor in taste and quality. One doctor stated emphatically: "We certainly cannot expect a sick person to eat the hospital food, which is not edible even for a healthy person; the money provided by the government for hospital food is not enough to prepare tasty and nutritious food."

The family usually emphasizes the patient's favorite food as well as food that is good for sick people. Mr. A's wife commuted every day with food from their home in Kobe to the hospital in Osaka, roughly a four-hour round trip. Prior to his hospitalization, in order to ease the man's ulcer, his wife kept a number of aloe plants, the popularity of which as a health food had once swept through Japan; she made every conceivable dish that could be made with aloe leaves, often in unrecognizable form. Now that her husband was in the hospital, she brought a dish of clams whenever she could; clams are a traditional *byōnin shoku* (food for the sick).

In accordance with this emphasis on family care of the sick, doctors often urge terminal patients to go home to die. When they observe that death is near, they usually tell the families to take patients home, so that they can breathe their last there.

Family members and others who take care of patients. So far I have referred to the family and family members without specifying exactly who participates in patient care. When a patient is someone other than the woman of the house (*shufu*), there is little question of who takes care of the patient – the woman takes care of her husband and children. This is the ideal pattern, and when possible, it is closely followed.

The role of women as caretakers of the sick overrides other roles dictated by the formal kinship structure. Japanese society used to emphasize patrilineal descent. Until the end of World War II, the law required that the oldest son inherit the major part of the property, in return for assuming the responsibility for taking care of the parents. Upon marriage, a daughter would leave her natal family and join the family of her husband. Not only did she acquire his family name, but she was also entered in his family registry and buried in his family plot. Ties with her own family remained secondary to ties with her husband's family. Even at that time, there were culturally sanctioned occasions when a married woman returned to her natal home; these occasions included childbirth and the times when her parents became sick.

Some of these traditional kinship rules still prevail, although the spirit has waned considerably. The emphasis now is the nuclear family and a stronger conjugal bond. There is much less pressure for younger women to give their primary allegiance to their husbands' families. Of the changes in kinship structure installed by the new constitution after World War II, the elimination of the primogeniture rule, accompanied by the institution of equal inheritance among offspring, has resulted in an unexpected problem for the aged in Japan: There is now no cultural rule that specifies who must take care of parents in their old age.

My own observations of case studies point to an increase in daughters taking care of their own parents, although a government survey in 1977 (quoted in *Asahi* April 1, 1979) reported more involvement of son's wives in care of the elderly. According to this survey, of the persons responsible for care of the aged, 37% were son's wives, 24.7% their own wives, 17.8% daughters, 5.7% their own husbands; daughter's husbands or sons were not involved. Whatever their kinship roles, then, women are in charge of the sick, and often they must care not only for their own elderly parents, but also for their husband's parents.

What if, then, the woman herself becomes sick? As noted earlier, the sick role or patient role assumed by women is somewhat attenuated. Pampering of the sick, long hospitalization periods, and all the other features discussed in this section apply in the case of women, but with considerable modification. Just as in the United States, a woman can ill afford to stay in bed all day, and must be hospitalized only as a last resort. "What do we do if mother gets sick?" was the title of a newspaper article published by the Kobe Municipal Government (*Kōbe* March 15, 1979). The article urged women to go for regular checkups to avoid becoming ill; the message is that women cannot "afford" to become sick.

When women do get sick, as the statistics above show, care is not always provided by male kin. In the case of the care by husbands, regardless of generation, the decision seems to depend on the individual; the role of a husband does not formally include the care of his wife (see *Asahi* May 16, 1979). I have seen many cases in which either a daughter or a mother came to help, even from a long distance. For example, when the wife of a physician at university hospital Y was hospitalized, her mother came all the way from the island of Shikoku, bringing an amulet from their community shrine, and took care of her grandchildren. One woman in her late forties at the obstetric-gynecology clinic at hospital X asked for immediate admission to the hospital for a partial hysterectomy; she had taken "a leave of absence" from her family for one month in order to undergo surgery at the hospital near her mother's house so that her mother could take care of her. Her own family resided in Kyūshū, indeed a very long distance from Kobe. In general, women choose hospitals with more nurses and other personnel to care for them, and rely less on family members.

Retention of identity as a social persona

Visitation (mimai). If the use of personal nightwear and other belongings signals the retention of the patient's individual identity, and if continued care by the family symbolizes maintenance of kinship identity, then the custom of *mimai* (visits to the patient) sustains the identity of the patient as a social persona. The patient role in Japan does not override these other three roles, which are the most basic as well as the most meaningful to the individual in most societies.

Mimai, or visitation, is a well-established cultural tradition with a long history. The term refers to visits during critical or uneasy times for an individual, such as during a serious illness. Visits are also made during seasonal rites of passage, such as midsummer or the end of the year. Offering a gift is such an integral part of *mimai* that the term is sometimes used to refer to the gift itself. In the past this gift was always food, and even now it is usually food. The food brought in to the patient is commonly called *sashiire*, as noted earlier. Traditionally, the visitor must share the food with the patient, with the idea that the vitality of the healthy visitor is transferred to the patient, aiding the process of recovery. Contemporary Japanese think of food as the source of energy in the literal sense, although food has always been considered the source of symbolic power (*chikara*) (Yanagita 1962).

I asked the doctors about damage done by food brought in by families or visitors to patients on special diets. They had all encountered cases in which food brought in did have negative effects on their patients. They also pointed out that even though the person to whom the food was brought might not be on a special diet, another occupant of the room might be. Because food is customarily shared by all those in the same room, it could cause harm to those on special diets. These doctors were quite convinced, however, that the benefits of providing good food to *chikara zukeru* (cheer up) the patient far outweighed the possible danger. Even though these doctors, thoroughly steeped in biomedical knowledge, do not believe in the literal interpretation of the traditional *mimai* custom, they acknowledge its psychological effect on the patient and, even though unconsciously, the symbolic meaning of food. This is the basis for their extreme lenience toward this custom; they did not seem to be offended by such violations of their instructions.

Shortly before I started to visit university hospital Y, the administration had moved up the starting time of visiting hours so that they would include both lunch and dinner. The sole purpose of this change was to accommodate feeding of the patients by families and visitors. One young doctor, however, suggested to me that, by allowing these practices, Japanese doctors showed too little concern about the entire body of the patient, and instead were concerned only about the ailing body part. This opinion was certainly in the minority, although some wards of larger hospitals, such as at university hospital Y or the National Center for Circulatory Diseases, where patients are on special diets, do have stricter rules. Most patients I talked to welcomed the food from outside. The extent to which patients cherish *sashiire* is vividly illustrated in the diary-report of two women journalists (Chiba 1981; Nakazato 1981). I might point out that this practice works quite well with Japanese foods, most of which are served at room temperature, unlike most Western main dishes, which must be served hot.

The importance of visitation to the retention of the social identity of the patient cannot be overemphasized. In addition to close family members, other people are expected to visit patients, including more distant relatives, friends, and people at work. Neglect of this custom is usually interpreted as a sign of unwillingness to associate with the patient, or even worse, of negative feelings toward the patient. Although some ignorance or neglect of social manners is tolerated, negligence by those who must pay a visit may bring grave social consequences.

In general, these rules are also applicable in the United States, where hospital visitation is increasingly less emphasized; however, the practice is assigned a great deal more importance in Japan. In the case of one elementary school boy, cited as an example by a doctor at university hospital Y, the teacher and the entire class came to see him after his surgery. The hospital has since adopted the policy of warning the family in order to prevent such occurrences. Usually, the higher the social status of the patients, the more visitors they receive. Mr. A's case again serves as an example. During his two-and-a-half-month stay in the hospital, he received a total of 114 visitors, the majority of whom were from his company. Some, like his immediate superior, visited him regularly, bringing news about the company and also about international trade and the stock market so that Mr. A, who had always worked in the export-import section of the company, would be kept abreast. Because he had taken good care of the men who worked for him, many of them also made repeated visits.

When the patient is a woman without her own social status, or a minor, the position of the husband or father is often reflected. For example, a nurse in the pediatric ward at university hospital Y recalled a recent incident involving the grandson of a well-known person in Osaka. On the first day of the boy's hospitalization, 36 visitors, most of whom did not know the boy himself, came to his room, leaving gifts and name cards to inform the grandfather of the visits.

As noted above, university hospital Y recently extended its visiting hours to accommodate carry-in food at lunch; the hours are now from 12 noon to 7 P.M. for all the wards. At hospital X, the hours are from 3 to 8 P.M. on weekdays and from 10 A.M. to 8 P.M. on Sundays and holidays – although the hospital was very lax, so that one could actually visit patients at almost any time. The National Center for Circulatory Diseases had the shortest hours: from 3 to 6:30 P.M. on weekdays and from 1 to 6:30 P.M. on Sundays and holidays. The enforcement of the rule was also more strict at this hospital. In the Keihanshin area there are a few hospitals operated by foreigners or Western religious organizations. These hospitals tend to follow the non-Japanese tradition of strict hours for visits. One such hospital, a Baptist hospital in Kyoto, has experienced a number of cases in which women come for prenatal care but choose another hospital for childbirth that has longer visiting hours.

The frequent presence of visitors in hospital rooms certainly generates ambivalent feelings on the part of doctors, patients, and their families. The possible harm done by the demands of visitors to a patient in need of rest has often been argued among people and in newspapers (*Asahi* March 25, 1979). Many people advocate a change in this custom. Indeed, the *mimai* custom runs contrary to the Japanese emphasis on the peace and quiet, or bed rest, that is recommended for almost all illnesses and for postpartum recovery. An apparent contradiction exists, then, between the medical value of bed rest and the value of social relationships. The predicament created by this contradiction was expressed by the director of hospital X: "It is indeed hard for us to refuse visitors when they come from far away or when their visits might cheer up the patient, even though most patients need a lot of rest."

The dilemma is worse when the patient becomes critically ill, because of yet another social custom. As a young doctor once explained to me, it is the duty of the doctor treating the patient to notify the family when death is approaching, and he or she often urges the family to take the patient home to die. In turn, it is the duty of the family to notify certain people who are expected to come and bid their last farewells. If the patient cannot be moved from the hospital, the doctor can put up a sign saying "No visitors" on the door. Ironically, this sign is read that the patient is in critical condition; consequently, it often increases the number of visitors. A doctor recalled one painful incident in which the medical staff set up an oxygen tent in the room of a critically ill patient and many visitors rushed to see him, defeating the purpose of the treatment and endangering the patient's life. One method sometimes employed by patients who are well known is to place another name on the outside wall of the room in the hope that most visitors will not be able to find the correct room. One large hospital discontinued posting the patient's name on the wall outside the room for the same reason.

The seemingly excessive lenience in allowing hospital visitors, however, must be analyzed in the context of Japanese society and Japanese views of human and social relationships. There is no question that in critical cases, the harm caused by visitors can be serious and sometimes devastating. On the other hand, in many cases the visits, although they tire patients in many ways, do have positive psychological effects. Most important, visitors enable patients to maintain their social identities, by reassuring patients that not only their friends and families, but also their co-workers perceive them as important. For people to whom work is important, and whose own self-images are derived largely from their identities as social personae, a flow of visitors prevents a sudden void in their own self-perception; otherwise, they might experience a feeling similar to the one at the time of retirement, when a person may go from "President Frank Smith of X Company" to simply "Frank."

The beneficial psychological effect of visitors was quite clear in the case of Mr. A. His immediate superior's daily visit not only kept him informed about happenings at his company and in world trade, but also reassured him that he was in good standing with his boss. His wife occasionally chided him, after his boss left, asking how her husband's condition could be expected to improve after hearing about the stock market, and so on. Given Mr. A's devotion to his work, however, and his personality, which is very sociable, the positive psychological effects seemed far to outweigh any adverse physical effects.

The involvement of the entire social group in Japanese hospitalization is curiously similar to the shamanistic healing process of so-called primitive or folk peoples. Many scholars point out that shamanistic healing is a communal event and that community involvement is a major source of moral encouragement for the patient, who can see and feel that others are concerned about his or her well-being (Ohnuki-Tierney 1981a:168–9). Thus hospitalization in industrialized Japan and shamanistic healing both emphasize the importance of involvement by the entire social group – the members of the community in shamanistic healing in a folk society, and the members of the social network in Japan.

The Japanese system, in which hospital patients are cared for by family and friends, has protected Japanese patients from the encroachment of the increasingly impersonal nature of modern life. However, the practice does exact a toll, especially on women, especially now that more women are working outside the home. In the cafeteria of hospital X, I met a woman who came every day to take care of her husband and spent a great deal of time at the hospital. She and her husband jointly operated a gas station, and she continued to supervise their employees and take care of the financial end of the business. A woman's perception of this system is described vividly in *Onna ga Shokuba o Saru Hi* (The Day When a Woman Leaves Her Work), by Okifuji (1979), who describes her final decision to quit work in order to care for her father, who became a victim of cancer. The system also works against individuals without families, although many do have friends and others who extend care as family members would do, as described in Chiba (1981) and Nakazato (1981).

Gifts. Hospital visits are almost always accompanied by gifts. Although the function of any gift is social, the choice of a specific gift derives almost exclusively from the symbolic meaning assigned to the item chosen, thereby rendering the immediate goal of the gift-giving not pragmatic or economic in nature. Based on my observation of Mr. A's case and several others, discussions with other people, and consultations at the gift departments of three large department stores, one in Osaka and two in Kobe, I see roughly four types of gifts that are considered appropriate for the occasion: food, items for personal cleanliness, flowers, and money.

In the past, food was the only gift item for the sick, and it is still the most common. Traditionally, uncooked fresh foods are chosen; because of their freshness (*nama, shinsen*), their vitality is supposed to be transferred from nature, via the healthy person, to the patients to invigorate them. Eggs used to be one of the most welcome presents for the sick (Embree 1958:214) and continue to be a health food among contemporary Japanese. However, eggs are no longer used as gifts, at least in urban areas. At present, fruits are chosen most often. Cantaloupe-type melons, originally an imported fruit, are one of the most prized gift items. Each melon comes in a gift box wrapped in soft white paper and is fairly expensive, ranging from ¥ 2,000 ($9) to ¥ 4,000 ($18). It seems luxurious, with its Western origin, and very different from more "mundane" apples or tangerines. Canned fruit juice, often packed in a gift box of two or three, is another popular present today, although it is not "fresh" fruit. The choice of fresh, natural food, and of such fruit as cantaloupes, which are of Western origin, reveals the link between the symbolic nature of the food selected for the patient and the clear-cut "outside," represented by nature and foreigners, both of which are associated with healing power (Chapter 2).

In urban areas today, visitors – especially those who know the patient well – often bring cooked food, either sweets or main dishes. They try to bring the patient's favorites. Extreme care is taken in choosing the food from a store known for that particular type of food. This concern reflects the Japanese emphasis on *shinise* (stores operating for generations, and known for certain kinds of food). In addition to regular dining halls, most department stores have a *meitengai*, which houses well-known restaurants, and in the basement they also feature famous manufacturers of food. The choice of the right food from the right store indicates not only refined taste on the part of the visitor, but also eagerness to please the patient. The selection of cheese or wine in many Western societies is somewhat similar, but in Japan the range of foods is quite remarkable; careful selection applies not only to some main dishes such as *sushi*, but also to seaweed, pickles, and almost every other food item.

The second major category of gifts includes *nemaki* (nightwear, either Western-style pajamas or the traditional kimono made of cotton or gauze), cakes of soap, and colognes. Common to all three items is their symbolic relationship to pollution and purification. Nightwear, as noted earlier, touches the sick body and thus must be changed frequently in order to get rid of the pollution. Relatives and friends who are fairly close to the patient sometimes give nightwear to facilitate these frequent changes. The symbolic association of soap and colognes to purification of the sick body is obvious. The popularity of soap as a gift item is illustrated by the 1979 spring-summer catalog from the gift section of the Daimaru department store in Kobe. The catalog lists thirty-one kinds of cake soap, all in gift boxes, and fourteen kinds of cakes of soap in different shapes (lemon, eggplant, cucumber, golf ball) in boxes and baskets, plus five kinds of laundry detergent in gift boxes. The price ranges from ¥ 500 ($2.30) to ¥ 3,000 ($13.60). In addition, it displays eighteen different combinations of imported cakes of soap and colognes, including the Chanels. The prices for these assortments are the highest, and range between ¥ 1,000 ($4.50) and ¥ 7,000 ($31.80). First introduced by the Portuguese, soap is a popular gift item for other occasions as well. However, when used as a gift for patients, its meaning as a purifying agent is perceived even by Japanese who describe their perception only in "scientific" terms.

The third type of gift is flowers. Flowers are pleasing to a bedridden patient, and the flowering process suggests growth and the vigor of nature. However, there are a number of taboos in choosing flowers. The most important is to avoid giving potted flowers, since the roots suggest a metaphor for the patient having roots in the hospital and never being discharged. Some Japanese, especially the young, are not fully aware of this taboo, and sometimes bring potted flowers; these are usually given to nurses and other hospital personnel. The choice of a particular flower also follows certain rules. Camellias must be avoided, since when the flower withers, the entire "head" falls off – an all-too-obvious analogy with death. The hydrangea is also taboo, since its flower changes color, suggesting a change for the worse in the patient's skin color. The Japanese are very sensitive about skin color, and the absence of luster and paleness are interpreted as symptoms of ill health. Lilies are also unwelcome, since their smell is too pungent. At present, according to nurses at university hospital Y, the two most welcomed flowers are roses and carnations, which were originally imported. Their symbolic implication is akin to that of the cantaloupes of Western origin.

The last type of gift is money. Many Japanese frown upon cash as a present, but it is used especially by distant friends and relatives who do not feel obliged to visit, but would rather ask another visitor to deliver a gift for them. The use of money as a gift has not been uncommon among the Japanese; money has always been used for *otoshidama* (New Year's gifts to children) and *kōden* (gifts at a funeral). However, one must be careful in choosing money as a gift lest it be interpreted as a sign of lack of thoughtfulness.

Since gifts express the wish for a speedy recovery, and not for "taking root," a feature common to all four types of gifts is their perishability. This idea is most conspicuous in fresh food and cut flowers, neither of which last very long. The pragmatic or economical nature of the gifts is secondary. In fact, the family of a patient with many visitors often experiences difficulty in disposing of all the perishable food. In Mr. A's case and in others I heard of, the family received so many expensive melons that they ran out of people to whom to give them. The choice of gifts, in summary, rests heavily on the symbolic meaning of the items chosen. Their function is social in nature; their economic or utilitarian value is secondary.

Return gifts. Just as certain people are obliged to visit a patient and to bring a gift with them, the patient usually is also obliged to give gifts in return. Because gifts of food are intended to transmit energy from the healthy person to the sick, return gifts must not be given until the sick person recovers completely; otherwise, the illness might be given to the healthy visitor. Although no formal ritual is usually involved today, the Japanese still mark the day when a person formally returns to health. The event is called *tokoage* (lifting of the bedding). As noted in Chapter 2, the beginning of the day for healthy Japanese is marked by folding the *futon* (bedding) and putting it in a closet. To have the *futon* laid out day and night is a sign of sickness; thus, the return to health is symbolically stated as the "lifting of the bed."

As custom requires, at the time of his *tokoage* Mr. A went to the gift section of a department store and chose return gifts for 114 of his visitors. For this purpose, he and his wife had kept a meticulous list of gifts throughout his entire hospital stay. He decided on three categories of return gifts based on the value of each gift received and the social relationship between himself and the visitor. He sat for over two hours on each of his two visits to the gift section of a large department store in Kobe and wrote his name on *noshi*, a covering specially made from rice paper that is always placed on a gift. This task of sending return gifts is often done by a woman, although in this case Mr. A undertook the task himself. Although all the gifts were delivered by the department store, he made an exception for his immediate superior, whom he and his wife visited with an expensive and carefully chosen gift in order to express their gratitude personally.

It should be noted here that anthropologists have assumed that gift exchange is an important characteristic of "primitive" societies (Mauss 1966; Lévi-Strauss 1969). Their studies also indicate that the items exchanged are usually of symbolic or nonutilitarian value (Ohnuki-Tierney 1976:317). The Japanese again share with the "primitives" both the importance of gift exchange and its symbolic nature.

Tsukisoi: Round-the-clock attendants

Tsukisoi refers to the practice in which an attendant, not a medical specialist, is hired to look after a patient around the clock (see Caudill 1961 for a discussion of this practice). These attendants are usually middle-aged or older women whose children are grown, widows, or women who are otherwise free from household duties. Although their official duty is to meet the basic physical needs of their patients, these women also provide psychological comfort to the patients, who are reassured that there is always someone beside them to provide exclusive attention. Although the job is demanding, it does not pay well.

In some cases, a family member staying with a patient will relieve the attendant during the day so that the latter can take care of the patient during the night. The *tsukisoi* system also works well for patients who do not have families or friends to care for them.

Until recently, the *tsukisoi* system had been an integral part of the Japanese system of hospitalization. It also operated informally; that is, the women were hired by the patients and their families and were paid directly by them. Hospitals willingly accommodated the women without establishing any formal relationship with them. Although the *tsukisoi* system has not changed a great deal in practice, recently a new regulation has been instituted by the Ministry of Health and Welfare which specifies that those hospitals with at least one nurse for every four patients may be certified as *kanzen kango* or *kijun byōin* (hospitals that provide complete care, or that meet the standard), but may not permit the employment of *tsukisoi* by patients. These certified hospitals, on the other hand, receive from the government an additional ¥ 2,240 ($10.20) to ¥ 2,360 ($10.70) per patient, depending on the gravity of the patient's condition. Patients who enter hospitals that are not certified in this manner are allowed to hire their own attendants, and the payment of these attendants may be reimbursed from the insurance if the doctor verifies the need for them. In 1979, the average payment to an attendant was between ¥ 7,000 and ¥ 10,000 per day (twenty-four hours). (The information on the new regulation is taken from *Asahi* February 21, 1979.)

In practice, as long as the patient or the family can afford it, an attendant can be hired even in a complete-care hospital by being disguised as a family member, since even at these hospitals family members can attend a patient, provided the doctor approves of their presence. The new regulation, however, has created a problem. The care provided by hospital personnel at the complete-care hospitals may be inadequate for some patients who are totally disabled, and yet the patients must pay out of their own pockets in order to have an attendant.

Doctor-patient relationships

In this final section on the patient role, I will review briefly some of the material presented earlier on the doctor's role, since the patient role cannot be fully understood without examining the ways in which doctors interact with patients.

The custom of "introduction," as I explained previously, is a means by which patients and their families choose the doctors, rather than being chosen by them. It also helps to establish a personal relationship between the two, since a doctor is chosen not by a simple match between the doctor's specialty and the patient's ailment, but because of a "vote of confidence" the patient has somehow given that particular doctor. At the time of hospitalization, each patient is assigned a *shujii* (the doctor primarily responsible for the patient). Both the doctor's and the patient's names are written on a tag and posted on the bed as well as in front of the patient's room. This custom institutionalizes a symbolic expression of the personal tie between the doctor and the patient.

Granted, there are many doctors who do not respond to the confidence and trust of the patient, and there are many patients who question the competence and sincerity of the doctor. There have been a number of observations that many Japanese patients entrust the doctor not only with their medical problems, but with their entire welfare. Caudill and Doi (1963:381) observed how patients with neuroses entrusted themselves completely to their doctors (*Sensei ni omakase shimasu*; I entrust everything to you, Doctor). This attitude is also found among patients with physical problems. Shortly after the spring *renkyū* (successive holidays, a long holiday weekend) one woman patient at the obstetric-gynecology clinic at hospital X told her doctor: "I tried my best not to move about during the holidays, since you might be gone for a vacation and I did not want to give birth during your absence." When the doctor told her he was going to Kyūshū for the weekend and suggested that he admit her the following day and artificially stimulate labor, she agreed to do so most readily.

The nature of the doctor-patient relationship also helps to explain why diagnoses of cancer are not given to patients. Long and Long (1980:15) observe :

To discuss a fatal prognosis not only depresses the patient, but would be asking the patient to accept part of the burden which has been assumed by the physician. It is an admission that the doctor, and scientific medicine, ultimately will fail. Many doctors sit up all night with a dying patient. Whatever they could do medically has been done, but other aspects of their role remain. One doctor drinks a final cup of *sake* with his dying patients.

Equally revealing is a statement made by Dr. Kajihara during the twentieth annual meeting of the Japanese Medical Association (quoted in *Asahi* April 19, 1979). He notes: "Human beings react indeed very strongly to the notion of death. We should let the patients spend the rest of their short lives without anxiety; we therefore should not inform the patient of the cancer verdict." He explains the need for announcing the cancer verdict in the United States in terms of the greater possibility of a malpractice suit if the information is not given to the patient.

Entrusted with such responsibility, then, the doctor is expected to take care of the patient not only as a patient, but also as a human being. Medical judgment is weighed against the psychological needs of the patient as an individual, and as a social being embedded in a network of kinship and social relationships. The doctor's tolerance or often encouragement of *sashiire* (food brought in for the patient), *mimai* (visiting), and patient care by a family member or even a *tsukisoi* (a round-the-clock professional attendant) are all mechanisms through which nonmedical aspects of the patient's needs are accommodated. The *satogaeri* custom, whereby a woman returns to her natal home for childbirth, often necessitating the change of a doctor, is another example along this line. These are, however, institutionalized as customs, so that not only are doctors exempt from making individual decisions, other than in critical cases, but they are also often unconscious of the implications of these customs for their roles as doctors. On the other hand, many Japanese doctors make a conscious effort to take the psychological needs of their patients into consideration.

Paradoxical though it may sound, doctors in Japan assume total responsibility for their patients, and yet remain nonauthoritative by accommodating "human factors," instead of adhering strictly to a more narrowly defined medical judgment.

Hospitalization as a "human drama"

The description so far has concentrated primarily on Japanese hospitalization as a cultural system comprised of various customary institutions, such as visitation, gift exchange, carry-in food, family care, professional attendants, and roles assigned to patients and doctors.

But hospitalization is also a serious, or even a crisis, situation not only for patients themselves, but also for all those close to them. It is a situation in which even the most rigorously suppressed emotions are revealed by the intensified interaction among the people involved. An interpretation of hospitalization, therefore, would be incomplete without an examination of the process from the perspectives of all the people, or, to put it in an anthropological framework, from the perspective of the actors in a social drama (see Turner 1975b). In this section, I will present such an interpretation of the case of Mr. A.

Mr. A certainly occupied center stage in the drama surrounding his hospitalization. Because of Mr. A's intense involvement with his work, the most prominent interactions during his illness were with the people with whom he worked. He was reassured of his good standing at work by the visits of his immediate superior and was flattered by the concern of those who worked for him, whom he and his wife referred to as *buka* (subordinates). On the other hand, if we examine the other people with whom he was interacting, it becomes immediately apparent that there was a second drama taking place simultaneously, centering on his wife. Mr. A, as noted earlier, was a college-educated middle-aged man who has followed, quite successfully, an upwardly mobile life style. In many ways, he fits all too well the stereotype of a category of men (and increasing numbers of women), both in Japan and elsewhere, who are married to their work. As a typical Japanese male "workaholic," he came home very late every day and spent weekends on the golf course with his business associates. Also, he had been overseas a number of times, often for extended periods of time.

In Japanese society, where traditionally there has been a sharp division of labor between husband and wife in terms of both activities and roles, many women take Mrs. A's type of life for granted. They develop their own network of friends, and do not rely on their husbands for socialization or various other psychological needs. This pattern helps when their husbands are assigned duties elsewhere in Japan or overseas, since the family does not always accompany the husband, especially when the move disrupts the children's schooling. Without a network of women friends, Mrs. A had had problems coping with her husband's absences. However, during his last tour of duty in an English-speaking country, his family had joined him. There Mr. A came home every evening, and his social engagements included Mrs. A, in contrast to the Japanese pattern, in which men's social activities often exclude wives. Mrs. A's superb command of English, coupled with her sophisticated knowledge of Western cultures and her remarkable ability as a hostess, in turn enhanced Mr. A's image among his associates, both Japanese and Western. His appreciation of his wife increased, and the couple's relationship was strengthened enormously.

To Mrs. A, then, Mr. A's hospitalization was a chance to relive that enjoyable overseas stay. She received all Mr. A's superiors and co-workers as they visited him in his hospital room. She was publicly recognized as the wife of a successful and well-liked executive. Her self-image not only was enhanced in her own view, but also was socially affirmed. In addition, the situation provided her with the greatest amount of time with her husband in their entire married life.

In almost any society, the status of a husband is also given to his wife. A conspicuous example of this pattern is the First Lady in the United States; the minute that a man becomes president, his wife automatically receives a greatly elevated status as First Lady. In the case of Mrs. A, this practice reveals an additional aspect peculiar to Japanese society. Mrs. A's daily presence at the hospital signified that her husband's work life had come under the domestic sphere, over which his wife had complete control, because tending to the sick is a woman's job.

Discussion

Through the crisis situation of hospitalization, the patient's entire social network becomes activated and reaches a new height of intensity, both positively and negatively. All the participants in the "drama" are forced to reexamine their human relationships. During the hospitalization, every fiber of the patient's social network is tested. Many relationships are strongly reinforced, while others prove too frail and are discontinued.

As patients, doctors, family members, relatives, and friends, all the actors in the drama act out their prescribed roles within the constraints of certain cultural rules. Sometimes the rules are manipulated or bent somewhat – or even purposely ignored. Hospitalization thus provides a setting in which individuals directly confront cultural rules. The dynamic relationship between them creates an intense human drama in which past experiences become extremely important in directing current behavior; past interactions with the patient determine an individual's decision about whether or not to visit, how to visit, or how to care for the patient. The decision on visitation or care, in turn, shapes the future relationship with the patient.

An analysis of hospitalization thus reveals norms in the value system and the formal Japanese social organization. In addition, it also uncovers the nonformalized power allocated to women and the nonformalized social network. It is important to point out that the nonformalized social network has seldom been given prominence in analyses of Japanese society – yet, as we have seen in this chapter, it is quite significant in understanding how Japanese society operates.

Being a microcosm of Japanese culture and society, hospitalization also presents rich intracultural variations. Thus, the ideal of generous sanctioning of illness and indulgent care of the sick must be modified when the patient is a woman or someone who cannot afford to take off from work. Intracultural variations are found not only along sex and socioeconomic lines, but also among individuals.

Individual variations are greatest when we consider how individuals perceive their own behavior and how they are motivated to act. Then we see a range of variation underneath the seemingly same overt patterns. For example, some people are aware of the symbolic meaning of the gifts, as well as reacting to them on an emotional level; they feel good about appropriately chosen gifts, and show a strong aversion to tabooed items, such as a potted flower. Some people react only at the emotional level, without realizing why; others understand the practice only intellectually, without accompanying feelings. Many people, in fact, follow the rules simply because it is customary, without any understanding, either intellecutal or emotional, of the nature of the gifts they choose or receive.

Individual variation is also apparent in the motivations of people who use the cultural systems. For example, some patients make a strenuous effort to be introduced to a doctor and give expensive gifts in order to ''bribe'' the doctor, whose acceptance of the gifts also may be based on a wide range of motivations, depending on the individual. To other people, a gift is a genuine expression of gratitude. As Dore (1973:262) concludes, ''Only a hair-line separates the 'mere token' of gratitude from the bribe. . . . ''

By studying the hospitalization process, we can learn a great deal about Japanese culture and society and about the actual interactions of individuals involved in the process. Conversely, we can never really interpret the hospitalization process without a thorough understanding of Japanese culture and society. Hospitalization in Japan is by no means a universal experience involving simply the biomedical treatment of a disease. Rather, it is a Japanese experience, *mutatis mutandis*.

10   Medical pluralism

The term *medical pluralism* or *pluralistic system of medicine* is somewhat misleading, in that it connotes that there are some societies with only a single
medical system and others with more than one. Most societies have a pluralistic
system of medicine, including the United States. If we include religious institutions, as I did in this book, priests and ministers have always actively practiced
a nonformalized medical system, including psychological counseling through
personal communication and holding services at times of stress, such as sickness
and death.

Perhaps the single most important factor in the success of medical pluralism
in Japan today is that each system has become so thoroughly embedded in
Japanese culture and society. Each system is a part of the total sociocultural
system. In Chapter 7 we noted that, from the perspective of ordinary people,
the meaning of buddhas and of Shinto and Taoist deities is derived from a single
symbolic structure – even though, except for folk Shinto, all the major religions
of Japan are foreign in origin. These supernaturals have served medical functions
as obstetricians, pediatricians, and the like within the cultural milieu of the
people.

We saw in Chapter 5 that *kanpō*, also of foreign origin, is thoroughly embedded
in popular folk notions of health and illness – so much so that some people
would find it difficult to apply the label of *kanpō* to moxibustion or some herbal
treatments, both of which are administered at home. *Kanpō* has been revived
even after legal oppression precisely because it has become so much a part of
Japanese culture and society, in which a common expression for telling someone
precisely what is wrong with something is *okyū o sueru* (to administer moxa).
An adult may also half-jokingly use the same expression to a misbehaving child.
It is for this reason that I share Leslie's (1975) skepticism about the adoption
of Chinese medicine in the United States, where the culture seems too alien for
it to succeed.

A thorough immersion in Japanese culture and society is also evident in the
case of biomedicine. In this chapter I will focus on a further interpretation of

the sociocultural nature of biomedicine, since biomedicine is a "cosmopolitan medicine" (Dunn 1976:135-6) and therefore can be compared by readers of any cultural background to the way in which it is practiced in their own countries. The sociocultural nature of Japanese biomedicine is especially pronounced because biomedicine was introduced from a vastly different Western culture only about a hundred years ago.

Biomedicine in culture and society

An examination of the sociocultural aspects of biomedicine starts with Japanese values and ideologies as incorporated in biomedicine delivery – the relationship of biomedicine to culture – and then proceeds to look at how these values are translated into patterns of social relationships. I will make frequent comparisons between Japan and the United States, perhaps overly stressing the differences.

Above all, biomedical delivery in Japan is firmly based on the cultural affirmation of illness. To use a Parsonian framework (Parsons 1979), illness in Japanese culture is assigned the positive values of legitimacy and desirability, which are institutionalized through the generous allowance of visitation at hospitals and other forms of "indulgence." Family members, friends, and even health specialists all pamper the sick. Patients are allowed to stay in the hospital for a long time, are fed their favorite foods, and receive visits and gifts. Similarly, Japanese workers who feel reluctant to take all their paid vacation readily take sick leave, and even the most dedicated wife and mother may take a month-long vacation from household chores and duties and return to her natal home for child delivery.

The cultural affirmation of illness is closely related to the cultural approval of the dependent state in which a sick person is placed. That dependent state is, in the Japanese view, an extension of the interdependent state of every person in Japanese society, in which "a self . . . can feel human in the company of others" (Plath 1982:120). This concept of self contrasts with the Western conceptual model, which Geertz (1976:225) points out as unique from a global perspective:

The Western conception of the person as a bounded, unique, more or less integrated motivational and cognitive universe, a dynamic center of awareness, emotion, judgement, and action organized into a distinctive whole and set contrastively both against other such wholes and against its social and natural background, is, however incorrigible it may seem to us, a rather peculiar idea within the context of the world's cultures.

Differences in cultural attitudes toward illness between Japan and the United States, then, are ultimately related to the concept of self in each culture.

Independence and individual freedom are two facets of the most cherished value in the United States. The sick, the handicapped, and the aged are people who must depend upon others; the healthy and the young must avoid becoming like them. One of the favorite ways to "brag" about an American child, I have often observed, is to say that the child is independent. Training for such independence must start right from the beginning; even a newborn infant has a crib or separate bed, and usually is placed in a separate room, rather than beside the mother. To cite only one other example, the label "Independent Living" is often used as the title of organizations and facilities that help the elderly and the handicapped in the United States. This label certainly minimizes or even hides the fact that these organizations and facilities are in existence because these people are in some way dependent. It also stresses the fact that they must become independent to be fully accepted members of American society. In contrast, Japanese parents brag about children being *amaeta*, amenable to letting the parents and others take care of them (see Doi 1978), and they often let children sleep beside their mothers until they are about twelve years old (Caudill and Plath 1966).

Values and attitudes toward illness are translated directly into the sick role and the patient role in the two cultures. In Japan, the patient role receives no negative sanction. Each patient continues to be a person (using personal belongings during hospitalization), a kin member (cared for by the family), and a member of a larger social group (receiving visitors from work). In fact, during hospitalization, these roles are tested and hence even more clearly articulated than usual. As a patient's social network becomes intensely activated, the social definition of the patient's self, as defined by multiple roles in the network, becomes clearly accentuated. In other words, the patient is not removed from the society; on the contrary, the patient is given an opportunity to feel and experience both individual and social identity, as well as importance as an individual and social persona. For patients who are reassured that they are cherished husbands, wives, fathers, or mothers, and desirable co-workers, the willingness to resume these roles certainly must be intensified.

Again, the contrast with the patient role in the United States is illuminating. An American patient becomes a number on a wristband, is clothed in a non-descript sterile gown, regardless of sex, fed institutional food, and almost completely isolated from the rest of society. The patient's role is a reflection of the idea that sickness is undesirable and that the sick must be removed from the society. As Parsons points out, the United States practices "insulation" of the sick from the healthy, as well as from other sick people, because both "motivationally as well as bacteriologically," illness may be contagious (Parsons 1979:133). It is feared that germs, or even worse, dependency will spread. Sterile gowns, then, are symbolic of sterilization to get rid of "American germs"; the biomedical justification for their sterility can hardly be taken seriously, because there are too many other objects patients come in contact with that are not sterile. The complete transformation of the sick individual into a patient also signifies the subordination of individuality to the "authority" of the medical personnel (see Blum 1960:esp. 220–9).

In the case of the Japanese, then, the legitimacy given to illness is the key to a successful fight against the encroachment of an impersonal institutionalization in the care of the sick. In contrast, in the United States the lack of legitimacy or the equating of illness with deviant behavior, as Parsons and Fox (1952) would put it, encourages the institutional care of the sick (see also Fox 1968:93). This is because the pampering of the sick by the family members would encourage a sick person to engage in "eating his cake and having it too" (Parsons and Fox 1952:35), thereby prolonging the illness-deviant behavior. In Japan the psychological support by the family and others motivates the patient to recover quickly, whereas in the United States, "punishment" by institutional-impersonal treatment motivates the sick to become healthy.

The Japanese fight against institutionalization in the care of the sick has historical continuity. Most revealing is a popular protest, called *korera ikki* (cholera riots), in 1879. During a cholera epidemic, the government isolated the victims to prevent its spread and also took care of the corpses, rather than returning them to their families (Koto, et al. 1967:76–7; Ono 1968:109–13; Tatsukawa 1979:177–206). These policies were directly contrary to the cherished tradition of the family continuing to care for the sick during hospitalization and allowing the sick to return home to die. They led people to believe that the hospitals were selling the victims' livers to Westerners, despite the fact that epidemics were brought into Japan by visitors from Asian countries (Ono 1968: 109), not by Westerners. The result was public protest.

It is ironic that in the United States, where individualism is valued so highly, the patient role denies individualism. Patients are denied their individual and social identities, are not permitted to make their own decisions, and must obey the medical judgments of their doctors who, in contrast to Japanese doctors, seem to place far less emphasis on "human factors." For Americans, therefore, in whose society individuals who defy the system and the authorities are treated as heroes in the public media (Hsu 1973:13–14), the hospital patient role is often a painful experience of dehumanization and the deprivation of individualism.

The role played by kin members in the care of the sick even after hospitalization is reported from many parts of the world. Janzen, in his study of Zairian health care, called attention to this phenomenon by stressing the "therapy managing group," who "rally for the purpose of sifting information, lending moral support, making decisions, and arranging details of therapeutic consultation," and who exercise "a brokerage function between the sufferer and the specialist" (Janzen 1978:13–14). The Zairian therapy managing group consists primarily of various maternal and paternal kin. In the case of the Japanese, a woman close to the patient (wife, mother, daughter) often becomes the primary person in patient care, although critical issues are sometimes discussed between the doctor and close male kin. Also, in the Japanese case the "broker" image would be inappropriate, because it suggests that the group mediates between the doctor and the patient. The Japanese family or an equivalent often act as "patient surrogates," who read the patient's wishes and speak for him or her, at times without explicitly consulting the patient. They are more than mediators; they are surrogates who almost become one with the patient.

To further illustrate this point, look at how the Japanese "individual" is defined within a network of heavily and intimately involved human relationships. Symbolic of this situation is the lack of an individual birth certificate. A person is born into a family and is recorded in the family registry as the first son, the fourth daughter, and so on, of the head of the family, who is usually a male. Thus, an individual is born into a family. Only later does one establish one's own family or marry into another family, as is the case with a woman. In Japanese kinship terminology, there is no word equivalent to "sister" or "brother"; both the address and reference terms for sibling include "younger" and "older." For example, *ane* (the reference term) or *onēsan* (the address form) means older sister, not simply sister. The same applies to the kinship terms for male siblings. In other words, a person in Japan is considered first and foremost a member of a family from birth, in contrast to the American pattern of recording each birth with an individual birth certificate and with little emphasis on position in the family.

A recent law governing cornea and kidney transplants provides yet another example of the concept of the individual and the pattern of the decision-making process in Japan. In 1979 a law was passed that legalized the transplantation of the cornea and kidney from a deceased person. The law specifies that the transplantation be done only after the deceased person's family gives its written consent. If, however, the deceased person has left written consent, the operation can be performed without the written consent of the family, provided that they do not object (*Asahi* May 24, May 28, 1979). The Japanese attitude toward the dead body and toward death itself must be taken into consideration in order to understand the meaning behind this law. The law clearly reveals a decision-making pattern in which the family has ultimate control over such important matters as the treatment of the body after death. Within this context, it is easier to understand why a cancer diagnosis is given to the family, and not to the patient; the family decides whether or not to tell the patient – that is, how the patient should live the rest of his or her life. Similarly, we can see why surrogate patients are accepted so naturally.

This interpretation of the cultural definition of the individual in Japanese society and the pattern of decision making must be taken cautiously, however. A Japanese individual, although defined in terms of a kinship network and deeply involved in interpersonal relationships, does not necessarily lack an independent mind or personality. The expectations and rules governing interpersonal relationships should not be translated directly into individual psychology. Furthermore, although most of the examples cited involved family members, it is human relationships in general, rather than just kinship ties, that have always been considered most important by the Japanese – even when their consideration results in a short-term loss of efficiency in individual or group activities.

If the meaning assigned to illness and the nature of the patient role both derive from Japanese culture and society in general, other aspects of hospitalization are embedded in Japanese culture as well. For example, the *mimai* custom, visitation with a gift, is only one of the many culturally prescribed gift-giving occasions. There are many occasions other than illness when the entire social network is activated through visits and gifts (for an extensive discussion of gift exchange in Japan, see Befu 1967, 1968, 1974). Most important of these occasions are *chūgen* and *kure* (midsummer and the end of the year), when one must pay visits to people important in one's social network. They include superiors at work, teachers, and important clients, as well as parents, parents-in-law, and other relatives. Most, but not all, gifts require return gifts. The amount (quality) and timing of gifts and return gifts are delicately prescribed by detailed cultural rules.

The general rule of thumb is that a social inferior must initiate the gift exchange. This rule is applicable even between the two sets of parents of a married couple. At any of the gift exchange times, the parents of a married daughter must give a gift to their daughter's husband's parents, who then must respond with a return gift. This gift exchange must be initiated by the woman's parents, because a wife in the traditional view is socially inferior to her husband. In some cases, a gift from a social inferior is an expression of gratitude and indebtedness that does not require a return gift. For example, teachers receive gifts from their students at certain times of the year or at graduation, but they are not expected to respond with return gifts. In other cases, such as people in the same organization, a superior may decide on an appropriate return gift at a little below half of the value of a gift received from a subordinate (for details of the rules governing gift exchange among equals and between people related hierarchically, see Befu 1967). Sending a gift, often via a store, is replacing the traditional practice of paying a visit to deliver the gift. There are certain individuals, however, to whom one must pay a visit, as we saw in the case of Mr. A, who paid a visit to his boss with a return gift.

Although some changes are taking place in this elaborate system of gift exchange, it is by no means declining. In a sense, it is even more conspicuous now than ever before, since the Japanese are more affluent and business establishments aggressively use the system to sell their products. Perhaps the most direct reflection of the enormous importance the Japanese place on the custom of exchanging visits and gifts is the fact that even in modern Japan – one of the most modernized and industrialized countries in the world – the monthly salary is calculated to include a sizable "bonus" (the Japanese use the borrowed English term, pronouncing it *bōnasu*), once at the end of the year and sometimes also in midsummer, when the entire nation becomes engulfed in *kure* and *bon* gift exchange. Thus, if an employee's stated salary is, for example, ¥ 300,000 ($1363.60) a month, the total annual salary is twelve times this amount plus a bonus, which ranges anywhere between two and ten months' salary; this makes the stated monthly salary figure misleading to non-Japanese. According to Dore's survey (1973:400–3) of seventeen households, expenditures on gifts ranged between 0.8 and 19.4% of total household expenses.

The importance of gift exchange is clear from the fact that it is culturally institutionalized, and that both public and private enterprises cooperate. In fact, this "bonus" system is practiced by every enterprise, both public and private, with at least one employee, indicating that the practice is actually an unwritten law. Historically, it should be noted, the standardization of this practice took place only around 1878, when the eight-hour work day, retirement age, amount of retirement pay, and various other labor laws were instituted (Tōkyō Hyaku-nenshi, ed. 1979:512–13). Modernization in Japan, in this respect as well as in others, was facilitated in part by the institutionalizing of traditional practices that previously had been left up to the individual employer. Today, one of the major functions of labor unions is to bargain for a larger bonus. The basis for their argument is now inflation, which necessitates cost-of-living raises. However, the contemporary bonus system derives historically from the custom of providing pocket money or an extra allowance at times of gift exchange – at the end of the year, at midsummer, and sometimes at other times as well (Ōkōchi 1968) – when the employees, like contemporary Japanese, went home for the holidays and bought gifts for their relatives.

Americans engage in gift exchange, even more than many realize, and there are some forms of payment in the business world comparable to the Japanese bonus. Such a thorough institutionalization as practiced in Japan, however, must seem somewhat alien to Americans, to whom the custom may be seen as an intrusion into an individual's right to make financial decisions and plans (even social security and retirement plans that operate on the same principle as the Japanese bonus system are only a recent invention in the United States).

As Mauss (1966, originally 1950) pointed out long ago, and Lévi-Strauss (1969) and others have elaborated, gifts are an important means of communication among individuals and groups, whose relationships are often strengthened by the gift exchange. The elaborateness of the Japanese system succinctly expresses the importance the Japanese place on human relationships.

This discussion illustrated how biomedical delivery in Japan is rooted in the basic values and patterns of social relationships. Many other aspects of biomedical health care demonstrate its deeply rooted sociocultural nature. In the examples of pregnancy and child delivery handled by biomedical hospitals and doctors, we saw that numerous traditional sociocultural features are institutionalized in contemporary practice. Such practices as the "ten month" duration of pregnancy, the use of the sash, and the *satogaeri* (return to one's natal home) are all intact. The rationale for the use of the sash is to prevent chilling of the stomach, and we recall that "chilling illness" is a culturally recognized illness (Chapter 3). In addition, placement of the sash over the abdomen is related not only to the fact that the fetus is in the abdomen, but also to the view of the stomach as the most important body part (Chapter 3).

The use of the sash, obtained from a temple or a shrine and still advocated by biomedical doctors today, provides evidence of syncretism. Biomedicine has adopted a part of traditional religious healing – although contemporary obstetricians would never consciously view it that way. As Leslie (1974, 1980) stresses, in a pluralistic medical system, the systems do influence each other.

In the delivery of biomedicine, we see a microcosm of Japanese society and culture. A thorough transformation of biomedical delivery holds the key to the successful penetration and growth of biomedicine in the pluralistic system of Japanese medicine. In it, each system shares with others basic values and patterns in human relationships, all derived from Japanese culture and society.[1]

Medical pluralism: A descriptive summary

Although the medical systems described so far in this book share common sociocultural aspects, at the institutional level they do operate as discrete systems. At the risk of oversimplification, I will portray schematically the relative importance of each of the three institutionalized medical systems, both in terms of the historical development of Japanese society and in terms of the "illness career" of a hypothetical contemporary individual (Figure 3). I include only the three institutionalized medical systems discussed in detail in this book. I repeat here that the functions provided by religious institutions may not be consciously perceived as "medical," but people nonetheless visit temples and shrines for general as well as specific problems of health, as noted in Chapter 6. Since the figure is drawn only schematically to suggest the major trends, the proportions of the relative importance of each system are simply approximations.

Although I do use the term "illness career," following Fabrega (1972:183),

---

[1] For this reason, I disagree with Lock (1980b), who not only views *kanpō* and biomedicine as discrete systems, but advocates a complete separation of the two so that *kanpō* grows as a viable medical system.

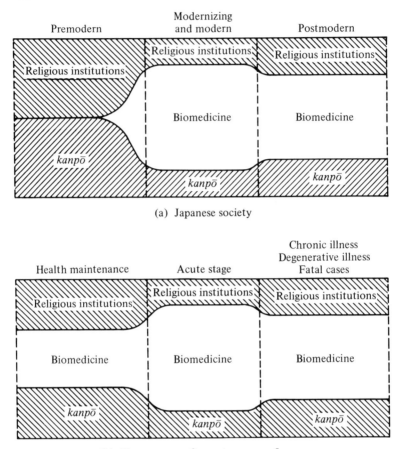

(a) Japanese society

(b) Illness career of a contemporary Japanese

Figure 3. A hypothetical picture of the relative importance of the three medical systems.

it is used only in a loose sense, postulating only two stages: acute and later. In the "later" stage in the figure, I have included other types of disease: chronic and degenerative, which often do not have an acute stage. Therefore, the picture is indeed a composite, squeezing different types of illness into one "illness career." My main point in this schema is to summarize the complementary practices of the medical systems detailed in Chapter 5. Biomedicine has been most effective in acute cases, and *kanpō* has been most effective in health maintenance and in cases where biomedicine has failed (chronic and degenerative illnesses, as well as new types of illnesses including those that are consequences of environmental pollution).

Here, attention will be focused on the complementary nature of the medical systems from a historical perspective in order to examine the broader and perhaps more general factors responsible for the development of medical pluralism. During premodern periods biomedicine was absent, and both institutionalized religions and *kanpō* played significant roles in health care. During the modernization period, promotion of biomedicine became a national policy, and at least at the institutional level it became the dominant system, and the practice of *kanpō* was officially discouraged. After the beginning of the postmodern period, the dominant role of biomedicine has eroded, especially with the revival of *kanpō* among the general public.

Although not shown in Figure 3, folk medicine (*minkanyaku*) occupied a significant place in health care during the premodern periods. Shamanism has long been a major nonformalized and noninstitutionalized medical system. Its decline may be closely linked to the rapid and continued development of new religions after World War II; many of the prophets of these new religions are "shamans" who were charismatic and successful enough to develop their individualistic practices into major religious organizations.

A significant point that emerges in the total picture of medical pluralism is the institutionalization of psychological care without it being labeled as such. All the medical systems incorporate the basic values of the legitimacy and desirability of illness, which are then translated into institutional allowance of the continued care of the sick by family or friends. Furthermore, even with the advent of biomedicine, the pluralistic system of medicine in Japan has always accommodated the medical role played by various religions, which have provided psychological comfort as well as counseling. In their conscious model of illness etiology, the Japanese tend to attribute illness to matter, including the body, rather than the mind (the physiomorphism of Chapter 4). On the other hand, the Japanese health care system has tacitly yet extensively incorporated psychological care into patient treatment. The nonformalized and nonverbalized method for dealing with the psychological dimension may be the result of cultural patterning – as Caudill (1976a:164) points out, the Japanese are reluctant to verbalize their feelings, although they can do so in writing. Thus, rather than vocally expressing their concerns to the sick, they take care of even minute discomforts, and feed patients their favorite foods.

Another significant point about the Japanese pluralistic system of medicine is that the cost of medical care does not determine its popularity. Unlike other "indigenous" systems of medicine, which are less expensive than biomedicine in many parts of the world, *kanpō* doctors' treatments and over-the-counter *kanpō* medicines are more expensive than biomedicine. In other words, through its bureaucratic expansion into the national health insurance system, biomedicine has made itself far less expensive and more available to the people. Nevertheless, *kanpō* is making an impressive comeback.

So far in this book I have offered an explanation for the revival of *kanpō* in terms of its "medical" efficacy in the types of medical problems for which biomedicine has proved ineffective. Although this is the argument offered by both Japanese laypeople and medical professionals, and its purely medical aspect sounds convincing, it bears further scrutiny. Doctors in Japan and elsewhere have been busy trying to isolate the pharmacologically active substances in *kanpō* herbs, as well as the medically effective physiochemical changes incurred by moxibustion and acupuncture. However, this research has yielded few findings; the psychosomatic factors in many illnesses make it exceedingly difficult to prove how a particular medicine really works. For this reason, Leslie (1974, 1976) is quite skeptical about evaluating medical systems on the basis of medical efficacy alone. He points to examples such as the disappearance of leprosy from Europe and the decline of tuberculosis in the nineteenth and early twentieth centuries, both of which are not traceable to medical developments at the time (Leslie 1974:77–8). Dubos' influential book (1979) makes the same point. Young (1976:5) also emphasizes that a "people's medical beliefs and practices persist because they answer instrumental *and* moral imperatives" [italics mine]. He further explains that the empirical effectiveness of the medical practices has "ontological consequences" of validating "ideas about the real world" (see also Maclean 1974:156).

We commit an error if we evaluate the contribution of *kanpō* to Japanese health care simply on the basis of narrowly defined "medical efficacy." The medical efficacy of *kanpō*, which has been emphasized by both laypeople and professionals in Japan, may be seen also as a way of validating their world view of the postmodern period, in which the Japanese people have regained their confidence as a people on the international scene. Primarily through economic success, Japan has risen from the ashes of the atomic bombs to a state in which it can comfortably see itself as a world power. It is for this reason that the revival of *kanpō* coincides with the resurgence of interest in Japanese culture, with temples and shrines attracting more people and their rituals receiving increasing popularity.

We noted in Chapter 2 that the Japanese have been always eager to tour "outside," to go to other countries, and that they have been exceedingly courteous to Westerners, who are symbolically equivalent to the ancient deities who brought rejuvenating energy to the villages. These outsiders were the absent "other" whose occasional presence was necessary for the Japanese to engage in self-reflexivity. Now that the Japanese have mastered the "outside" and "outsiders," they have room to engage in collective self-reflexivity.

Ancient Chinese civilization was once "the other" lying outside Japan, providing medicine, technology, a writing system, city plans, and a host of other advances. These introduced elements have long been digested in Japan, becoming part of "the self." In the age of *Roots*, a book and an idea that have become exceedingly popular in Japan, we may speculate that the Japanese are turning their focus from Western civilization to ancient Chinese civilization as the source of their "roots." It may not be accidental, therefore, that the *kanpō* boom has coincided with the *Chūgoku* boom (China boom). The Japanese are eager to visit the People's Republic, and numerous exhibitions of ancient Chinese civilization, including medicine, now attract a large number of people. The revival of *kanpō*, accompanied by a more critical attitude toward biomedicine, must be seen within the broader context of the changing world view of the Japanese. It symbolizes a significant change in the self-reflexive process of the Japanese during the postmodern era.

In short, any evaluation of *kanpō* should not be based strictly on its medical efficacy. The unsuccessful attempt to find pharmacologically effective substances should not lead to the conclusion that it is nothing but a placebo. As noted in Chapter 5, I am convinced that *kanpō* treatments do have a narrowly defined medical efficacy. On the other hand, to judge a particular medical system solely by its medical efficacy would be a grave error, since no system can be truly medically effective without being responsive to the ontological concerns of the people. An evaluation of any medical system must always be two-pronged.

Summary

If the portrait of the Japanese presented in this book is quite different from the more familiar ones described in other works on the Japanese and their civilization, it is due primarily to the fact that this book is written from the perspective of the ordinary Japanese. It is also different because of its emphasis on the symbolic dimensions of Japanese daily life. Rather than examining formalized public rituals, events, or institutions themselves, I examined the perspectives and involvement of people in them, together with the management of daily hygiene and general body and health maintenance.

The urban Japanese as seen in this book are people who have maintained well-delineated symbolic categories of thought, or to use a more fashionable term, a structure of "consciousness." Although couched today in the language of biomedical germ theory, Japanese concepts of hygiene are deeply embedded in symbolic categories of thought (Chapter 2). Their thought patterns also include physiomorphism, often attributed to magical thoughts, and their urban life is full of magical rites (Chapters 4, 6, and 7). Nervously attempting to expel pollution from their universe, they nevertheless live in a dualistic universe in which death and evil coexist with life and good, although the former are always placed in ritual contexts (Chapter 3). The urban Japanese notion of the self is not that of the "individual," isolated and free from other members of the society (Chapters 8, 9, and 10). Assigning legitimacy to illness, performing magical rites, and living in a densely intertwined network of human relationships, the Japanese nonetheless manage to limit the impersonal institutionalization of their lives – at least so far, they have done so more successfully than many other peoples in the industrialized sectors of the world. They have accomplished this feat in the face of repeated government pressure to the contrary. In this postindustrial era, they have even revived the "folk" medicine of kanpō, whose theoretical foundation runs counter to that of biomedicine (Chapter 5).

Magic, as well as its conceptual counterpart of physiomorphism, the symbolic notion of pollution, and the concept of a dualistic universe all have been considered hallmarks of the structure of thought of "premodern," "primitive," or "tribal" peoples. Likewise, Japanese hospitalization is akin to shamanistic healing in that in both cases the entire social group is involved in the healing process. Again the primordial ties and close links between individuals and their social group have often been seen to characterize the folk society.

The presence of these features in contemporary Japanese culture and society, then, contradicts some of the major theories of social scientists on the impact of modernization, a process characterized by industrialization as its economic core, as well as associated developments, such as modern Western science. Although the concept of "modernization" is too broad and vague to be meaningful, and a satisfactory critique of modernization theories would require another book, I would point out here that reliance on unsatisfactory models of modernization is due to two related factors. First, the models have been based solely on the modernization process in Western societies. Second, they are based on only a small segment of Western society – primarily the thought structure of the intellectual-professional elite and urban patterns of social relationships. Therefore, these models are unsatisfactory even as comprehensive models of Western modernization. They are not based on the daily folk life of Western societies, or for that matter, the daily life of even the intellectuals. Such a model would consider Kant only in his role of writing philosophy, and not his daily routine of dining and otherwise functioning within the German popular culture.

Leach (1963:124–36, 1966, 1968, 1976, 1982) has been the most articulate in emphasizing the presence of symbols and rituals in the behavior of all of us. Recent emphasis on secular rituals (Babcock and Myerhoff, ed. 1978) or the perceptive work by Barthes (1979, 1981) on symbolic dimensions of French daily life indicate that anthropologists have become increasingly reflexive in regard to their own cultures (see Chapter 1). They are realizing the active roles taken by particular cultures in shaping such processes as industrialization and scientific development – processes that are far from immune to cultural patterning and that rarely follow a unilinear course of development. As Sahlins pointed out, it is not that the economy "objectively" is the core of human activities; it is the symbolic structure of Western culture which places the economy in "the main site of symbolic production," thereby producing Economic Man and Woman. Thus, *la pensée bourgeoise* (Sahlins 1976:211, and the title of his Chapter 4) is far richer in symbolic elements than some social scientists have led us to believe. The uniqueness of a culture, however, does not lie in its specific features. Many of the features of Japanese culture described in this book, when taken individually, are found in other cultures. It is the particular combination of these features and their synthesis that make Japanese culture distinct from others.

References

Ariyoshi, Kenji, ed. 1978. *Shōjō kara Mita Katei no Igaku Hyakka* (Home Manual of Medicine – Diagnosis of Symptoms). Tokyo: Hoken Dōjinsha.

Azumi, Koya. 1968. The mysterious drop in Japan's birth rate. *Trans-action* 5(6):46–8.

Babcock, Barbara A. 1980. Reflexivity: Definitions and discriminations. *Semiotica* 30(1/2):1–14.

Babcock, Barbara A., and Barbara Myerhoff, ed. 1978. *The Reversible World*. Ithaca, N.Y.: Cornell University Press.

Barnhart, C. L., ed. 1961. *The American College Dictionary*. New York: Random House.

Barthes, Roland. 1979. *Elements of Semiology*. New York: Hill and Wang. (Originally published in French in 1964.)

1981. *Mythologies*. Selected and translated from the French by Annette Lavers. New York: Hill and Wang. (Originally published in French in 1957.)

Bartholomew, James R. 1981. Review of *East Asian Medicine in Urban Japan* by Margaret M. Lock. *Journal of Japanese Studies* 7(1):195–200.

Basso, Keith H. 1979. "Wise words" of the Western Apache: Metaphor and semantic theory. In *Language, Culture and Cognition*, Ronald W. Casson, ed. New York: Macmillan. Pp. 244–67.

Beardsley, Richard K. 1965. Religion and philosophy. In *Twelve Doors to Japan*, R. K. Beardsley and J. W. Hall, eds. New York: McGraw-Hill. Pp. 310–47.

Beardsley, Richard, John W. Hall, and Robert E. Ward. 1969. *Village Japan*. Chicago: University of Chicago Press. (Originally published in 1959.)

Befu, Harumi. 1967. Gift-giving and social reciprocity in Japan, an exploratory statement. *France-Asie/Asia* 188:161–77.

1968. Gift-giving in modern Japan. *Monumenta Nipponica* 23:445–6.

1971. *Japan – An Anthropological Introduction*. San Francisco: Chandler.

1974. Power in exchange: strategy of control and patterns of compliance in Japan. *Asian Profile* 2(5–6):601–22.

1979. Review of *The Japanese* by E. Reischauer. *Journal of Asian Studies* 39 (1):164–6.

Benedict, Ruth. 1967. *The Chrysanthemum and the Sword*. New York: New American Library. (Originally published in 1946.)

Berger, Peter L., and Thomas Luckmann. 1967. *The Social Construction of Reality*. Garden City, N. Y.: Doubleday.

226

Blacker, Carmen. 1975. *The Catalpa Bow: A Study of Shamanistic Practices in Japan.* London: George Allen & Unwin.

Blum, Richard H. 1960. *The Management of the Doctor-Patient Relationship.* New York: McGraw Hill.

Boon, James A. 1977. *The Anthropological Romance of Bali 1597–1972 – Dynamic Perspectives in Marriage and Caste, Politics and Religion.* Cambridge: Cambridge University Press.

Bowers, John Z. 1965. *Medical Education in Japan: From Chinese Medicine to Western Medicine.* New York: Harper & Row.

Bunkachō (Ministry of Cultural Affairs, Government of Japan), ed. 1976–80. *Shūkyō Nenkan, Shōwa Gojūnenban-Gojūyonnenban* (Annals of Religion, 1975–9). Tokyo: Ōkurashō Insatsukyoku.

Buraku Kaihō Kenkyūjo, ed. 1978a. *Buraku Mondai Gaisetsu* (Introduction to *Buraku* Problems). Osaka: Kaihō Shuppansha.

1978b. *Buraku Mondai Yōsetsu* (Outline of *Buraku* Problems). Osaka: Kaihō Shuppansha.

Bureau of Statistics, Office of the Prime Minister, ed. 1977. *Population Census of Japan.* Vol. 3, Part 28 (Hyōgo-ken). Tokyo: Bureau of Statistics, Office of the Prime Minister.

Carstairs, G. M. 1977. Medical anthropology. *Royal Anthropological Institute News* No. 22:1–2.

Caudill, William. 1961. Around the clock patient care in Japanese psychiatric hospitals: The role of *tsukisoi*. *American Sociological Review* 26(2):204–14.

1976a. The cultural and interpersonal context of everyday health and illness in Japan and America. In *Asian Medical Systems*, C. Leslie, ed. Berkeley: University of California Press. Pp. 159–77.

1976b. Social change and cultural continuity in modern Japan. In *Responses to Change*, G. DeVos, ed. New York: Van Nostrand. Pp. 18–44.

Caudill, William, and Takeo Doi. 1963. Interrelations of psychiatry, culture, and emotion in Japan. In *Man's Image in Medicine and Anthropology*, I. Galdston, ed. New York: International University Press. Pp. 374–421.

Caudill, William, and David W. Plath. 1966. Who sleeps by whom? Parent-child involvement in urban Japanese families. *Psychiatry* 29:344–66.

Chiba, Atsuko. 1981. Nyūgan nanka ni makerarenai (I cannot afford to be overcome by breast cancer). *Bungei Shunjū* 59(5):264–94.

Cohen, A. 1974. *Two-Dimensional Man: An Essay on the Anthropology of Power and Symbolism in Complex Societies.* London: Routledge & Kegan Paul.

Cole, Robert E. 1979. *Work, Mobility and Participation.* Berkeley: University of California Press.

Crapanzano, Vincent. 1980. *Tuhami – Portrait of a Moroccan.* Chicago: University of Chicago Press.

Davis, Winston. 1980. *Dōjō: Magic and Exorcism in Modern Japan.* Stanford: Stanford University Press.

De Craemer, Willy, Jan Vansina, and Renée C. Fox. 1976. Religious movements in Central Africa: A theoretical study. *Comparative Studies in Society and History* 18(4):458–75.

DeVos, George, and H. Wagatsuma, eds. 1966. *Japan's Invisible Race – Caste in Culture and Personality*. Berkeley: University of California Press.

Doi, Takeo. 1978. *Amae no Kōzō* (The Structure of *Amae*). Tokyo: Kōbundō.

Donohue, John. 1966. The social persistence of an outcaste group. In *Japan's Invisible Race*, George DeVos and Hiroshi Wagatsuma, eds. Berkeley: University of California Press. Pp. 137–52.

Dore, Ronald P. 1973. *City Life in Japan – A Study of a Tokyo Ward*. Berkeley: University of California Press. (Originally published in 1958.)

Douglas, Mary. 1966. *Purity and Danger*. London: Routledge & Kegan Paul.

1975. *Implicit Meanings*. London: Routledge & Kegan Paul.

Dubos, René. 1979. *Mirage of Health: Utopias, Progress, and Biological Change*. New York: Harper & Row. (Originally published in 1959.)

Dumont, Louis. 1970. *Homo Hierarchicus*. Chicago: University of Chicago Press. (Originally published in French in 1966.)

Dumont, Jean-Paul. 1978. *The Headman and I: Ambiguity and Ambivalence in the Fieldworking Experience*. Austin: University of Texas Press.

Dunn, Fred L. 1976. Traditional Asian medicine and cosmopolitan medicine as adaptive systems. In *Asian Medical Systems: A Comparative Study*, Charles Leslie, ed. Berkeley: University of California Press. Pp. 133–58.

Durkheim, Emile, and Marcel Mauss. 1963. *Primitive Classification*. Chicago: University of Chicago Press. [Originally published in *Année Sociologique* 1901–2(1903).]

Embree, John F. 1958. *Suye Mura: A Japanese Village*. Chicago: University of Chicago Press. (Originally published in 1939.)

Fabrega, Horacio, Jr. 1972. Medical anthropology. In *Biennial Review of Anthropology, 1971*, B. Siegel, ed. Stanford, Calif.: Stanford University Press. Pp. 167–229.

1975. The need for an ethnomedical science. *Science* 189:969–75.

Fernandez, James W. 1974. The mission of metaphor in expressive culture. *Current Anthropology* 15:119–46.

1980. Reflections on looking into mirrors. *Semiotica* 30 (1/2):27–39.

Fox, Renée. 1968. Illness. In *International Encyclopedia of the Social Sciences*, Vol. 7, pp. 90–96. New York: Macmillan.

Frake, Charles O. 1961. The diagnosis of disease among the Subanun of Mindanao. *American Anthropologist* 63:113–32.

Frankenberg, Ronald. 1957. *Village on the Border: A Social Study of Religion, Politics and Football in a North Wales Community*. London: Cohen & West.

1981. What Manchester does today . . . ? *Royal Anthropological Institute News* No. 45:6–8.

Freedman, Maurice. 1969. Geomancy. *Proceedings of the Royal Anthropological Institute of Great Britain and Ireland for 1968*. Pp. 5–15.

Fujita, Shinichi. 1978. Usoga ooi jinkō chūzetsusū (Unreliable figures for abortions). *Asahi* November 21, 1978. In the series called "Osan Kakumei" (Revolution in Childbirth).

Fuse, Shōichi. 1979. *Ishi no Rekishi* (A History of Medical Doctors in Japan). Tokyo: Chūō Kōronsha.

Geertz, Clifford. 1973. *The Interpretation of Cultures*. New York: Basic Books.

1976. "From the native's point of view": On the nature of anthropological understanding. In *Meaning in Anthropology*, K. H. Basso and H. A. Selby, eds. Albuquerque: University of New Mexico Press. Pp. 221–37.

Genji, Keita. 1982. Mizuko kuyō (Memorial service for aborted fetuses). *Shōsetsu Shinchō* 36(2):46–7.

Glick, Leonard B. 1977. Medicine as an ethnographic category: The Gimi of the New Guinea Highlands. In *Culture, Disease and Healing*, David Landy, ed. New York: Macmillan. Pp. 58–70.

Good, Byron J. 1977. The heart of what's the matter: The semantics of illness in Iran. *Culture, Medicine and Psychiatry* 1(1):25–58.

Graburn, Nelson H. H. 1977. Tourism: The sacred journey. In *Hosts and Guests: The Anthropology of Tourism*, Valene L. Smith, ed. Philadelphia: University of Pennsylvania Press. Pp. 17–31.

Hall, Edward T. 1969. *The Hidden Dimension*. Garden City, N.Y.: Doubleday Anchor Books. (Originally published in 1966.)

Harada, Tomohiko. 1978a. Buraku no zenshi (An early history of *buraku*). In *Buraku Mondai Yōsetsu* (Outline of *Buraku* Problems), Buraku Kaihō Kenkyūjo, ed. Osaka: Kaihō Shuppansha. Pp. 16–23.

1978b. Kinsei hōken shakai to buraku keisei (The feudal society and the formation of *buraku*). In *Buraku Mondai Yōsetsu* (Outline of *Buraku* Problems), Buraku Kaihō Kenkyūjo, ed. Osaka: Kaihō Shuppansha. Pp. 24–33.

Hayashiya, Tatsusaburō. 1980. *Nihon Geinō no Sekai* (Japanese Performing Arts). Tokyo: Nihon Hosō Shuppan Kyōkai.

Higo, Kazuo. 1942. *Nihon Shinwa Kenkyū* (Research in Japanese Mythology). Tokyo: Kawade Shobō. (Originally published in 1938.)

Hori, Ichirō. 1968. *Folk Religion in Japan*. Chicago: University of Chicago Press.

1977. *Minkan Shinkō* (Folk Religion). Tokyo: Iwanami Shoten. (Originally published in 1951.)

Horton, Robin, and Ruth Finnegan, eds. 1973. *Modes of Thought: Essays on Thinking in Western and Non-Western Societies*. London: Faber & Faber.

Hsu, Francis L. K. 1973. Prejudice and its intellectual effect in American anthropology: An ethnographic report. *American Anthropologist* 75(1):1–19.

Hyōgo-ken Eiseibu. 1979. *Eisei Tōkei Nenpō* (Annual Report of Health Statistics). Kobe: Yamato Shuppan Insatsu Kabushiki Kaisha.

Ikeda Shoten Katei Igaku Henshūbu. 1977. *Katei Igaku Shin Jiten* (A New Manual for Human Medicine). Tokyo: Ikeda Shoten.

Ikemi, Yūjirō. 1978. *Zoku Shinryō Naika* (Internal Medicine for Psychosomatic Illnesses), Vol. 2. Tokyo: Chūō Kōronsha. (Originally published in 1973.)

1981. *Shinryō Naika* (Internal Medicine for Psychosomatic Illnesses). Tokyo: Chūō Kōronsha. (Originally published in 1963.)

Imamura, Michio. 1979. Minkan ryōhō (Folk medicine). In *Kōza Nihon no Minzoku Shūkyō* (Folk Religions of Japan), S. Gorai, T. Sakurai, T. Oshima, and N. Miyata, eds. Tokyo: Kōbundō. Pp. 198–215.

Inoue, Hisashi, et al. 1978. *Shinpojūmu Sabetsu no Seishinshi Josetsu* (Introduction to a Spiritual History of Discrimination – A Symposium). Tokyo: Sanseidō.

Inoue, Kazuko. 1979–81. Personal communication.

1981. Gan kenkyūkai fuzoku byōin de no toshokan sābisu (Voluntary work at the library at the hospital attached to the National Institute of Cancer Research). *Byōin Toshokan* 3(2):3–6.

Inoue, Kiyoshi. 1967. *Tennō-sei* (Emperor System). Tokyo: Tōkyō Daigaku Shuppan-kai.

Inoue, Kiyoshi, ed. 1979. *Kenkō Kazoku* (The Healthy Family), No. 18. Tokyo: Shufu to Seikatsusha.

Ishihara, Akira. 1962. *Kampo* [*sic*]: Japan's traditional medicine. *Japan Quarterly* 9:429–37.

――― 1978. *Kanpō* (Chinese-Derived Japanese Medicine). Tokyo: Chūō Kōronsha.

Ishikiri Kyōhonchō, ed. 1980. *Ishikiri* No. 34. Osaka: Ishikiri Kyōhonchō.

Itoh, Mikiharu. 1976. Shinkō seikatsu (Religious life). In *Nihonjin no Seikatsu* (Life of the Japanese) (Kōza Hikaku Bunka, Vol. 4), T. Umesao, ed. Tokyo: Kenkyūsha. Pp. 212-38.

Jacobson, Avrohm, and Albert N. Berenberg. 1952. Japanese psychiatry and psychotherapy. *The American Journal of Psychiatry* 109:321–9.

Janzen, John M. 1978. *The Quest for Therapy in Lower Zaire*. Berkeley: University of California Press.

Jingū Shichō, ed. 1967. *Koji Ruien Vol. 5 – Shingi bu* (Ancient Matters, Vol. 5 – Deity of Heaven and Deity of Earth). Tokyo: Yoshikawa Kōbunkan.

Jung, Carl G. 1971. *Jung*. New York: Viking.

Kailasapathy, K. 1968. *Tamil Heroic Poetry*. Oxford: Clarendon Press.

Kaneoka, Shūyū. 1970. *Koji Meisatsu Jiten* (A Dictionary of Ancient and Famous Temples). Tokyo: Tokyodō Shuppan.

Katō, H., J. Iwasaki, K. Kata, and S. Gotō. 1967. *Meiji Taishō Shōwa Sesōshi* (A History of Social Conditions during the Meiji, Taishō and Shōwa Periods). Tokyo: Shakai Shisōsha.

Katō, Hidetoshi, Toshinao Yoneyama, Mikiyaru Itō, Tadao Umesao, Noritada Kubo, Chōshū Takeda, and Tatsusaburō Hayashiya. 1972. Kamigami no bungyō (zadan kai) (Division of labor among deities – A roundtable discussion). In *Nihon Bunka to Sekai* (Japanese Culture and the World), T. Umesao and M. Tada, eds. Tokyo: Kōdansha. Pp. 60–113.

Katz, Pearl. 1981. Ritual in the operating room. *Ethnology* 20(4):335–50.

Kenmochi, Takehiko. 1980. *"Ma" to Nihon Bunka* (Japanese Culture and *Ma*). Tokyo: Kōdansha. (Originally published in 1978.)

Kimura, Harumi. 1978. Shin kōsai kō 4 (Thoughts on new manners, No. 4). *Asahi Shinbun* (Nagoya ban) March 18.

Kindaichi, Haruhiko. 1966. *Nihongo* (The Japanese Language). Tokyo: Iwanami Shoten.

Kindaichi, Kyōsuke. 1967. *Nihon no Keigo* (Japanese Honorifics). Tokyo: Kadokawa Shoten.

Kindaichi, Kyōsuke, ed. 1953. *Meikai Kokugo Jiten* (Concise Dictionary of Japanese). Tokyo: Sanseidō.

Kleinman, Arthur. 1980. *Patients and Healers in the Context of Culture: An Exploration of the Borderland Between Anthropology, Medicine, and Psychiatry*. Berkeley: University of California Press.

Kōbe-shi Eiseikyoku (Department of Health, City of Kobe), ed. 1978. *Kōbe-shi Eisei*

Tōkei Yōran – Shōwa 53-nen (1978 Health Statistics for the City of Kobe). Kobe: Kōbe-shi Eiseikyoku.

Kokuritsu Gengo Kenkyūjo (National Institute for Language Studies). 1957. *Keigo to Keigo Ishiki* (Sociopsychological Survey of Japanese Polite Expression). Tokyo: Kokuritsu Gengo Kenkyūjo.

Kōseishō, ed. 1978. *Shōwa 53-nen ban Kōsei Hakusho* (Report on Health and Welfare for the Year 1978). Tokyo: Ōkurashō Insatsukyoku.

Kōseishō Tōkei Jōhōbu, ed. 1979. *Shōwa 52-nen Iryō Shisetsu Chōsa – Byōin Hōkoku* (A 1977 Survey of Medical Facilities). Tokyo: Tōkei Insatsu Kōgyō Kabushiki Gaisha.

Kubo, Noritada. 1961. *Kōshin Shinkō no Kenkyū: Nicchū Shūkyō Bunka Kōshōshi* (Research on Belief in Kōshin – A History of Cultural-Religious Exchange between Japan and China). Tokyo: Nihon Gakujutsu Shinkōkai.

Kuhn, Thomas S. 1962. *The Structure of Scientific Revolutions*. Chicago: University of Chicago Press.

Kurihara, Minoru, Midori Tahara, Misako Okada, Michiko Okazawa, and Sachio Maeda. 1979. Zadankai – Gan o norikoeta hitotachi (Roundtable discussion – Those who survived cancer). *Hōmu Dokutā* (March, 1979):14–21.

Landy, David. 1977. Role adaptation: Traditional curers under the impact of Western medicine. In *Culture, Disease and Healing*, D. Landy, ed. New York: Macmillan. Pp. 468–81.

Leach, Sir Edmund. 1963. *Rethinking Anthropology*. London: Athlone Press.

1966. Ritualization of man. In *Philosophical Transactions of the Royal Society of London* (Series B: Biological Sciences), Vol. 251, No. 722, pp. 403–8.

1968. Ritual. In *International Encyclopedia of the Social Sciences*. Vol. 13, pp. 520–6. New York: Macmillan.

1976. *Culture and Communication*. Cambridge: Cambridge University Press.

1982. *Social Anthropology*. London: Fontana.

Lebra, Takie Sugiyama. 1976. *Japanese Patterns of Behavior*. Honolulu: University Press of Hawaii.

Leonard, George. 1976. The holistic health revolution. *New West* 1(10):40–9.

Leslie, Charles. 1974. The modernization of Asian medical systems. In *Rethinking Modernization: Anthropological Perspectives*, J. J. Poggie, Jr., and Robert N. Lynch, eds. Westport, Conn: Greenwood Press. Pp. 69–108.

1975. Pluralism and integration in the Indian and Chinese medical systems. In *Medicine in Chinese Cultures*, A. Kleinman, P. Kundstadter, E. R. Alexander, and J. L. Gale. Washington, D.C.: National Institutes of Health DHEW Publication No. (NIH) 75–653. Pp. 401–17.

1976. The ambiguities of medical revivalism in modern India. In *Asian Medical Systems*, Charles Leslie, ed. Berkeley: University of California Press. Pp. 356–67.

1980. Medical pluralism in world perspective (1). *Social Science and Medicine* 14B(4):191–5.

Lévi-Strauss, Claude. 1960. On manipulated sociological models. *BIJDRAGEN – Tot de Taal-, Land- en Volkenkunde* 116(1):45–54.

1966. *The Savage Mind*. Chicago: University of Chicago Press. (Originally published in French in 1962.)

1967. *Structural Anthropology*. Garden City, N.Y.: Doubleday. (Originally published in French in 1958 and in English in 1963.)

1969. *The Elementary Structures of Kinship*. London: Eyre & Spottiswoode. (Originally published in French in 1949.)

Lewis, I. M. 1981. What is a shaman? *Folk* 23:25–35.

Lieban, R. W. 1977. *Cebuano Sorcery: Malign Magic in the Philippines*. Berkeley: University of California Press.

Lock, Margaret M. 1980a. *East Asian Medicine in Urban Japan*. Berkeley: University of California Press.

1980b. The organization and practice of East Asian medicine in Japan: Continuity and change. *Social Science and Medicine* 14B(4):245–53.

Long, Susan O., and Bruce D. Long. 1980. Curable cancers and fatal ulcers: Attitudes toward cancer in Japan. Paper presented at the Midwest Regional Seminar on Japan, held at Knox College, Galesburg, Illinois, September 27, 1980.

Maclean, Una. 1974. *Magical Medicine*. Middlesex, Eng.: Penguin Books.

Manabe, Kōsai. 1959. *Jizōson no Sekai* (The World of *Jizō*). Tokyo: Aoyama Shoin.

1960. *Jizōbosatsu no Kenkyū* (Research on *Jizōbosatsu*). Kyoto: Sanmitsudō Shoten.

Manaka, Yoshio. 1972. *The Layman's Guide to Acupuncture*. New York: Weatherhill.

Mann, Felix. 1973. *Acupuncture: The Ancient Chinese Art of Healing and How It Works Scientifically*. New York: Vintage Books.

Martin, Samuel. 1964. Speech levels in Japan and Korea. In *Language in Culture and Society*, Dell Hymes, ed. New York: Harper & Row. Pp 407–15.

Matsuda, Michio. 1979. *Nihon-shiki Ikujihō* (Japanese Ways of Childrearing). Tokyo: Kōdansha. Revised edition.

Matsudaira, Narimitsu. 1977. *Matsuri – Honshitsu to Shosō – Kodaijin no Uchū* (Festivals – Their Essence and Multiple Dimensions – The Universe of Ancient Japanese). Tokyo: Asahi Shimbunsha.

Mauss, Marcel. 1966. *The Gift – Forms and Functions of Exchange in Archaic Societies*. London: Cohen & West. (Originally published in French in 1950.)

Minami, Hiroshi. 1961. *Nihonjin no Shinri* (Psychology of the Japanese). Tokyo: Iwanami Shoten. (Originally published in 1953.)

Misumi, No. 149 (March 1979).

Miura, Momoshige, and Shinichi Usa. 1974. A psychotherapy of neurosis: Morita therapy. In *Japanese Culture and Behavior*, T. S. Lebra and W. P. Lebra, eds. Honolulu: University Press of Hawaii. Pp. 407–30.

Miyata, Noboru. 1975. *Kinsei no Hayarigami* (Popular Deities in the Early Modern Period in Japan). Tokyo: Hyōronsha.

Mizobe, Ryō. 1970. Gendai jiin to gensei riyaku (Temples and their efficacies today). In *Nihon Shūkyō no Gensei Riyaku* (Practical Benefits of Japanese Religions), Nihon Bukkyō Kenkyūkai, ed. Tokyo: Okura Shuppan. Pp. 408–23.

Moore, Sally F., and Barbara G. Myerhoff. 1977. Introduction: Secular ritual: Forms and meanings. In *Secular Ritual*, S. F. Moore and B. G. Myerhoff, eds. Amsterdam: Van Gorcum. Pp. 3–24.

Mori, Yūsai. 1977. Chūi Gakuin no genkyō – Chūigaku no gendai igaku ni taisuru igi (The present state of Chinese medicine – Contributions by Chinese medicine to modern medicine). *Kanpō Kenkyū* 10:388–93.

Morisue, Yoshiaki, and Suketaka Hinonishi, eds. 1967. *Fūzoku Jiten* (A Dictionary of Customs). Tokyo: Tōkyōdō.

Moriya, Katsuhisa. 1978. *Kyō Ishi no Rekishi: Nihon Igaku no Genryū* (Research on Doctors in Kyoto: A Study of the Source of Japanese Medicine). Tokyo: Kōdansha.

Morris, Ivan. 1975. *The Nobility of Failure: Tragic Heroes in the History of Japan*. New York: New American Library.

Morse, Edward S. 1961. *Japanese Homes and Their Surroundings*. New York: Dover Publications.

Murase, Takao. 1974. Naikan therapy. In *Japanese Culture and Behavior*, T. S. Lebra and W. P. Lebra, eds. Honolulu: The University Press of Hawaii. Pp. 431–42.

Myerhoff, Barbara. 1980. *Number Our Days*. New York: Simon and Schuster.

Myerhoff, Barbara, and Jay Ruby. 1982. Introduction. In *A Crack in the Mirror*, J. Ruby, ed. Philadelphia: University of Pennsylvania Press. Pp. 1–35.

Nakajima, Kiichi. 1978. Current situation of and prospects for Oriental medicine. Presidential address delivered at the 29th Congress of Oriental Medicine in Japan, May 20, 1978, Nishiyama Memorial Hall, Kobe. Transl. T. Matsumoto. Published as a booklet. 56 pp.

Nakamura, Hajime. 1978. *Ways of Thinking of Eastern Peoples: India-China-Tibet-Japan*. Honolulu: University Press of Hawaii.

Nakane, Chie. 1970. *Japanese Society*. Berkeley: University of California Press.

Nakazato, Tsuneko. 1981. Yūshū ki: Gan byōtō yori kaerite (Notes on sadness: Reflections on a cancer ward). *Chūō Kōron* 1134:298–319.

Needham, Joseph. 1969. *Science and Civilization in China*. Vol. 2, *History of Scientific Thought*. Cambridge: Cambridge University Press.

Needham, Joseph, F. R. S., in collaboration with Wang Ling, Lu Gwei-Djen, and Ho Ping-Yü. 1970. *Clerks and Craftsmen in China and the West*. Cambridge: Cambridge University Press.

Needham, Rodney. 1963. Introduction. In *Primitive Classification*, by Emile Durkheim and Marcel Mauss. Chicago: University of Chicago Press. Pp. vii–xlviii.

Ninomiya, Shigeaki. 1933. An inquiry concerning the origin, development, and present situation of the *eta* in relation to the history of social classes in Japan. *Transactions of the Asiatic Society of Japan* 10:47–154.

Noguchi, Michihiko. 1978. Chūsei no shomin seikatsu to hisabetsumin no dōkō (The life of common people and discrimination against *Burakumin* during the Middle Ages). In *Buraku Mondai Gaisetsu* (Introduction to *Burakumin* Problems), Buraku Kaihō Kenkyūjo, ed. Osaka: Kaihō Shuppansha. Pp. 86–99.

Norbeck, Edward. 1952. Pollution and taboo in contemporary Japan. *Southwestern Journal of Anthropology* 8(3):269–85.

1955. *Yakudoshi*, a Japanese complex of supernaturalistic beliefs. *Southwestern Journal of Anthropology* 11(2):105–20.

1970. *Religion and Society in Modern Japan: Continuity and Change*. Houston: Tourmaline Press.

1976. *Changing Japan*. New York: Holt, Rinehart & Winston. Revised edition.

Obeyesekere, Gananath. 1976. The impact of Āyurvedic ideas on the culture and the individual in Sri Lanka. In *Asian Medical Systems*, C. Leslie, ed. Berkeley: University of California Press. Pp. 201–26.

Ochiai, Shigenobu. 1972. *Mikaihō Buraku no Kigen* (Origin of Discrimination against *Buraku*). Kobe: Kōbe Gakujutsu Shuppan.

Ogawa, Hiroshi, and Kunio Aoki. 1978. Igan ni taisuru taido no igaku shakai shinri-gakuteki kenkyū (A medicosocial psychological study on attitudes toward stomach cancer). Dai Ippō (Report 1): Igan no chishiki no naiyō bunseki (Content analysis of knowledge on stomach cancer). *Nihon Kōeishi* 25(7):349–56.

Ogawa, Teizō. 1982. *Igaku no Rekishi* (History of Medicine). Tokyo; Chūō Kōronsha. (Originally published in 1964.)

Ohara, K., and David Reynolds. 1970. Love-pact suicide. *Omega* 1(2):159–66.

Ohnuki-Tierney, Emiko. 1971. The system of speech levels as social behavior in Japan. Paper delivered at the 70th Annual Meeting of the American Anthropological Association, New York, November 18, 1971.

1976. Regional variations in Ainu culture. *American Ethnologist* 3(2):297–329.

1981a. *Illness and Healing among the Sakhalin Ainu – A Symbolic Interpretation.* London and New York: Cambridge University Press.

1981b. Phases in human perception/cognition/symbolization processes: Cognitive anthropology and symbolic classification. *American Ethnologist* 8(3):451–67.

1984. Monkey performances – A multiple structure of meaning and reflexivity in Japanese culture. In *Text, Play and Story: The Construction and Reconstruction of Self and Society*, Edward Bruner, ed. 1983 Proceedings of the American Ethnological Society. In press.

Okazaki, Kanzō. 1976. *Kusuri no Rekishi* (A History of Medicines). Tokyo: Kōdansha.

Okifuji, Noriko. 1979. *Onna ga Shokuba o Saru Hi* (The Day When a Woman Leaves Her Work). Tokyo: Shinchōsha.

Ōkōchi, Kazuo. 1968. Rinji kyūyo (Extra allowance). In *Gendai Yōgo no Kiso Chishiki* (Basic Knowledge of the Modern Japanese Language). Tokyo: Jiyū Kokuminsha. P. 431.

Ōkuma, Miyoshi. 1973. *Seppuku no Reikishi* (History of *Seppuku*). Tokyo: Yūzankaku.

Okuyama, Kenji. 1976. *Nihon no Iryō* (Medical System of Japan). Tokyo: Shin Nihon Shuppansha.

Ōmori, Yasuhiro. 1981. Pari no nihonjin gakkō ni okeru bunka haikei no kotonaru seito o megutte (Interpersonal problems caused by diverse foreign experiences among pupils of the Japanese school in Paris). *Kokuritsu Minzokugaku Hakubutsukan Kenkyū Hōkoku* 6(3):597–628.

Ono, Hideo. 1968. *Meiji Wadai Jiten* (A Dictionary of Events during the Meiji Period). Tokyo: Tokyodō Shuppan.

Origuchi, Shinobu. 1965a. *Origuchi Shinobu Zenshū, Dai Ikkan* (Collected Papers of Shinobu Origuchi, Vol. 1). Tokyo: Chūō Kōronsha.

1965b. *Origuchi Shinobu Zenshū, Dai Nikan* (Collected Papers of Shinobu Origuchi, Vol. 2). Tokyo: Chūō Kōronsha.

1966. *Origuchi Shinobu Zenshū, Dai Nanakan* (Collected Papers of Shinobu Origuchi, Vol. 7). Tokyo: Chūō Kōronsha.

Ōshima, Tatehiko, et al. 1980. *Nihon o Shiru Shōjiten Vol. 3: Ishokujū* (A Concise Dictionary of Japan, Vol. 3: Clothing, Food, and Housing). Tokyo: Shakai Shisōsha.

Ōtsuka, Yasuo. 1976. Chinese traditional medicine in Japan. In *Asian Medical Systems*, Charles Leslie, ed. Berkeley: University of California Press. Pp. 322–40.

Ouwehand, C. 1958–59. Some notes on the god Susano-o. *Monumenta Nipponica* 14(3–4):138–61 (384–407).

1964. *Namazu-e and Their Themes: An Interpretative Approach to Some Aspects of Japanese Folk Religion*. Leiden: E. J. Brill.

Parsons, Talcott. 1979. Definitions of health and illness in the light of American values and social structure. In *Patients, Physicians, and Illness*, E. Gartly Jaco, ed. New York: Free Press. Pp. 120–44.

Parsons, Talcott, and Renée Fox. 1952. Illness, therapy and the modern urban American family. *Journal of Social Issues* 8(4):31–44.

Peacock, James. L. 1975. *Consciousness and Change: Symbolic Anthropology in Evolutionary Perspective*. New York: Halsted Press.

Philippi, Donald L., transl. 1959. *Norito: A New Translation of the Ancient Japanese Ritual Prayers*. Tokyo: The Institute for Japanese Culture and Classics, Kokugakuin University.

1969. *Kojiki*. Princeton, N.J.: Princeton University Press. Tokyo: University of Tokyo Press.

Plath, David W. 1966. Japan and the ethics of fatalism. *Anthropological Quarterly* 39(3):161–70.

1980. *Long Engagements: Maturity in Modern Japan*. Stanford, Calif.: Stanford University Press.

1982. Resistance at forty-eight: Old-age brinkmanship and Japanese life course pathways. In *Aging and Life Course Transitions*, T. K. Hareven and K. J. Adams, eds. New York: Guilford Press. Pp. 109–25.

Porkert, Manfred. 1974. *The Theoretical Foundations of Chinese Medicine: Systems of Correspondence*. Cambridge, Mass.: MIT Press.

Press, Irwin. 1978. Bureaucracy versus folk medicine: Implications from Seville, Spain. In *Health and the Human Condition*, Michael H. Logan and Edward E. Hunt, eds. North Scituate, Mass.: Duxbury Press. Pp. 376–87.

Price, John. 1966. A history of outcaste: Untouchability in Japan. In *Japan's Invisible Race*, G. DeVos and H. Wagatsuma, eds. Berkeley: University of California Press. Pp. 6–30.

Rabinow, Paul. 1977. *Reflections on Fieldwork in Morocco*. Berkeley: University of California Press.

Rappaport, Roy A. 1980. Concluding comments on ritual and reflexivity. *Semiotica* 30(1/2):181–93.

Reynolds, David K. 1976. *Morita Psychotherapy*. Berkeley: University of California Press.

Rohlen, Thomas. 1974. *For Harmony and Strength: Japanese White-Collar Organization in Anthropological Perspective*. Berkeley: University of California Press.

Romanucci-Ross, Lola. 1977. The hierarchy of resort in curative practices: The Admiralty Islands. In *Culture, Disease and Healing*, D. Landy, ed. New York: Macmillan. Pp. 481–7.

Sahlins, Marshall. 1976. *Culture and Practical Reason*. Chicago: University of Chicago Press.

Schechner, Richard. 1982. Collective reflexivity: Restoration of behavior. In *A Crack in the Mirror*, Jay Ruby, ed. Philadelphia: University of Pennsylvania Press. Pp. 39–81.

Schonberg, Harold C. 1982. Championing Japanese music. *The New York Times* February 21, 1982. Pp. 17–18.

Schutz, Alfred. 1971. *Collected Papers. Vol II: Studies in Social Theory.* Ed. and introduced by Arvid Brodersen. The Hague: Martinus Nijhoff.

Shanghai Chūigakuin, ed. 1978. *Chūigaku Kiso* (The Foundation of Chinese Medicine). Kōbe Chūigaku Kenkyūkai, transl. Tokyo: Ryōgen Shoten.

Shimonaka, Yasaburō, ed. 1941. *Shintō Daijiten* (Encyclopedia of *Shinto*), Vol. 1–3. Tokyo: Heibonsha.

Simmel, Georg. 1950. *The Sociology of Georg Simmel.* Translated, edited and with an introduction by Kurt H. Wolff. Glencoe, Ill.: Free Press.

1978. *The Philosophy of Money.* London: Routledge & Kegan Paul.

Smith, Robert J. 1974. *Ancestor Worship in Contemporary Japan.* Palo Alto, Calif.: Stanford University Press.

Sono, Ayako. 1980 a and b. *Kami no Yogoreta Te* (Soiled Hands of God), Vol. 1 and 2. Tokyo: Asahi Shimbunsha.

Sontag, Susan. 1979. *Illness as Metaphor.* New York: Random House.

Sōrifu Tōkeikyoku (Statistics Bureau, Prime Minister's Office), ed. 1980. *Nihon Tōkei Nenkan* (Statistical Yearbook of Japan). Tokyo: Nihon Tōkei Kyōkai and Mainichi Shinbunsha.

Stein, Howard F. 1977. Commentary on Kleinman's "Lessons from a clinical approach to medical anthropological research." *Medical Anthropology Newsletter* 8(4):15–16.

Sunahara, Shigeichi. 1977. *Kusuri sono Anzensei* (Risks of Medication). Tokyo: Iwanami Shoten.

Suzuki, Mitsuo. 1974. *Marebito no Kōzō – Higashi Ajiya Hikaku Minzokugaku Kenkyū* (The Structure of *Marebito* [Visitors] – Comparative Folklore of East Asia). Tokyo: Sanichi Shobō.

1979. *Marebito* (Visitors). In *Kōza Nihon no Minzoku* (Folk Cultures of Japan), Vol. 7 – *Shinkō* (Belief Systems), T. Sakurai, ed. Tokyo: Yuseidō Shuppan. Pp. 211–39.

Swanger, Eugene R. 1981. A preliminary examination of the *omamori* phenomenon. *Asian Folklore Studies* 40(2):237–52.

Takenaka, Shinjō. 1977. *Tabū no Kenkyū* (Research on Taboo). Tokyo: Sankibu Busshorin.

Tambiah, Stanley J. 1973. Form and meaning of magical acts: A point of view. In *Modes of Thought: Essays on Thinking in Western and Non-Western Societies*, R. Horton and R. Finnegan, eds. London: Faber and Faber. Pp. 199–229.

Tatsukawa, Shōji. 1976. *Nihonjin no Byōreki* (A Medical History of the Japanese). Tokyo: Chūō Kōronsha.

1979. *Kinsei Byōsōshi – Edo Jidai no Byōki to Iryō* (History of Medicine – Illness and Medical Treatment during the Edo Period). Tokyo: Heibonsha.

Thomas, Keith. 1971. *Religion and the Decline of Magic.* New York: Charles Scribner's.

Tōkei Sūri Kenkyūjo Kokuminsei Chōsa Iinkai, ed. 1970. *Dai-Ni Nihonjin no Kokuminsei* (The National Character of the Japanese, No. 2). Tokyo: Shiseidō.

Tōkyō Hyakunenshi Henshū Iinkai, ed. 1979. *Tōkyō Hyakunenshi* (One Hundred Year History of Tokyo), Vol. 4. Tokyo: Gyōsei.

Tominaga, Shigeki. 1977. *Kenkōron Josetsu* (Introduction to the Theory of Health). Tokyo: Kawade Shobō Shinsha.

Tomosada, Keiko. 1976. Genshōgakuteki hoiku kenkyū (A phenomenological approach to childrearing). In *Hoiku Genshō no Bunkaronteki Tenkai* (Cultural Interpretations of Childrearing), Kazuko Honda and Shin Tsumori, eds. Tokyo: Kōseikan. Pp. 94–126.

Topley, Marjorie. 1976. Chinese traditional etiology and methods of cure in Hong Kong. In *Asian Medical Systems*, C. Leslie, ed. Berkeley: University of California Press. Pp. 243–65.

Tsurumi, Kazuko. 1972. *Kōkishin to Nihonjin* (Curiosity and the Japanese). Tokyo: Kōdansha.

Turner, Victor. 1967. *The Forest of Symbols*. Ithaca, N.Y.: Cornell University Press.

1975a. Symbolic studies. In *Annual Review of Anthropology*, Vol. 4, B. J. Siegel, A. R. Beals, and S. A. Tyler, eds. Palo Alto, Calif.: Annual Reviews, Inc. Pp. 145–61.

1975b. *Dramas, Fields, and Metaphors: Symbolic Action in Human Society*. Ithaca, N.Y.: Cornell University Press.

Ueda, Kazuo. 1978a. Buraku no bunpu to jinkō (Distribution of *buraku* settlements and population). In *Buraku Mondai Gaisetsu* (Introduction to *Buraku* Problems), Buraku Kaihō Kenkyūjo, ed. Osaka: Kaihō Shuppansha. Pp. 3–10.

1978b. Kodai senminsei to buraku kigensetsu ("The lowly people" in ancient Japan and the origin of *buraku*). In *Buraku Mondai Gaisetsu* (Introduction to *Buraku* Problems), Buraku Kaihō Kenkyūjo, ed. Osaka: Kaihō Shuppansha. Pp. 73–85.

1978c. Kinsei hōken shakai to mibunsei (The caste system during the feudal period). In *Buraku Mondai Gaisetsu* (Introduction to *Buraku* Problems), Buraku Kaihō Kenkyūjo, ed. Osaka: Kaihō Shuppansha. Pp. 100–18.

Umehara, Takeshi. 1967. Jō to yū kachi (Purity as a value). In *Bungaku Riron no Kenkyū* (Research on Literary Criticism), T. Kuwahara, ed. Tokyo: Iwanami Shoten. Pp. 78–97.

Umesao, Tadao. 1980. *Chikyū Jidai no Nihonjin* (The Japanese in the Space Age). Tokyo: Chūō Kōronsha.

1981. *Biishiki to Kamisama* (Aesthetics and Deities). Tokyo: Chūō Kōronsha.

van Gennep, Arnold. 1961. *The Rites of Passage*. Chicago: University of Chicago Press. A Phoenix Book. (Originally published in 1909.)

Vansina, Jan. 1970. Cultures through time. In *A Handbook of Method in Cultural Anthropology*, R. Naroll and R. Cohen, eds. Garden City, N.Y.: Natural History Press. Pp. 165–79.

Whorf, Benjamin L. 1952. *Collected Papers on Metalinguistics*. Washington, D.C.: Department of State, Foreign Service Institute.

Wunderman, Lorna E. 1980. *Physician Distribution and Medical Licensure in the U.S., 1979*. Chicago: Center for Health Services Research and Development, American Medical Association.

Yamaguchi, Masao. 1977. Kinship, theatricality, and marginal reality in Japan. In *Text and Context: The Social Anthropology of Tradition*, Ranvindra K. Jain, ed. ASA

Essays in Social Anthropology. Philadelphia: Institute for the Study of Human Issues. Pp. 151–79.

1978a. *Bunka to Ryōgisei* (Culture and Ambiguity). Tokyo: Iwanami Shoten.

1978b. Yamai no uchūshi (Illness and world view). In *Chi no Enkinhō* (Distant and Close Views of Rationality), by M. Yamaguchi. Tokyo: Iwanami Shoten. Pp. 221–53.

Yamazaki, Toyoko. 1978–79. *Shiroi Kyotō* (The White Giant Tower). 3 vols. Tokyo: Shinchōsha.

Yanagita, Kunio (Minzokugaku Kenkyūjo), ed. 1951. *Minzokugaku Jiten* (Dictionary of Ethnology). Tokyo: Tokyodō.

1962. *Teihon Yanagita Kunio Shū* (Selected Papers of Kunio Yanagita), Vol. 14. Tokyo: Chikuma Shobō.

1963. *Teihon Yanagita Kunio Shū* (Selected Papers of Kunio Yanagita), Vol. 12. Tokyo: Chikuma Shobō.

1964. *Teihon Yanagita Kunio Shū* (Selected Papers of Kunio Yanagita), Vol. 29. Tokyo: Chikuma Shobō.

Yokoi, Kiyoshi. 1975. *Chūsei Minshū no Seikatsu Bunka* (The Life of the Common People during the Middle Ages). Tokyo: Tōkyō Daigaku Shuppan Kai.

Yoneyama, Toshinao. 1979. *Tenjinsai – Osaka no Sairei* (*Tenjin* Festival – A Ritual in Osaka). Tokyo: Chūō Kōronsha.

Yoshida, Shūji. 1970. Iseebi to hashika: Minzoku yakugaku e no apurōchi (Lobster and measles – An approach to ethnopharmacology). *Kikan Jinruigaku* 1(4):46–75.

Yoshida, Teigo. 1978. *Nihon no Tsukimono: Shakai Jinruigakuteki Kōsatsu* (Possession in Japan: A Social Anthropological Perspective). Tokyo: Chūō Kōronsha.

1981. The stranger as god: The place of the outsider in Japanese folk religion. *Ethnology* 20(2):87–99.

Young, Allan. 1976. Some implications of medical beliefs and practices for social anthropology. *American Anthropologist* 78(1):5–24.

Zborowski, Mark. 1952. Cultural components in responses to pain. *Journal of Social Issues* 8:16–30.

Index